CONTESTED ADOPTIONS

Contested Adoptions

Research, law, policy and practice

edited by
Murray Ryburn

arena

© Murray Ryburn 1994

Published by
Arena
Ashgate Publishing Limited
Gower House
Croft Road
Aldershot
Hants GU11 3HR
England

Ashgate Publishing Company
Old Post Road
Brookfield
Vermont 05036
USA

British Library Cataloguing in Publication Data

Contested Adoptions: Research, Law,
  Policy and Practice
  I. Ryburn, Murray
  362.734
  ISBN 1 85742 188 4 (pbk)
       1 85742 187 6 (hbk)

Library of Congress Cataloging-in-Publication Data

Contested adoptions: research, law, policy and practice / edited by Murray
  Ryburn.
     p. cm.
  Includes bibliographical references and index.
     ISBN 1–85742–187–6 (hardback): $55.95. – ISBN 1–85742–188–4 (pbk):
  $39.95
     1. Adoption – Research – Great Britain.   2. Adoption – Government
  policy – Great Britain.   3. Adoption – Law and legislation – Great
  Britain.   I. Ryburn, Murray.
  HV875.58.G7C65   1994
  362.7'34'0941–dc20   94–30650
                                                                        CIP

Typeset in 10pt Palatino by Photoprint, Torquay and printed in Great
Britain by Hartnolls Ltd, Bodmin.

Contents

Notes on contributors

Nick Banks is a lecturer in social work at the University of Birmingham and a chartered clinical psychologist. He is often asked to appear as expert witness in cases concerning parents with learning difficulties and child care, and the care of black children.

Bill Jordan is the author of many texts on social policy and social work, and is reader in social studies at the University of Exeter and principal lecturer in social work at the University of Huddersfield.

Phil King is a freelance social worker and trainer based in the West Midlands. He is a highly experienced guardian *ad litem* and also provides expert evidence for other parties in court proceedings. As a partner in Independent Training Agency, he is involved in providing training services to a wide range of professionals.

Lydia Lambert has been involved with adoption issues for many years as a researcher at Edinburgh University, National Children's Bureau and BAAF and as a diocesan social worker.

Gerison Lansdown is currently director of the Children's Rights Development Unit, established to promote the fullest possible implementation of the UN Convention on the Rights of the Child in the UK.

Elizabeth Lawson is a barrister and Queen's Counsel who for many years has specialised in adoption and child care work.

Mary Ryan is a solicitor and the co-director of the Family Rights Group. She has extensive experience of work with families involved in contested adoptions.

Murray Ryburn is Director of Social Work Courses at the University of Birmingham. Adoption and child placement are his specialist fields of research and publication, and he often appears as an expert witness in contested adoption hearings.

Jill Smart is a social worker by training who now works in the children's law department of Young and Lee solicitors in Birmingham.

June Thoburn is a professor in social work at the University of East Anglia in Norwich and has previously worked as a social worker in England and Canada. Her research and publications are in the fields of child protection, family social work and child placement. Professor Thoburn is frequently asked to give expert evidence in care and adoption cases.

Noreen Tingle is the National Secretary of the Grandparents' Federation and was formerly a school teacher. Her experience of the care system stems from nearly losing two grandchildren to adoption and from her work with the Federation.

Ian Young who specialises in the law relating to children, is a solicitor and partner in Young and Lee, Birmingham. He is a member of the Law Society's Family Law Committee and a member of the Law Society's Children Panel.

1 Contested adoptions in context

Murray Ryburn

Introduction

Adoption and freeing for adoption are, apart from death, the only events that extinguish permanently and absolutely parental responsibility and all of the rights and duties of parenthood. This book is about situations where there are applications to dispense with the rights of birth parents or guardians to the adoption of their children, whether this is by way of application for an adoption order or to free for adoption. Where such an application succeeds it is the most forceful of interventions by the state into family life. Yet compulsory orders in adoption – Draconian though they are – have attracted very little attention in literature or research. This book is the first to focus exclusively on contested adoption proceedings. Its contributors share a common belief that if compulsory adoption is ever justified, this is only where it is genuinely a decision of last resort which demonstrably follows the most rigorous and exacting examination of all the alternatives.

Compulsory adoption proceedings require, routinely, that distinctions be made between the interests of children and those of their parents. In making such distinctions, social workers, guardians and the courts must answer crucial questions. They must decide, for example, what degree of parental neglect, incapacity or culpability justifies the removal of all rights to a say in their child's future. They must weigh up the long- and short-term interests of children and where these are not mutually inclusive they must decide which to attempt to safeguard. Compulsory adoptions require courts to make decisions for children and young people that will profoundly affect their futures, but with only a 'best guess' at what the future may bring. The finality of an adoption order on the other hand – there has

been but one recorded instance of revocation – means there is no mechanism to renegotiate and to alter decisions in the light of future knowledge.

Adoption – and contested adoption in particular – is fundamentally out of step with other areas of family law. While the inalienable status of parenthood has always been a foundation-stone of English family law, in adoption the complete extinction of parental responsibility, especially in circumstances where this is forced, creates an anomaly. Another guiding principle for decision-making in family law is the importance of negotiated settlements, yet in contested adoptions perhaps the most major decision in the life of a child is made as the result of an adversarial process.

Contested adoptions also raise crucial questions in relation to how the state should discharge its duty of welfare to children, and how far the voices of children should shape the decisions made on their behalf. It must lead us also to question the effectiveness of the state in constructing families, and to what extent it is reasonable to seek to build nurture from conflict. Finally, we should ask whether the very existence of compulsory adoption, as an alternative to prevention, saps the will of practitioners to work collaboratively and their commitment to partnership.

How many contested adoptions are there?

There are no national statistics concerning the number of adoption or freeing applications that are contested by birth parents. We do, however, have data from the recent *Pathways to Adoption* survey (Murch et al., 1993). These researchers found (p.28) that of 393 agency adoption applications concerning non-relative placements 26 per cent (101) were contested, while of 102 freeing applications 75 per cent (77) were contested. We cannot assume that all the remainder were not contested, however, since here the figures include situations where it was not known if an adoption order or freeing application was contested. Nor do these figures give any indication of how many birth parents were deeply unhappy with an agency's plan for adoption but lacked the will, ability or resources to contest it.

Contested adoption proceedings are common where children have been committed to care. Care orders often follow from situations of considerable conflict between professionals and families, and a previous history of conflict about the placement of a child probably presages continuing conflict where an adoption order is subsequently sought. In the *Pathways* study (p.55) 48 per cent of children compulsorily adopted and 72 per cent of those freed for adoption were in compulsory care. Given the association between being in care and contested adoption, any rise in the number of

children adopted from care would be likely to constitute evidence of increasing adversarialism in adoption. The number of children in England committed to care who were subsequently adopted shows a 35 per cent increase from a figure of 1029 in 1988 to 1386 in 1991. This increase in adoptions from care can not be explained by higher overall numbers of adoption orders. It also occurred during a period when there were not significant changes in the number of children committed to care. This seems therefore to indicate a greater tendency to compulsion in adoption than in other areas of child care. The likely trend to compulsion and adversarialism is also supported by the evidence of the numbers of children adopted following (voluntary) reception into care. Here there was a reduction of 17 per cent from 1272 in 1988 to 1053 in 1991 (DoH, 1988, 1991).

Contents

Contested Adoptions places compulsory adoptions within a broad social policy analysis, and examines the research and the law, the issues for practice, and, most importantly, the views of those who have experienced them. It questions whether decisions as complex as those made in adoption should ever be made by way of an adversarial process. It is a book which challenges readers to consider if the forced adoption of children is likely ever to serve their best interests and, if it is, in what circumstances this may be so.

In chapter 2 *Bill Jordan* asks why adoption should be an area where adversarialism persists, whilst co-operative decision making and negotiated agreements are encouraged in other areas of the law and practice. He locates contested adoptions in the broader social policy framework that has developed in the Thatcher years and beyond. He offers a thought-provoking analysis of the place that adoption occupies in child care services and of the potential danger to partnership that is posed by the existence of a residual model of adversarial decision-making.

Mary Ryan in chapter 3 brings together extensive knowledge of adoption law and the Children Act with experience of working with families facing contested proceedings. She considers the reasons why birth parents decide to oppose the plans of social workers for the adoption of their children and examines in terms of justice and equity, current adoption law and the proposals for its reform. She argues cogently for new steps and procedures in relation to the dispensation of parental consent to adoption which could contribute significantly to a system where fairer decisions would be made.

Elizabeth Lawson in chapter 4 brings to her review of ways that the courts have interpreted the law in contested proceedings many years' experience as a barrister and Queen's Counsel, specialising in adoption work. She examines critically the welfare test in adoption, the grounds in law for the dispensation of parental consent and how these have been interpreted in case law. She considers issues of post-adoption contact, and the vexed question of what is a 'reasonable parent'. She concludes with a discussion of procedural changes and alterations to the grounds for dispensing with consent which might diminish the number of contested hearings.

Jill Smart and *Ian Young* work in a large law firm which specialises in family law. They have between them many years' experience of work in adoption, and they bring to their chapter many examples from their current practice to illustrate the issues and dilemmas that contested proceedings raise. Contact between children and their birth families following adoption is, they argue, the single most critical issue in creating the context in which a bitter struggle between birth parents, and social workers and adopters, is probably inevitable.

Gerison Lansdown in chapter 6 examines the usefulness of the United Nations Convention on the Rights of the Child as a framework for amending both law and practice in situations of conflict in adoption. She argues that without an approach to adoption matters that is informed by a rights perspective, decisions will be made that are not in the best interests of children. She considers an approach to contested situations which would be consistent with Britain's ratification of the Convention.

In chapter 7 the focus shifts from the law to research. *Lydia Lambert*, an experienced adoption researcher, reviews the available research on contested proceedings, and highlights areas where further research would be helpful. Her review offers an historical perspective beginning before the last major amendments to adoption law which followed the Houghton Report. She addresses such matters as the rise in contested proceedings since that time, the research in relation to freeing for adoption, the procedural problems that attend contested proceedings, the difficult issue of what constitutes a contested adoption, and the findings on the perspectives of practitioners.

In contested adoptions, research findings are often relied on by professionals in order to lend support to their views. In chapter 8 *June Thoburn*, who contributed the survey of research on adoption to the adoption law review, draws on her knowledge both of research and research methodology as well as her experience as a witness in contested adoptions. She highlights not only the ways research can be helpful in informing judgments in contested cases, but also how it can be misused so that far more is claimed from research in support of a particular view or conclusion than is justified. Her chapter offers a particularly helpful

framework for professionals who are seeking to analyse the usefulness of research findings or wishing to challenge the ways in which they are used.

Many of the decisions and claims about what will be best for children in contested cases draw upon psychological theories of attachment and child development. Some knowledge of these and the relevant research is therefore essential for those engaged in decision-making in contested adoptions. In chapter 9 *Nick Banks*, an experienced clinical and educational psychologist, examines a number of issues likely to be of key concern to professionals in contested cases. He considers, for example, models of attachment and the importance of attachment for healthy identity formation. He discusses the possible effects of broken attachments and how remediable the negative effects of broken attachments can be.

Chapter 10 is contributed by *Phil King*, an experienced guardian *ad litem* with wide experience of contested adoptions. In it he draws on his own practice to tease out how the various elements of the guardian's role and task can fit together to provide an approach which is focused on the child's interests. His discussion ranges over issues such as the duties of the guardian, giving evidence, determining what is in conflict, understanding the wishes of children, working in partnership, managing negotiations and determining issues of contact.

In chapter 11 I draw on the findings of a research project which considered the views of adopters in seventy-four adoption placements finalised after contested adoption hearings. This chapter offers an overview of the effect of contested proceedings on adopters. It considers in detail issues such as how contested proceedings shaped the attitudes of adopters to birth families, and the effects they were perceived to have had on the availability of information. This chapter offers new information about such matters as the effects of contested proceedings on post-adoption contact, and the effects of contested proceedings on the wider families of adopters.

Chapter 12 is based on a small qualitative research study of the views of twelve families who experienced the compulsory adoption of their children. This study of birth parents' views in contested adoptions is to date unique, and many of those to whom I spoke expressed such anger with social workers and the courts that the lack of inclusion of their views in other studies is not surprising. Interwoven with the summary of birth families' views is an analysis of how far current proposals for the reform of adoption law in consultation documents and the White Paper might address some of the key issues which they raise.

In chapter 13 *Noreen Tingle*, founder of the United Kingdom Grandparents' Federation, offers a personal perspective on contested adoption which has been widened over many years by contact with other grandparents and birth relatives. Her chapter raises many important consider-

ations, not least the extent to which grandparents and other relatives are a largely neglected resource when plans are made for new placements for children. Her chapter represents a plea for a more compassionate and sensitive service in contested cases, and for new placements to incorporate children's vital links from the past.

In the final chapter, drawing particularly on experience as a witness in contested adoptions, I explore the use of an adversarial process in order to make long-term decisions about what will be best for children. Adversarial proceedings, I maintain, push professionals to exceed justifiable conclusions in both the process of making plans and of giving evidence. They create a context for decision-making in which 'winning' matters more than anything else, and they are likely to lead to rigid and inflexible decisions that are not in the best interests of children and their futures.

This book questions much of what is currently perceived as best practice where plans for compulsory adoption are formulated. It challenges the idea that in contested adoptions a different set of values and assumptions for practice should be applied compared with those required by the law, good practice and research findings in other areas of work with children, young people and their families. It calls for practice in adoption that promotes negotiated agreements and collaborative working and which seeks, most crucially, in all circumstances, the maintenance of significant links for children with their past.

References

Department of Health (1988), *Children in Care 1988, England*, A/F 88/1, London: HMSO.
Department of Health (1991), *Children in Care 1991, England*, A/F 91/1, London: HMSO.
Murch, M., Lowe, N., Borkowski, M., Copner, R. and Griew, K. (1993), *Pathways to Adoption Research Project*, Bristol: Socio-Legal Centre for Family Studies, University of Bristol/DoH.

2 Contested adoptions and the role of the state in family matters

Bill Jordan

Introduction

This chapter sets out the social policy background to the issue of contested adoptions. It aims to provide a context for the contributions by lawyers, researchers, practitioners and those involved in such proceedings, indicating some of the reasons why adoption is a field in which adversarialism still persists in Britain, and may be growing.

In the first part of the chapter I shall consider the British government's general position on the relationship between the state and the family. This involves examining the theoretical basis of government policies in the 1980s, and how this was reflected in legislation at the end of that decade.

The second part considers why legislation, policy and practice on parents and children have not fitted easily into the mould set by the government's overall approach. I will argue that the Children Act 1989 (and especially government guidance associated with it) reflects an alternative approach to state intervention in family matters – the attempt to sustain partnership and shared responsibility between a public agency and parents having difficulties bringing up their children.

Finally, I shall speculate about why adoption does not readily fit this alternative paradigm, and why it has become the focus of tension and conflict between professionals and parents. This involves analysing the contradictions between the overall basis of government policy on the family, and the aims of the Children Act.

The family in social policy: the 1980s

The British government's project in the decade of Margaret Thatcher's premiership was extremely ambitious. It aimed to reconstruct social relations, weakening ties to a set of institutions (such as trade unions, local authorities and public sector agencies) which had flourished in the social democratic era after the Second World War, and strengthening the sense of responsibility of individuals and families for providing their own income and welfare. In the first half of the decade, this was attempted through economic policies (monetarism, the restraint of trade union power, the deregulation of the labour market, the privatisation of public utilities, etc.), and through ideological persuasion. In the second half, the government restructured all social service agencies according to new principles, and redefined their tasks. The enormous volume of new legislation (over 50 Acts affecting local authorities alone) and the complexity of the task masked the essentially simple theoretical basis of all this activity.

This lies in Hayek's (1973) distinction between society as spontaneous order and as constructed, rational order. Margaret Thatcher's favourite intellectual considered that the most reliable and enduring social institutions were those that had adapted through evolutionary trial-and-error processes, not created by planning and state design. In social interaction, our decisions are co-ordinated with those of others through those institutions which allow individuals to accommodate to each other in mutually beneficial ways. Markets and families have adapted successfully to the more diverse and complex purposes now pursued by individuals, and are able to provide order and prosperity without detailed knowledge of the projects of others (which is in any case unattainable). According to this view, when people align their practices to these two institutions (markets and families) they are unconsciously and unintentionally benefiting society as a whole, without having to be directed by government.

The Thatcher regime's policies were not so much directed against collectivist socialism, as against any attempt to plan society or co-ordinate complex human activity by rational design. This explains why Thatcher was as opposed to the essentially Christian Democratic (i.e. continental conservative) institutions of the European Community as to the British welfare state. Following Hayek (1960; 1976), this analysis insists that no planner could possibly have the knowledge to organise and direct the dispersed, local and practical activities that make up a society, and that the attempt to do so (whether in the name of economic efficiency or social justice) is counterproductive. Thus the search for a rationally constructed order is misguided: government should seek instead to frame universal

rules, providing a framework of laws within which individuals and agencies can pursue their various purposes (Hayek, 1967). All this has important implications for family policy. First, it implies that families – as part of the spontaneous order – are better at planning and organising their own lives than the state could possibly be at providing for their welfare. Hence collective responsibility should be kept as narrow as possible, and family responsibility extended as widely as possible. Families are a 'natural' unit, based on instinct and sympathy. They form, organise and care for each other without official sanction, and should be encouraged to do these things for themselves across the broad range of their needs.

Second, in this view families are 'naturally' private, independent and exclusive. They shun intervention by state officials, even when this is well-meant. Ferdinand Mount (1983, p.174), in his influential book, wrote of such professional visits:

> what is always affronting, offensive and distressing is the simple fact of their intrusion into our private space. Our feelings are mixed even in the case of the most helpful of all public visitors [Health Visitors] . . . The Visitor – grim symbolic title – remains an intruder . . . In all the revolts against big government and high taxes . . . resentment has played its part . . . the feeling that the state is intruding into private space more and more and ought to be stopped is growing. The Visitor is being made to feel unwelcome. His or her claim to moral superiority is being disputed.

The critique of collectivism (symbolised by the centrally-planned socialism of the Soviet Union) was that it tried to substitute rational design for the spontaneous order of families and markets. The agenda of the Thatcher years was to allow households the greatest possible freedom to accumulate property, but to make members responsible for each other's needs. Collective provision may be needed where families fail to provide for themselves, but it should be carefully targeted so as to avoid weakening the independence and self-reliance of the family, or intruding into its sphere.

It follows from all this that the aim of social policy should be to distinguish families' from the state's responsibilities, strengthen the privacy and independence of families, and define the limited role of the state quite precisely. This is to encourage families to provide for themselves by saving, insurance, etc., and by supplying unpaid care: as has often been pointed out, 'family' here is a term that cloaks the expectation that women will perform this role (see Baldwin and Twigg in MacLean and Groves, 1991). In order to deny those that might be tempted to transfer the costs associated with dependence (childhood, illness, disability, old age) onto the state the opportunity to do so, benefits and services should be:

1 Targeted so as to exclude those who can afford to buy them

2   Assessed so as to meet needs precisely, rather than provided in a generalised way to a wider community
3   Businesslike, so as to eliminate waste and inefficiency, and thus keep down the high taxes that penalise prudence and self-sufficiency.

All these principles are clearly recognisable in the community care legislation, with its emphasis on assessment for individualised packages of care, to be purchased by care managers, working in a mixed economy of local services. The aim of enabling maximum 'independence' for those who need care means independence of public agencies: the assumptions behind policy are that elderly and disabled people prefer to live in their own homes, and that they will buy their own services, or have them bought for them if they lack the means, in such a way as to supplement family care.

In other areas of social policy, family responsibility has been enforced. This is clearest in the field of social security, where benefits for 16- and 17-year-olds have been withdrawn, unemployed claimants have been required to demonstrate their willingness to take insecure low-paid work, and the maintenance payments of absent parents have been more strictly enforced.

The paradox of this policy orientation is that its overstated contrast between spontaneous and constructed order becomes a kind of self-fulfilling prophecy. The attempt to define separate spheres of responsibility for the family and the state requires public agencies to be far more regulative and restrictive in their practices than would be necessary under a more inclusive, universalist regime. Since the primary task is to avoid intruding into the territory of family responsibility, or usurping its self-sufficiency, practice tends to become formal, rule-bound and arm's-length. The so-called 'enabling authority' is primarily concerned with assessing, enforcing and purchasing, and thus emphasises its bureaucratic and official features. At the same time, the 'spontaneous' care given by families becomes largely invisible – it is relegated to the private sphere, with only 'family failure' (including a rising number of desperate acts, such as carers abandoning old people, or parents rejecting unemployed teenagers) being recognised in the public sphere, and triggering intervention.

The Children Act 1989 cannot readily be analysed in terms of these features. A number of scholars (David in MacLean and Groves, 1991; Parton, 1991) have tried to interpret it as following the same principles, but I do not find their accounts convincing on this point. Clearly the Act has to be implemented at a local level, and in a public sector culture which has been heavily influenced by the government's other social legislation. Even so, it is far easier to see the continuity between the themes of the Short Report (Social Services Select Committee, 1984), the government-commissioned research reports on child care issues (Packman et al., 1986; Millham et al., 1986), the Interdepartmental Committee Review of Child

Care Law (DHSS, 1988), the 1987 White Paper (DHSS, 1987), and the Act, than it is to recognise the features which are common to the rest of the Thatcher regime's programme. In particular:

1 There is almost nothing in the Act, regulations or guidance about markets, value for taxpayers' money, purchasers and providers, or packages of care. Thus, although the 'contract culture' may well influence those services which are located in the same organisational system as community care provision, the Act does not push services for children and their families in this direction.

2 Far from narrowing the state's sphere, Part III of the Act widens it, for instance in relation to holiday and after-school care, provision of accommodation for homeless 16- and 17-year-olds, and continuing responsibility for young people leaving care at 18.

3 Instead of defining the respective responsibilities of the family and the state, and distinguishing more sharply between them, the Act emphasises shared responsibilities over children in need, and partnership between parents and the public agency. While it is certainly true that the Act is concerned to specify that birth parents are responsible for their children, this definition does not of itself limit the scope for help from the local authority. Rather, it limits the authority's power to exclude parents from decisions about children.

4 The Act more clearly delineates the scope and purposes of court orders, and promotes voluntary agreements where possible in issues over the care of children in need.

It seems, therefore, that the Act encourages a rather different kind of relationship between the state and the families of children in need than the one promoted by the rest of the social policy legislation of this period. In emphasising that local authorities should, where possible, reach agreements with parents over services for families, and by encouraging the sharing of care, it enables a style of practice which is informal and negotiated, rather than formal and regulatory. The emphasis is on partnership between the public agency itself and such families, rather than the purchasing of services from voluntary organisations and commercial providers. Why should there be this important inconsistency between the Children Act and other legislation of the Thatcher years?

Child care policy, 1975–88

One reason for this difference can be traced to the policy failures of the period leading up to the new legislation. Following the Maria Colwell

scandal and the subsequent child abuse tragedies and inquiries, policy took a turn which anticipated the Conservative approach in many ways. The Maria Colwell case coincided with the beginnings of cutbacks in local authority spending, and the attempt to focus child care expenditure more effectively. The issue of child abuse provoked an attempt to set up rules, procedures and practices which would better protect children, and to use the courts as the main forum for decision-making in such cases (Parton and Martin, 1989).

This shift towards legalism encouraged practitioners to rely on technical expertise in identifying children at risk and removing them from their parents, and to define public care in terms of the need to protect such children from danger within their families. Research exposed the weaknesses in this approach, and these criticisms were underlined in the Cleveland Report (Secretary of State for Social Services, 1988), where the legalistic and procedural methods of social services staff were criticised. Thus the period leading up to the passing of the Children Act was one in which the overall principle of other legislation – a stronger distinction between the spheres of the state and the family, and the task of identifying situations in which families had 'failed' – was by then discredited. There was already a new intellectual culture among the relevant civil servants and an influential policy-making community which moved in the opposite direction from that of the other government legislation.

This new intellectual culture must also be seen as something of a reaction against the strongest policy lobby of the late 1970s and early 1980s, the Permanence Movement. Deriving much of its inspiration from the United States, this set of ideas about child care practice put strong emphasis on distinguishing between children needing permanent placement outside their birth families (and strongly favoured adoption for such children as the most secure form of placement), and children who could quickly be 'rehabilitated' with their parents after a short admission to public care (Fahlberg, 1981). The policy drive of this period was emphatically towards implementing this distinction, with important consequences for the kinds of provision for care available in the public sector, and the kinds of expertise cultivated by aspiring professional staff. The new focus on quick and accurate assessment and planning, and on achieving the legal authority to carry out plans through court orders, moulded the careers of staff, giving status to a kind of expertise in assessment and procedural competence, at the expense of more informal negotiation skills.

Of course, this set of principles, for all its intellectual dominance in that period, never achieved the goals – in terms of policy and practice – to which its strongest advocates aspired. However, its identifiable priorities made it vulnerable to criticism when researchers began to investigate the field of child care decision-making during this period (DHSS, 1985). The

following features of practice in the early 1980s were identified and questioned by the research studies published in the middle of the decade:

1 A tendency to see the aim of 'preventive' work with families as being to keep children out of public care, and with their birth families. This led to a reluctance to arrange voluntary admissions to local authority facilities, and the perception of the public system of child care as a 'last resort'. It implied that parents should be required to care for their children with little support even when they were requesting assistance – a kind of enforced responsibility (Packman et al., 1986).
2 Increased use of court orders (especially place of safety orders) as a route into the public child care system. Even when this was quickly followed by 'rehabilitation', researchers pointed to the adverse effects of these methods, with their stigmatising implications of public failure by parents, and tendency to polarise family and official views of the issues (Packman et al., 1986). The emphasis on court decisions in child care matters promoted an adversarial, coercive practice, which was strongly criticised in the Cleveland Report as unsuited to the complex and difficult relational problems in child protection cases: children's own wishes and feelings were not sensitively handled.
3 The goal of legal and administrative control over decisions by professionals tended to exclude families, disempower already disadvantaged parents, and reduce the scope for co-operation and sharing. The research finding that a large proportion of children returned to their families of origin on leaving care led to criticisms of practices which severed or weakened links with families during placements (Millham et al., 1986).
4 Research suggested that security and the sense of permanence were at least as likely to be promoted by well-planned agreements for sharing responsibility between birth parents and carers as by adversarial action to exclude parents from care arrangements, and to prevent contacts (Thoburn, 1989).
5 Research on placements found that the dualism of the Permanence Movement's principles was far too simplistic. While many admissions of children were for family crises (often surrounding material problems like homelessness) and were therefore appropriately organised on a voluntary basis, others involved longer-term relational problems (Rowe et al., 1989). Child care decisions could not be categorised as starkly as the popularised versions of this orthodoxy seemed to argue.

The new analysis that emerged in the mid-1980s saw statutory child protection as a more limited part of the child care field, and its methods as more appropriately confined to cases where parents were identifiably

dangerous and unco-operative. New principles were developed under which a more negotiated style of work, seeking to maximise areas of agreement and shared responsibility, and offering practical support to families, was seen as much more effective for the great proportion of child care work. Thus the directions in which government ideology might have pushed policy were already foreclosed by the recent history of developments in this field.

Public and private law

The other important factor influencing the shape of the Children Act was the priority given to bringing together public and private law about children. This was seen as desirable, given the increasing volume of issues arising through divorce, and the considerable overlap between these matters and public child care decisions (DHSS, 1985). It was recognised that a single definition of parental responsibility could greatly clarify the common ground between these decisions about children, and avoid inconsistencies between the way in which courts dealt with divorcing parents, and with families who had dealings with local authority services.

If the tendency of social work policy and practice in the previous period was to polarise the spheres of the family and the state, the trends in private law disputes were in the opposite direction. Both research (Wallerstein and Kelly, 1980; Murch, 1980) and practice innovations (such as conciliation agencies) pointed towards the benefits of agreements and shared responsibilities, and the dangers of contests and exclusionary orders, for children. The goal of consistency between public and private law thus pointed towards an inclusive view of parental responsibility, one which emphasised the enduring nature of the rights, duties and powers associated with parenthood, and the necessity to exercise these by co-operation and agreement, even where other issues had led to irreconcilable differences between partners. In reaching its definitions of parental responsibility, and setting the terms for residence and contact for children whose parents divorced, the Act therefore moved public child care law in the direction of partnership and shared care, and away from exclusivity and polarisation between the family and the state.

It could also be argued that the stark realities of life for families with children in 1980s Britain pushed policy and practice in the same direction. The 'natural and spontaneous' order of the family and the market that underpins government social policy is highly idealised. The real world of families with children is one which has experienced a rapid economic deterioration in relative terms. Within the growing sector of the population

living in poverty, this group has emerged as the largest component. One in three marriages end in divorce, with a consequent growth in both single-parent and reconstituted families. Hence the pieties of government ideology bear little relation to the experiences of a large proportion of families.

If children are to achieve secure identities and a sound basis for adult relationships within this fragmented pattern of social relations, they can only do so through fairly complex processes of identification and support, sustained by networks of friends, extended family kin, step-parents, teachers and so on. If this is so for the wider sphere governed by private law, it must also be reflected in law, policy and practice in the sphere of public child care. It makes sense for the law and professional practice to encourage parents to exercise as much responsibility as they beneficially can, and to supplement their care by as many other positive influences as possible. Conversely, it makes little or no sense to try to force decisions into a mould in which parental responsibility is either total and exclusive, or removed altogether. The changes reflected in the Children Act mirror those in wider society, and bring this sphere of professional practice more closely in line with developments in divorce court welfare work.

What (if anything) is special about adoption?

If my analysis is accepted up to this point, it remains for me to try to explain why law, policy and practice in the field of adoption have for the most part been insulated from these changes, and remain largely in the paradigm of the earlier period, as concerned with contested issues of exclusion. This part of the chapter is necessarily more speculative: whether it is convincing must be judged partly by reference to the other chapters in this book.

Clearly, adoption has a special status within the new legislation. Parental responsibility can, according to the Children Act, only be extinguished by death or an adoption order. Thus adoption is treated as having a legal status that is different from any other power or order. It has a special significance, for this reason, for birth families, because it alone can exclude them from decisions about and influences upon their children; it can also exclude other kin from these matters.

From my argument above, it might be expected that adoption orders would have peaked in the period when the Permanence Movement was most dominant, the early 1980s. In fact, adoption orders are still rising, at a time when other kinds of public law orders about children (emergency protection orders and care orders) are showing a marked fall, following the

Children Act. Adoption as a reason for leaving care has increased steadily since the 1960s, and now stands at about 6 per cent of children leaving care (DoH, 1992).

There are a number of possible reasons for this trend. One is that the proportion of younger (pre-school) children in care is rising again, after a decline in the later 1980s. Such children are seen as particularly appropriate for adoption orders, especially where there has been abuse of one child in a family containing a number of children. Another factor is that a higher proportion of black children in care, including children of mixed ethnic origin, are adopted than white children: this may also be influencing the statistics.

Whatever the explanation, this tendency is significant. It means that there is an enclave of child care decision-making that continues to hold much potential for contested, adversarial processes in which families' and public officials' views are polarised through orders which are exclusive, and which carry heavy stigma. The fact that orders which extinguish parental responsibility are continuing to rise should be of concern for those who consider that compulsory, adversarial methods should be minimised. Adoption represents a still-expanding, though perhaps residual, sector of child care policy and practice that reflects older orthodoxies.

The fact that these processes may disproportionately concern black children should also cause concern. In the past, the adoption of black children by (predominantly better-off) white parents was strongly challenged by black staff, and led to changes in policy. But an important issue remains, even where transracial adoptions are no longer so readily approved. Exclusive adoption as a legal procedure is less likely to be endorsed by black birth parents than white (Ryburn, 1992), as legal adoption is not a family form that is part of Caribbean or African culture. The growth of adoption orders for black children is therefore an important unresolved issue.

The other chapters in this book explore the details of contested adoptions more fully than this chapter attempts. However, there appear to be some links between the three elements of my analysis – the ideological basis of Conservative social policy, the changes introduced in the Children Act 1989, and the continued growth in adoption orders. Where there is greatest tension between ideals of family life and the messy, fragmented, impoverished world of children in need, the appeal of adoption is strongest. Paradoxically, although adoption is the most artificial, legally constructed family form (the least spontaneous, and hence the form least like the Hayekian version of family life it would be possible to imagine), it is perhaps the one most likely to attract the idealisations and fantasies that government social policy promotes.

As the law stands – and even as it will largely remain if the changes

currently being canvassed are introduced – the approach to practice which is enabled (if not encouraged) is to identify the feature of birth parents' care which makes them uniquely unsuitable, and the features of prospective adopters' potential which make them especially promising, and to argue for the total substitution of the former by the latter through the order of a court. Thus adoption is potentially set up as adversarial, and as counterposing the avoidable harm children will suffer in their families of origin with the potential gain of such a placement. There may well be situations where these two stark alternatives are the only ones available, but it is a matter for concern if the law and policy offer this option too readily to practitioners. At a time when so many official and cultural influences idealise the 'successful' family, and scapegoat family failure, a whole culture of practice could develop around adoption which is at odds with the central – partnership-based – thrust of the Children Act. It could continue to attract those professionals who prefer the status-giving simplicities of the past age of child care decision-making to the messy negotiations that make up everyday work with disadvantaged families.

What would be dangerous about such a development would be the fantasy element in it. Research indicates that adoptive families are as prone to the insecurities and calamities of modern life as any other families. There is no clear-cut group of 'wonderpeople' waiting to be identified who will give children in need the total experience of love and security that all child care workers wish. Adoption work, like other child care work, is approximate and uncertain, and can almost certainly benefit from the kind of flexibility and inclusiveness that characterises the rest of this field. Thus – for instance – practice which aims to include natural grandparents in the lives of children placed for adoption seems likely to be generally beneficial.

The partnership approach to child care and child protection is an ambitious and difficult one. The Children Act sets an agenda which is quite different from the policy direction of the other social services: it aims to bridge the growing division in living standards and cultures between families in need and wider society by a process of negotiated exchanges, co-operatively agreed. In rejecting the rule-bound formalism of the other legislation, this development is required to make its values and practices explicit, and to change the attitudes and methods used by professionals in the previous period.

All this may ask too much for under-resourced practitioners, working under enormous pressure with an increasingly deprived and alienated group of parents. The danger is that the existence of a residual, adversarial sector of court-based practice will increasingly offer an alternative to the partnership approach. The dualism rejected in the Children Act could, as it were, return through the back door. Parental responsibility could be interpreted as requiring families to care for their children without support

se<u>rvices from the</u> state and, if they fail to do so, as requiring <u>professionals</u>
to <u>rescue their children</u> and find them permanent substitute placements. In
order for the spirit of the 1989 Act to survive in a hostile social policy
climate, the issues raised by contested adoptions will have to continue to
be debated.

References

Baldwin, S. and Twigg, J. (1991), 'Women and Community Care: Reflections on a
    Debate', in MacLean, M. and Groves, D. [eds], *Women's Issues in Social Policy*,
    London: Routledge and Kegan Paul.
David, M. (1991), 'Putting on an Act for the Children?', in MacLean, M. and
    Groves, D. [eds], *Women's Issues in Social Policy*, London: Routledge and Kegan
    Paul.
Department of Health (1992), *Child Care Statistics*, London: HMSO.
DHSS (1985), *Social Work Decisions in Child Care: Recent Research Findings and Their
    Implications*, London: HMSO.
DHSS White Paper (1987), *The Law on Child Care and Family Services*, Cmnd. 62,
    London: HMSO.
DHSS (1988), *Review of Child Care Law: Report of an Interdepartmental Working Party*,
    London: HMSO.
Fahlberg, V. (1981), *Helping Children When They Must Move*, London: BAAF.
Hayek, F. (1960), *The Constitution of Liberty*, London: Routledge and Kegan Paul.
Hayek, F. (1967), *Studies in Philosophy, Politics and Economics*, London: Routledge
    and Kegan Paul.
Hayek, F. (1973), *Rules and Order*, London: Routledge and Kegan Paul.
Hayek, F. (1976), *The Mirage of Social Justice*, London: Routledge and Kegan Paul.
Millham, S., Bullock, R., Hosie, K. and Haak, M. (1986), *Lost in Care: The Problems of
    Maintaining Links between Children in Care and their Families*, Aldershot: Gower.
Mount, F. (1983), *The Subversive Family*, Harmondsworth: Penguin.
Murch, M. (1980), *Justice and Welfare in Divorce*, London: Sweet and Maxwell.
Packman, J., Randall, J. and Jacques, N. (1986), *Who Needs Care? Social Work
    Decisions about Children*, Oxford: Blackwell.
Parton, N. (1991), *Governing the Family: Child Care, Child Protection and the State*,
    London: Macmillan.
Parton, N. and Martin, N. (1989), 'Public Inquiries, Legalism and Child Care in
    Britain', *International Journal of Law and the Family*, 3(1), 21–39.
Rowe, J., Hundleby, M. and Garnett, L. (1989), *Child Care Now: A Survey of
    Placement Patterns*, London: BAAF.
Ryburn, M. (1992), *Adoption in the 1990s: Identity and Openness*, Birmingham:
    Leamington Press.
Secretary of State for Social Services (1988), *Report of the Inquiry into Child Abuse in
    Cleveland*, Cmnd. 412, London: HMSO.
Social Services Select Committee (HC 360) (1984), *Children in Care*, London: HMSO.
Thoburn, J. (1989), *Success and Failure in Permanent Placement*, Aldershot: Avebury.
Wallerstein, J. and Kelly, J. (1980), *Surviving the Breakup: How Children and Parents
    Cope with Divorce*, New York: Grant MacIntyre.

3 Contested proceedings: justice and the law

Mary Ryan

Introduction

This chapter analyses justice and injustice in the ways adoption law presently works, and may work in the future, and discusses the reasons why people contest adoption proceedings.

Why do people contest adoption proceedings?

The extensive experience of advocacy groups such as the Family Rights Group, which deals with over 350 inquiries a year in relation to contested adoption situations, indicates that there are four common reasons why people withhold consent to adoption. These reasons are important for they offer us the clearest indicators of perceived injustices in the law. The four principal explanations for the contesting of adoption orders are as follows:

1   The effect of adoption: complete legal severance
    Parents withhold consent simply because the effect of adoption, complete legal severance from their child, is something they cannot consent to, often because they worry that in later life their child will think they were rejecting them. This is despite the fact that, in many cases, the parents agree that the child cannot return to live with them.
2   Wanting still to care for their child
    Parents withhold consent because they would like their child to return to live with them, or alternatively to live with relatives or friends in the extended family, but the local authority has refused to agree to this.

3   **Wanting continuing contact**
    Parents withhold consent because they wish to have continuing contact
    with their child, or they would like their child to remain in contact with
    relatives or friends. Where the prospective adopters do not agree to this
    or the local authority is opposed to continuing contact, the parents
    know that a condition of contact, or a contact order, will not be attached
    to the adoption order and they see no alternative but to oppose it.
4   **A sense of injustice**
    Parents withhold consent to adoption because they believe, often
    correctly, they have been given inadequate support and services in the
    past, and treated unjustly.

Elizabeth Lawson, in chapter 4, looks at some of the procedural changes
that might lead to a reduction in the number of contested adoption
hearings, but what of the law itself? There are several aspects of the current
legislation which are likely almost automatically to create contested orders
in some circumstances. Each of the four categories of explanation listed
above for the opposing of orders can be related to aspects of injustice in
this legislation. It is possible that the Adoption Law Review proposals
(DoH, 1992) and resulting White Paper, *Adoption: The Future* (DoH, 1993),
may make a difference but, as we shall see, there are a number of significant omissions.

The effect of adoption: complete legal severance

The legal effect of an adoption order or a freeing order is to extinguish
entirely any parental responsibilities that existed before the granting of an
order and to transfer these in their entirety to the new parents. It is the fact
that legally the former life of an adopted child is entirely extinguished that
provokes many birth relatives to oppose adoption.
    The Adoption Law Review Consultation Document stated that:

> The fundamental purpose of adoption is to secure a permanent home for a child
> by transferring the child, for virtually all purposes, from the birth family to a
> new adoptive family and severing the legal links with the first. We propose that
> adoption should continue to have this effect (para 3.1).

The Review recommends that adoption should continue to be distinguished
from other orders about where a child should live, and specifically states:
'The current legal effects of adoption should by and large be retained' (para
3.5).
    This recommendation that adoption should continue to exist in its
current form, and the government's belief expressed in the White Paper
that the basic structure is sound, is disappointing. The enforced 'ampu-

tation' of the family of origin in legal terms, in addition to losing the child in physical terms, is something which families find particularly distressing.

Recognising that there are cases where children need to be cared for on a long-term basis by a new family, and, in some of those cases, that an order must be permanent and irrevocable, does not lead logically to the conclusion that such children have to lose their legal relationship with their families of origin in order for permanence to be established.

Legal status and permanence The overview of research issued with the first series of Adoption Law Review consultation papers (DoH, 1990) underlines that it is not the legal status of the child which is important in securing permanence, but rather a sense of permanence felt by the child and the new family. In addition, adoptions do break down despite the existence of an irrevocable court order, and other scenarios, such as the separation of the adoptive parents or the death of either or both of them, may complicate the adoption placement or cause disruption. Furthermore, the Review acknowledges (para 31.3) the importance of openness and continuing links for adopted children. Where there is an open adoption, adopters – particularly those with older children – will find it far easier to explain the child's history if legal severance has not taken place. Finally, it should be noted that legal severance contradicts a key principle of the Children Act – that of continuing parental responsibility.

Retention of parental responsibility A more just form of adoption order would change the nature and effect of adoption so that a permanent irrevocable legal relationship was created with the adopted family, without the severance of the legal ties with the family of origin. This would enable an adopted child to acquire a new family in legal terms, without having to lose their legal relationship with their family of origin. It would be achieved by allowing the parental responsibility of the parents of origin to continue after the adoption order has been made, in the same way that it does for other orders, except for freeing.

The Children Act 1989 provides mechanisms for limiting the exercise of parental responsibility, such as residence orders, prohibitive steps orders and the provisions of section 33(3), which allow a local authority to limit the exercise of parental responsibility when a child is in care. There is also provision in section 91(14) for courts to restrict applications for certain orders, such as contact orders, that would otherwise have existed as of right.

A mechanism similar to that which exists under the Children Act should be introduced so that the court would have the ability to restrict the right of parents of origin to exercise parental responsibility, where this was considered necessary in order to safeguard and promote the welfare of the

child. Thus the adopters would gain parental responsibility and exercise it either *alongside* the parents of origin, where appropriate, or *exclusively*, where this had been ordered by the court. It is important to remember that there are established cases of open adoption where adopters and parents of origin have shown themselves capable of consulting with each other and sharing responsibility for the child. Such an arrangement may well be the most appropriate where openness and contact are an integral part of the placement.

Legal status and inheritance   Another possibility, which would help to mitigate the effects of adoption if the current legal effects were retained, is to amend section 39(1–2) of the Adoption Act 1976. That section declares, in relation to the status of the adopted child, that:

> An adopted child shall be treated in law as if he were . . . the child of the (adopters') marriage . . . (and) not the child of any person other than the adopters.

This provision exists solely so that adopted children can inherit from their adoptive relatives under the intestacy rules. The section is misleading and must be confusing to children who are adopted and to their families. It does not seem right that the status of an adopted child should be framed around the rules relating to intestacy. Instead, property and inheritance law should be amended to deal with the specific rights of an adopted child, and adoption legislation should be amended to show that an adopted child becomes part of the adopted family from the date of the adoption order and not before.

Welfare checklist   The only proposals in the Adoption Law Review dealing with the issue of the legal effect of adoption are that the welfare checklist, which applies to court proceedings under the Children Act, should also apply to adoption proceedings and that, in addition, the court should be required to look at the 'likely effect on the child's adult life of any change in his legal status'. While this is a helpful addition to the welfare checklist in relation to adoption proceedings, it does not address the key problem of the distress caused to families by the effect of legal severance.

Wanting still to care for their child

The development of the 'permanency' philosophy in this country has led to adoption being placed at the top of a hierarchy of orders. Adoption is seen as *the* way to secure permanence. There are many birth relatives who feel that the blinkered focus on adoption ignores the fact that with the right help children could return to their parents or be placed within the

extended family, or live long term in another family as a foster child or under a residence order.)

Effect of a hierarchy of orders   The development of a hierarchy of orders has led to social workers and other child care professionals focusing exclusively on getting children adopted rather than considering all possible options. As research shows, however (see for example Lahti, 1982; Thoburn et al., 1986; Thoburn, 1989; Trent, 1989; Fratter et al., 1991), there are many different arrangements that can provide permanence for children. The focus on adoption as *the* way to secure permanence is compounded by the lamentable lack of skills and resources applied to the work of returning children to their homes or to their extended families. Despite the requirements in the Children Act that local authorities should first look to the extended family for a placement for children before looking to stranger carers, the experience of relatives and friends is often that they are overlooked or marginalised, or have their views and suggestions on placement ignored.)

An addition should be made to the welfare checklist to require the court to consider whether all possibilities of placement within the wider family have been explored in accordance with section 23(6) of the Children Act 1989. The court should only make an adoption order if it is satisfied that there are no such possibilities for placement within the wider family and are not likely to be any in the foreseeable future. Research shows that placements within the wider family are likely to be more successful than stranger placements, and it is important that there should be a court check on compliance with that duty, to ensure that all such placements are fully explored before a long-term placement with a stranger family is pursued.

While the White Paper reiterates the key principles of the Children Act 1989, it does not provide detail of how 'the importance of keeping children in their birth families whenever possible and of supporting them if necessary' (para 3.14) would operate in adoption cases.

Implications for black children   The place of adoption at the top of a hierarchy of orders to secure permanence has particular implications for black children and children from other minority ethnic groups. The legal effect of adoption and the frequently exclusive nature of the order are in conflict with cultures and child-rearing practice which are not in the white Euro/American tradition. This can make it difficult to recruit adopters for black children and other children from minority ethnic groups. People from black and other minority ethnic groups may well be prepared to be foster carers, possibly with a view to obtaining a residence order in the future. Such placements are often able to offer children security, permanence and, most importantly, a sense of identity, yet they are seen

as a 'second best' to adoption. (See also chapter 9, 'Issues of attachment, separation and identity in contested adoptions'.)

Additions to the welfare checklist to address issues of race and culture and returning children to the wider family should be made in adoption legislation. This would help to ensure that the courts give proper consideration to all the alternatives available for children other than adoption. Thus the checklist should include a requirement for courts to have regard to the child's racial origin, cultural and linguistic background, and religious persuasion when deciding an adoption case. In view of the large numbers of black and mixed-race children placed with substitute families on a long-term basis, it is important that practice in the courts and in agencies needs to be led by legislaton to ensure that this important factor is not overlooked. It will also ensure that the courts will be checking on whether the requirements contained in section 22 of the Children Act 1989 in relation to race, culture, language and religion have been complied with.

The White Paper promised to introduce a 'broad requirement' to consider ethnicity and culture in matching children and parents (para 4.31), in line with the Children Act, but goes on to stress that ethnicity and culture are 'amongst the issues to be considered and they should not necessarily be more influential than any other' (para 4.32). Clearly, much will be left to the judgment of those conducting assessments.

Changes to the hierarchy of orders   The only way that families who feel that they have been ignored as a potential resource for their children are likely to feel differently is if there is an effective challenge in law to the idea of a hierarchy of orders. The Adoption Law Review recognises the existence of this hierarchy: 'adoption is too often regarded as the only way of securing permanence' (para 6.3). The Review itself stresses that permanence for children can be achieved in a number of different ways:

> It is also important that adoption is not seen as the only or best means of providing a child with a permanent home. Permanence can only be achieved in a number of ways: for instance working with the child's family to enable the child's return home, care by other relatives, or other long term foster care (para 6.1).

It points out that in many cases a residence order:

> will generally provide the necessary permanence for the family concerned, as once a child is settled the courts are reluctant to disturb the status quo and are most unlikely to discharge the order in favour of another party (para 6.3).

Inter vivos guardianship orders   The Review's proposals for challenging the hierarchy of orders are first, to give the court a duty to consider all the alternative orders and the full range of powers available under the Children Act 1989 and under adoption legislation (para 6.3 and para 7.5),

and also to make residence orders more attractive where it is intended that they should be permanent orders by introducing something called an 'inter vivos guardianship order' (paras 6.4–6.5).

The advantage of this new order would be that it would provide the child and the family with a greater sense of permanence but would not legally sever the child from the family of origin. Such an alternative order is referred to as a guardianship order in the White Paper. Guardianship already exists as a legal concept, currently under section 5 of the Children Act 1989. It is also a concept which is generally familiar to most people. Referring to someone as 'my guardian' is far less strange than referring to 'the person who has a residence order in relation to me'. These orders, as proposed in the Adoption Law Review, would last until the child was 18 as opposed to residence orders which generally last only until the child is 16.

The proposals for the introduction of inter vivos guardianship, whether adoption remains in its present form or not, are to be welcomed. Guardianship does not carry with it any stigma, is a perfectly logical explanation of the status of the substitute carer and has the important ingredient of irrevocability, without cutting out the family of origin completely.

It is unlikely, however, that inter vivos guardianship will be promoted as a realistic alternative to adoption (unless the adopters/carers request it themselves) because so many practitioners, and indeed so many members of the judiciary, are currently committed to adoption as the best and only way of achieving permanence with a new family. Inter vivos guardianship would have a much better chance of becoming a real alternative to adoption if it were possible to make the order last for life and not just until the child is 18, so that the extent of commitment required from the new family, and the degree of permanence, is matched by the order. The proposed age limit of 18 sits oddly with the government's commitment in the White Paper to 'consider the child's welfare into adulthood' (para 4.2).

An additional way of ensuring that alternatives to adoption are properly considered by practitioners and the court woud be to require the court, when it is considering making an adoption order, not to make such an order unless it is satisfied that doing so would be significantly better for the child's welfare than making an order for an inter vivos guardianship. Thus, legislation would raise a presumption in favour of inter vivos guardianship over adoption by modifying the 'no order principle', currently in section 1(5) of the Children Act 1989, which the Adoption Law Review suggests should become part of adoption legislation.

Wanting continuing contact

The absence of any presumption in favour of continuing contact in adoption probably does more than anything else to lead original families

to contest adoption orders in the courts. The research on adoption points very clearly to the benefits of contact (see for example Ryburn, 1992a).

Proposals for change   The Adoption Law Review accepts the research findings on the importance, for children living permanently away from home, of information about their history and the maintenance of continuing links between those children and their families and friends.

The Consultation Document expressed somewhat ambivalent views about continuing contact, but stresses that it is an issue which should be considered, and that courts should have the power to make a contact order together with an adoption order. It also emphasises that the issue of continuing links should be something addressed in the welfare checklist, as follows:

> The relationships which the child has with his parents, his siblings, other relatives and any other relevant persons, the value to the child of them continuing, and the likelihood of them continuing if the order is or is not made (para 7.6).

The White Paper would appear to back-track on contact: 'the Government considers that once an adoption order is made, the most important objective is to support the new family relationship' (para 4.14).

Families' experiences of openness   While there is considerable talk about open adoptions, the experience of families is that continuing contact is not viewed enthusiastically, or even positively, either by social workers or by the courts. Family members have great difficulty in persuading agencies and/or prospective adopters to agree to the most limited forms of contact such as sending occasional photographs or exchanging written information. Case reviews indicate that some judges seem to be implacably opposed to continuing contact, while others are more in favour of it, but there is no consistency of approach.

The reasons for these professional attitudes are interconnected. Social workers do seem often to hold the view, though there is no research evidence to support it, that continuing contact is not of benefit to children, that prospective open adopters cannot be found and that children or their adopters will be unsettled by contact. In addition, there is a widely held view that courts will not make an adoption order if contact is continuing. Certainly judges, perhaps because they have listened so frequently and for so long to social work and psychiatric opinion that contact is unsettling and therefore bad for children, do seem, as Elizabeth Lawson indicates in chapter 4, to find the idea of adoption with continuing contact particularly difficult.

It is difficult to see how professionals' attitudes will change when the White Paper states that contact 'should generally' be allowed where the adopters consent, but 'the most important objective is to support the new family relationship' (paras 4.14–4.15). A similar indication that contact is not to be encouraged is apparent from *Placement for Adoption*, the consultation paper on placement orders published after the White Paper, which states that when a court has decided in favour of an adoption plan:

> it should grant other orders only when it considers these would increase the chances of a future adoption being successful. A contact order, for example, should only be made when a court believes such contact would help rather than hinder the child to settle permanently with a potential new family (para 4.30).

Despite the Review's recognition of the research findings on the importance of continuing links and its proposals to ensure that contact is an issue which is considered, there is a danger that contact after adoption will always be in the most minimal form, such as an exchange of written information or photographs, or the occasional and very infrequent visit.

Changes in law   The experience of past changes to legislation in relation to contact between children in care and their families and friends (see for example Millham et al., 1989) has indicated clearly that this is an area where change in attitude and practice needs to be led and encouraged by legislative change, rather than by relying on guidance and developments in practice. In addition to the Adoption Law Review recommendations that contact orders be available when an adoption order is being made, a much stronger addition to the welfare checklist would ensure that practitioners and the courts take the issue of contact seriously. This could take the form of a requirement that the court make orders which enable the child's relationships with her or his family of origin, which are important to her or him, to continue *unless* the court is satisfied that such an order is not necessary and/or that it would be detrimental to the child's welfare.

In addition, regulations and guidance should encourage agencies to recruit long-term carers who are in favour of openness. They should require pre- and post-adoption services to disseminate research on why maintenance of links is important and to provide support and conciliation for adoptive families of origin where contact is continuing.

A sense of injustice

As research by Ryburn (1992b) and the chapter in this book by a grandparent indicate, many are left with a burning sense of injustice about how they have been treated in relation to their children. It seemed briefly,

as Elizabeth Lawson writes, that court agreement that such injustice existed might become a legitimate ground for parents not to consent to adoption. As she states, however, this was one of a number of arguments advanced on behalf of parents which have only 'glimmered fitfully before being put out'. The sense of grievance that birth relatives bear centres on a number of different but related issues.

Lack of adequate consultation   Although the Adoption Agencies Regulations require agencies to consult with families of origin as well as prospective adopters and children, this is frequently done in a very cursory way, if at all, in contested proceedings. The proposals in the Adoption Law Review that legislation similar to sections 22(4) and (5) of the Children Act 1989 be incorporated in adoption legislation and the emphasis upon soliciting the views of birth families, are to be welcomed. Agencies, however, already have too great a tendency to dismiss the views and wishes of families of origin as contrary to the welfare of the child.

Family meetings   Adoption legislation needs to be more specific about the involvement of the wider family and friends. Once it has become apparent to the agency concerned that long-term plans need to be made for the child to secure a permanent home it should be a legal requirement for the agency to hold a meeting, as Murray Ryburn suggests in chapter 14, with *all* family members who are contactable to explore possible alternatives to adoption *before* a substitute care/adoption plan is proposed. Such a meeting should ask the family to make proposals for the child's long-term care within the family, if at all possible, in the knowledge that if they cannot come up with a satisfactory proposal, then a permanent substitute care/adoption plan will be pursued. If they are unable to make any proposals regarding the former, then they should be invited to make known their views regarding the latter.

The convening of a meeting of the whole family is the necessary precursor to their effective involvement in planning for their child. The current tendency to consult by letter or to have discussions with individual members of the family does not give the family any real opportunity to take responsibility or have any influence on decisions made by the local authority. Such a family meeting would ensure that the provisions of section 23(6) had been complied with. It would also enhance the possibility of children being brought up by their own families, if at all possible.

Non-married fathers   Non-married fathers are often significantly disadvantaged in trying to play any role in the life of their children when adoption is under consideration. The Adoption Law Review expresses somewhat conflicting views about the involvement of non-married fathers.

The proposal that adoption legislation include something similar to sections 22(4) and (5) of the Children Act 1989 would indicate a desire to consult and involve non-married fathers without parental responsibility (who come within the definition of 'parent' in the 1989 Act). The Review also recommends that agencies and guardians *ad litem* should be under a duty to 'make all reasonable efforts' to inform the non-married father of adoption proceedings and ascertain his views and wishes (para 9.3).

However, as well as talking about fathers without parental responsibility being consulted 'in general', the Review also talks about adoption being put at risk and the possibility of harm to the child's welfare if non-married fathers are sought out. In addition, the Review proposes that the agreement of a non-married father to adoption should not be required unless he has acquired parental responsibility under section 4 of the Children Act 1989.

It is unjust to exclude unmarried fathers from a decision as crucial as adoption. This approach does not tie in with the definition of 'parent' in the Family Law Reform Act 1987, or the requirements in the Children Act 1989 on local authorities and other agencies to consult with parents (including non-married fathers) before making any decision about a child. Nor does it take account of the duty on local authorities to allow parents reasonable contact with children in care, or the court rules requiring notice of care proceedings to be served on fathers without parental responsibility, thus enabling them to be joined as parties if necessary. While there may be practical difficulties in tracing non-married fathers, this should not be a reason for excluding them.

In relation to the possibility of non-married fathers disrupting the process, surely whether or not adoption is in the child's best interests is something for the court to decide. It should do so having heard all the relevant evidence, which should include the father's objections, if he has any, and any proposals that he may have for the child's future.

While the White Paper remains curiously silent on the subject of non-married fathers, the Law Commission Review on illegitimacy distinguished between fathers with a 'genuine familial link' with the child and fathers who have displayed 'no concern either for the child or for his or her mother' (para 18). Fathers with a genuine familial link may nevertheless, and for whatever reason, including lack of or poor legal advice, not have acquired parental responsibility for the child. It seems unfair to expect them to obtain such an order before they can even be in a position to give or withhold consent to their child's adoption. The fact that an unmarried father has not applied for parental responsibility could also arise from ignorance about the need to apply for such an order. In some cases fathers are aware of their legal position but are reluctant to jeopardise what is otherwise a satisfactory relationship with the child, and the child's mother,

because the mother was opposed to their acquiring parental responsibility for her own reasons.

Fathers with a genuine familial link may have cared for their children for all, or a good part of, their lives. The fact that they have no legal responsibility does not mean that they have not shown complete responsibility as parents, both financially and in terms of care, love and commitment. To continue to exclude such fathers from the adoption process and to disregard the fact that they do not consent to the adoption is an abuse of power by the state. Moreover, Article 18 of the United Nations Convention on the Rights of the Child, which the United Kingdom ratified in December 1991, states that 'parties shall use their best efforts to ensure recognition of the principle that both parents have common responsibilities for the upbringing and development of the child'. To disregard unmarried fathers' lack of consent to adoption would seem to constitute a fundamental breach of this article.

If the duties in the Children Act in relation to looked-after children are complied with, unmarried fathers should be sought out at an early stage, which would reduce the risk of their appearing suddenly on the scene when adoption was raised as an option. This would make it all the more illogical not to give them the right to give or withhold consent.

In summary, there should be no distinction between the position of married and unmarried fathers with regard to their agreement to adoption, and the term 'parent' for the purposes of adoption legislation should include those who do not have parental responsibility.

Placement arrangements   One of the greatest areas of injustice for birth relatives in current law and practice is the way placements are made. Often there is delay that means, as Murray Ryburn discusses in chapter 12, that decisions are made by default and the capacity of birth relatives actively to dispute them is greatly diminished. In addition, since the introduction of freeing for adoption procedures it has been possible to dispense with the consent of parents to an adoption without any specific adoption plan and placement in mind.

The Adoption Law Review recognises the problems that attach to freeing for adoption proceedings: the delays; the courts contrasting the apparent shortcomings in the care offered, or likely to be offered, by a child's parent with the care likely to be offered by hypothetically perfect adoptive parents; the danger of a child being left without a family once freed for adoption (para 14.4); and the distancing of the prospective adopters from the freeing process, which prevents the possibility of any negotiations about continuing contact or openness (para 14.5). The Review's proposal that freeing in its present form should be abolished is to be welcomed (para 14.8), as is the proposal that the court should look at the case at the earliest

possible stage once it has been proposed that a long-term substitute placement is required for a child.

Placement orders   The Adoption Law Review Consultation Document made proposals about placement orders – orders designed to ensure an early court hearing so that courts were not dealing with a *fait accompli* when hearing an adoption or freeing for adoption application.

The proposals met with considerable criticism and a subsequent consultation document, *Placement for Adoption* (DoH, 1994), was issued after publication of the White Paper. The proposals in *Placement for Adoption* replace one unjust system with another.

In uncontested cases, it is proposed that there should not be a hearing prior to placement, but there is a failure to establish a fair or adequate mechanism for eliciting whether the child's family approves adoption (paras 4.2–4.3), which may result in serious miscarriages of justice for children and their families of origin.

In contested cases, the proposals do not substantially differ from the current, much criticised, freeing proceedings. It is proposed that there should be two possible orders – an order endorsing a general adoption plan (GAP) or a specific placement order (SPO).

The problem with an order endorsing a general adoption plan is that, at an early stage, before a placement has taken place and, in many cases, before possible carers have been identified, the court will be deciding that there is a significant advantage in the child being adopted, as opposed to any other long-term placement arrangement, such as a residence order or inter vivos guardianship. It would be far better to have a pre-placement hearing which simply authorised the agency to seek a long-term placement for the child.

It is also proposed that parental consent could be dispensed with when an order endorsing a GAP is made. Parents would retain their parental responsibility but they would not be able to exercise it. The intention seems to be to eliminate the family of origin from the picture as soon as possible, to make it easier for the prospective adopters and the agency.

The specific problems with freeing, identified in the Adoption Law Review referred to above (see p.30), have not been addressed and the proposal is far from being 'significantly different from the present freeing order' (para 4.29), as is claimed.

Specific placement orders, allowing a placement for adoption with a specific family, do have the advantage of dealing with a particular placement, but the proposals raise the possibility of the hearing occurring after placement, in which case the possibility of the courts dealing with a *fait accompli* arises again.

It is proposed that parental consent could be dispensed with when a

SPO is made, so if the hearing takes place *before* placement there then remains the problem of measuring the parents against hypothetically perfect adoptive parents.

If enacted, these proposals would not achieve the stated objective of 'providing a fairer deal to birth parents and others contesting the adoption' (para 3.6).

Alternative proposals   A better system would be that the agency should make the application to the court without the prospective carers/adopters being involved, or even identified. The court's decision should be based on an application of the welfare principle with the amended checklist. If an order were made it would be an order giving 'authority to proceed' with a plan for placement with a new family, rather than sanctioning a specific placement, or identifying adoption as the preferred legal status for the child.

Although the government does not wish to place courts in the role of scrutinising local authority practice where a care order exists, such scrutiny at *this* stage is essential because once introduction or placement is made, the case becomes almost a *fait accompli* in favour of adoption. The Review accepts this point in its criticism of freeing for adoption proceedings (para 14.2) and indeed this is the reason behind its proposals for pre-placement hearings. It is recognised in the Children Act that courts should be involved in major decisions concerning children in care, for example contact, and whether or not the order should be discharged or a residence order made. The decision not to pursue reunification of the child with his/her family is another crucial decision which requires the court's scrutiny and permission.

Bringing the pre-placement hearing forward to the pre-introduction stage would not leave the child without a family as is suggested by the Review. Instead, it would clarify the position with regard to possible options within the family and the kinds of factors to be considered by the panel in the matching and recruitment process.

The court would not need to dispense with the parents' consent in contested cases at this stage, but the parents would be parties to the application and would be entitled to oppose it.

The wider family should be given notice of the application (which would follow logically from the consultation process) and would be entitled to be joined as parties on request without having to obtain leave. Parents should remain parties to the main adoption application and their consent would be dealt with when the adoption application was heard.

Conditions to an 'authority to proceed' order   Having looked at the issue in relation to the welfare of the child and having applied the welfare

checklist with the proposed amendments, the courts should be able to attach conditions to an 'authority to proceed' order. Thus the birth family, the prospective carers, and the agency would all know what sort of plan had been sanctioned by the court and what were the expectations of each party. This kind of clarification in the court order would increase the chances of the plan being followed through smoothly by all concerned, in the same way that a written agreement assists practice when children are looked after. Although the Review does recommend that the agency should be required by regulations to draw up a written plan (para 10.1), this would not be sufficient as there would be no guarantee that the birth family's views and requests would be incorporated in the plan or complied with.

A mechanism for a court to attach conditions to a plan for long-term substitute care, which the agency had to abide by, would have two advantages:

- There would be far fewer adopters/carers dissatisfied with the service they receive from the placing agency (in not being given all the information about the child and his/her family), and
- More birth parents would be likely to give consent to a plan for substitute care/adoption if they knew they had no realistic chance of caring for their children again and the agency had to comply with their preferences when looking for a placement.

If the agency could not comply, then it would be open to the agency to apply again to the court for such conditions to be varied, and the parents would be able to make representations. Court applications would be reduced in a way that they would not if the Review's proposal were followed that parents merely be asked whether or not they agree with an unconditional placement order.

It may be argued that attaching conditions to an order authorising a substitute care plan or placement will make it more difficult to place children. This cannot be established until it is attempted, but the more commonplace it becomes for conditions to be attached to reflect the child's needs, the more ready carers or adopters will be to accept conditions. Indeed, researchers such as Fratter (1991), Thoburn and her colleagues (1986), Thoburn (1990) and Berridge and Cleaver (1987) found that new families were willing to consider placements with continuing contact if it was perceived to be of benefit to the child's welfare. Such findings suggest that carers or adopters are willing to consider placements with conditions attached, providing the importance to the child of the factors concerned are highlighted in the advertising, recruitment, and preparation process.

Proposed procedure on agency placements

1   Consultation with child, parent, family and friends. Where adoption is being considered, Family Group Conference called.
2   Consideration of race, culture, language and religion; issues of contact, alternative orders.
3   Application by agency for court approval to begin process of finding long-term placement for the child. Proposed adopters not involved.
4   Parents parties. Parental agreement not dealt with at this stage. Wider family given notice, entitled to become parties.
5   Authority to proceed given if only way to promote and safeguard child's welfare, applying checklist with amendments (including requirement that court satisfy itself that all possible placements within extended family have been investigated). Court may attach conditions to authority to proceed order.
6   Panel involved in matching process only. Parents and wider family to attend and make representations.
7   Parents and prospective adopters to meet, unless there is evidence that this would be detrimental to child's welfare (guidance).
8   Application to adopt. Parents (including unmarried fathers) parties, and their agreement required or dispensed with.
9   Court considers agreement, welfare checklist, other orders available, contact, and must show that adoption is significantly better than inter vivos guardianship.
10 Effect of adoption:
    ● *Either* parents of origin retain parental responsibility, but limited in ability to exercise it;
    ● *Or* child becomes adopters' child as from date of adoption order – amend Section 39 (1)–(2), Adoption Act 1976.

Grounds for dispensing with consent   The Review expresses concern that 'insufficient weight is given to a parent's lack of agreement' (para 12.1) and comments that this is often due to the courts having been presented with a *fait accompli* arising from the child having settled with prospective adopters. As the Review and the White Paper point out, this frequently negates the parent's theoretical right to argue for an alternative to adoption.

This concern relates specifically to the 'unreasonably withholding consent' grounds for dispensing with agreement. In relation to this particular ground, which is the most commonly used one, it seems very clear from reviewed judgments that this objective test is approached in a very subjective way by individual judges, as Elizabeth Lawson outlines in chapter 4.

The Review is proposing new grounds for dispensing with parental agreement, but it is surprising that, having stated that the paramountcy principle should not apply to the issue of whether or not to dispense with agreement, the Review has come up with a proposal (para 12.6) which is entirely concerned with weighing up the relative advantages to the child of adoption against any alternative options.

The proposed new test for dispensing with consent is thus a welfare test, and is also open to very subjective interpretation by judges. Those who have an ideological belief that adoption is at the top of a hierarchy of permanence orders will be far less likely to explore other possible orders, such as residence orders or inter vivos guardianship orders. Moreover, if judges need no longer concern themselves with the parents' reasonableness (or lack of it) in withholding agreement, it is likely that many parents will still find their consent being dispensed with.

The Review proposes three specific grounds for dispensing with consent:

- That the parent cannot be found, or is incapable of giving agreement.
- A test which should:
  a) address the question of the advantages of becoming part of a new family and having a new legal status (rather than the question of where the child should reside);
  b) focus on the needs of the child rather than any parental shortcomings;
  c) require the court to be satisfied that adoption is significantly better than other available options and that parental wishes should therefore be overridden.
- Where a parent who has agreed to adoption when a placement order is made withdraws that agreement, and the court considers that there have not been any significant changes since then such as would justify a different outcome (para 12.6).

It is very hard to see how this last proposed ground can be reconciled with another view contained in the Review – that parental agreement can be withdrawn at any time up until the adoption order is made. Parents should not be punished for changing their minds and their children denied a renewed chance to be brought up by their families.

The new test for dispensing with consent would remedy much of the injustice suffered by families under current legislation only if the following proposals were taken up alongside it:

- Changing the effect of adoption so as not to sever legal ties.
- Empowering the court to make authority to proceed orders with conditions attached instead of placement orders.

- Including in the welfare checklist requirements to look at placements within the wider family, race, and culture, and contact and openness with a presumption of continuing contact..
- Introducing a presumption of an inter vivos guardianship order instead of an adoption order.

If these proposals were incorporated, it is likely that more birth parents would agree to adoption. Those that did not would be less distressed than under the present system at finding their consent dispensed with on the basis of the proposed welfare test. The wording of the test might be changed slightly so that part (a) of the new test read 'Address the question of the advantages of being adopted' and at point (c):

> The court must be satisfied that the advantages to the child of adoption are so significantly greater than the advantages to the child of any alternative order as to justify overriding the wishes of the parent or guardian.

Conclusion

While it may be possible to agree that there has to be some mechanism for dispensing with consent, it must be hoped that the mechanism will in future only need to be used in exceptional circumstances and in a minority of cases. We may hope that the greater emphasis in the Children Act on the involvement of children and families in planning and decision-making, and on the importance of contact, will lead to fewer cases of contested adoption. While adoption remains in its current form and continues to be seen as the best way of obtaining a substitute family for a child, this is, unfortunately, unlikely to be the case.

If we return to the four factors that were listed at the beginning of this chapter as the reasons why parents contest adoptions, there are four corresponding sets of legal changes that would be likely greatly to reduce the number of contested cases. They are:

- Introducing changes to the legal effect of adoption.
- Ensuring consideration of a placement within the wider family.
- Ensuring a presumption of openness.
- Involving the court at the earliest possible stage in approving a local authority's long-term plan.

Improvements in practice are also important. There needs to be a substantial improvement in relation to returning children to their parents

or to the wider family or friends. Such work needs to be adequately resourced, planned and supported, and recognised as skilled work. Attitudes need to shift so that social workers genuinely work to promote contact between children and their families and, where children cannot return home to their parents, actively look within the extended family for possible placements. Changes and improvements in practice will not in themselves be sufficient but need to be accompanied by changes in the legislative framework.

Contested adoptions cause considerable stress and pain for all those involved. It is a matter of great regret that currently their number is rising both numerically and proportionally. A crucial aim of changes to legislation must be to reduce this number substantially.

References

Berridge, D. and Cleaver, H. (1987), *Foster Home Breakdown*, Oxford: Blackwell.

DoH/Welsh Office (1990), *Inter-Departmental Review of Adoption Law, Discussion Paper 2, Agreement and Freeing*, London: DoH.

DoH/Welsh Office (1992), *Review of Adoption Law: Report to Ministers of an Interdepartmental Working Group: A Consultation Document*, London: DoH.

DoH/Welsh Office/Home Office/Lord Chancellor's Department (1993), *Adoption: The Future*, Cmnd. 2288, London: HMSO.

DoH/Welsh Office/Lord Chancellor's Department (1994), *Placement for Adoption: A Consultation Document*, London: DoH.

Fratter, J. (1991), 'Adoptive Parents and Open Adoption in the UK', in Mullender, A. [ed.], *Open Adoption: The Philosophy and the Practice*, London: BAAF.

Fratter, J., Rowe, J., Sapsford, D. and Thoburn, J. (1991), *Permanent Family Placement: A Decade of Experience*, London: BAAF.

Lahti, J. (1982), 'A Follow-up Study of Foster Children in Permanent Placements', *Social Service Review*, **56**(4), 556–71.

Millham, S., Bullock, R., Hosie, K. and Little, M. (1989), *Access Disputes in Child-Care*, Aldershot: Gower.

Ryburn, M. (1992a), *Adoption in the 1990s: Identity and Openness*, Birmingham: Leamington Press.

Ryburn, M. (1992b), 'Contested Adoption Proceedings', *Adoption and Fostering*, **16** (4), 29–38.

Thoburn, J. (1989), *Success and Failure in Permanent Placement*, Aldershot: Avebury.

Thoburn, J. (1990), *Review of Research Relating to Adoption*, London: Dept of Health/Welsh Office, (also Appendix C in (DoH 1992), *Review of Adoption Law, A Consultation Document*, London: HMSO).

Thoburn, J., Murdoch, A. and O'Brien, A. (1986), *Permanence in Child Care*, Oxford: Blackwell.

Trent, J. (1989), *Homeward Bound: The Rehabilitation of Children to Their Birth Parents*, Ilford: Barnardos.

4 Contested adoption proceedings: a barrister's perspective

Elizabeth Lawson

Introduction

This chapter aims to draw out some of the key legal issues confronting the courts when they must reach decisions in contested adoption matters. The law, of course, cannot be divorced from adoption policy and custom, and the analysis of legal issues is set in the context of current adoption practice.

The bias towards adoption

Over the past 20 years the number of adoptions has fallen from around 23 000 in 1974 to just over 7 000 in 1991 (*Adoption: The Future*, DoH, 1993). For those practising the law in adoption, however, this may not be their impression. During that period, for the vast majority of children in the care of local authorities, there has been a significant shift away from placement in residential homes in favour of placement in substitute families. The long-term plan for the vast majority of children who were unable to return home was that they should be placed for adoption, and have no contact with their natural family. By the end of the 1980s, there was a significant number of local authorities that no longer had any long-term foster parents available. The prevailing wisdom was that if rehabilitation was not possible, there was no value for the child in having contact with his or her natural family. He or she could learn all they needed to know from a life story book. Any parent who wished to have contact was inevitably perceived as unable to put the child's needs before his or her own.

To some extent this was an extension of the general attitude towards

parents, that once their children were in care, they had no role to play, no insights to offer into their children's behaviour, indeed no valid point of view. They were seldom, if ever, consulted about the decisions made concerning their children, including the decision that they should be adopted. This is beginning to change. The Children Act 1989, with its presumption of continuing contact between a child in care and his or her natural family, and its emphasis on partnership between parents and local authority will, it is to be hoped, in time change these attitudes. Similarly, the evidence from research, and the practice in other jurisdictions, are beginning to call into question our traditional process of closed adoption.

At present, however, the tendency is to accept the research findings in theory, but to justify traditional closed adoption for this particular child, relying on the familiar arguments that contact would confuse the child or undermine his or her security. There is also the very real difficulty that very few adopters have been or are being recruited on the basis that there will be continuing contact with the natural family. Many of those seeking to adopt children do so because they are unable to have children of their own. It is often they, rather than the children, who need the security of adoption. Understandably, they find it hard to cope with anything which reminds them that this is not their biological child. Despite their own big emotional investment in the making of an adoption order, however, the prospective adopters are almost invariably presented as looking at the issue only from the point of view of the child's welfare. This contrasts with the attitude towards the natural family, who are said to be putting their own needs before the child's.

This is one example of the lack of appreciation within our present system of the bias in favour of adoption. Both child care and adoption law are largely framed and administered by those who have no expectation that their own children will ever be taken into care or adopted against their will. They are much more likely to have friends and acquaintances who have adopted children than to know people socially whose children have been removed from their care and adopted. Adoption agencies, and the fostering and adoption sections of local authorities, are largely staffed by those who believe in the benefits of adoption. Most agencies have a financial interest in an adoption order being made, even if the adopters themselves do not.

The welfare test in adoption

It is important to emphasise these matters at the outset, because the basic test which the courts have to apply in deciding whether or not to make an

adoption order is essentially a value judgment, rather than a legal one. Section 6 of the Adoption Act 1976 provides that:

> In reaching any decision relating to the adoption of a child a court . . . shall have regard to all the circumstances, first consideration being given to the need to safeguard and promote the welfare of the child throughout his childhood; and shall so far as practicable ascertain the wishes and feelings of the child regarding the decision and give due consideration to them, having regard to his age and understanding.

It has been the received wisdom for many years that adoption is the best, if not the only means of really securing a placement and that any other form of order or combination of orders is second best. Indeed this has been so much the case that it has become almost axiomatic in practice that if the child is to remain in a substitute family, it is in his best interests to be adopted by them.

Similarly, although the child's wishes and feelings are usually ascertained, the process of doing so tends to be very superficial. Most children, if asked, will say that they want to stay where they are, but whereas in a dispute between parents over a child's residence that statement would be probed, in adoption proceedings it seldom is. Adoption is equated with 'staying for always'. For the child, there is no realistic alternative to remaining living where he or she is. The child will probably have been told that this is to be his or her permanent home. If the issue is probed at all, it is likely to be on the basis of moving back to live with the natural family. There is seldom any real explanation of the difference between going on living where he or she is and not being adopted, and being adopted. Also, there is seldom any appreciation of the extent to which the child is likely to be influenced by the present carers' strong wish to adopt.

Parental consent in adoption

It is not enough, however, for the court to be satisfied that adoption would safeguard and promote the welfare of the child throughout childhood. The law also requires that the parents should consent to the adoption or that the court should dispense with that agreement on specified statutory grounds. For this purpose 'parent' does not include the father of an illegitimate child, unless he has parental responsibility either as a result of an agreement between the parents or by virtue of a court order giving it to him. The statutory grounds in section 16(2) of the Adoption Act 1976 are:

that the parent or guardian:
- (a)   cannot be found or is incapable of giving agreement;
- (b)   is withholding his agreement unreasonably;
- (c)   has persistently failed without reasonable cause to discharge his parental responsibility for the child;
- (d)   has abandoned or neglected the child;
- (e)   has persistently ill-treated the child;
- (f)   has seriously ill-treated the child (subject to sub-section (5)).

Section 16(5) of the Act states that 'Sub-section (2)(f) does not apply unless (because of the ill-treatment or for other reasons) the rehabilitation of the child within the household of the parent or guardian is unlikely.'

Of these grounds the one most commonly relied on, in practice, is that the parent is unreasonably withholding his consent, and it is on that ground that this chapter will concentrate.

It is important to remember that the issue of whether the parent is withholding his agreement unreasonably only arises once the court has concluded that adoption is in the child's best interests. If the court decides that adoption is not in the child's interests, while that conclusion may actually be due to the parent's objections, the question of whether or not the parent is unreasonably withholding consent does not fall to be considered.

The history of the courts' approach to the reasonableness of the parent's refusal parallels the developments outlined above. Passages in some of the older cases indicate starkly the shift in the courts' approach over the years. Thus in *Re K* [1953] 1 QB 117, p. 129, Jenkins L.J. says:

> Prima facie it would seem to me eminently reasonable for any parent to withhold his or her consent to an order thus completely and irrevocably destroying the parental relationship. One can imagine cases short of such misconduct or dereliction of duty as mentioned in Section 3(1)(a) in which a parent's withholding of consent to an adoption might properly be held to be unreasonable, but such cases must, in our view, be exceptional . . . We would say, first, that the withholding of a parent's consent to an adoption order cannot be held unreasonable merely because the order if made would conduce to the welfare of the child. Secondly, we would say that such withholding of a parent's consent cannot be held unreasonable merely because the parent has . . . placed the child in the care of foster parents, without in any sense abandoning it . . . Otherwise the remarkable consequence would ensue that foster parents entrusted for reward with the care of a child by a parent not for the time being able to provide it with a suitable home could in due course confront the parent with an application to adopt the child which the parent would be unable to oppose.

The watershed decision on this issue is the case of *Re W* [1971] AC 682. The case concerned a baby placed within a few days of birth with temporary foster parents who applied to adopt him when he was just

under a year old. The child was illegitimate and the mother had had no contact with him after he was placed. She was living in one room with her two older children, who were also illegitimate, and was dependent for her subsistence on state benefits. There was no chance of her marrying the father.

The County Court judge formed the opinion that there was a grave risk that she would have another unplanned child, and that her inner resources were of doubtfully adequate strength to enable her to cope with the difficulties which the addition of W to her household would bring. He also considered that to remove W from the only home which he had ever known would disturb him emotionally and perhaps also psychologically. He accordingly held that the mother was unreasonably withholding her consent. The Court of Appeal allowed the mother's appeal, holding that the judge had wrongly based his decision on considerations of the welfare of the child and that the Act envisaged a degree of unreasonableness which did not fall far short of positive misconduct.

The House of Lords allowed the appeal and held that the test was not culpability or callous or self-indulgent indifference, or failure of parental duty, but of reasonableness in all the circumstances. Although welfare in itself was not the test, the fact that a reasonable parent paid regard to his child's welfare made welfare in any particular case a more or less relevant or decisive factor, depending on how the reasonable parent would regard it. But reasonableness was to be judged by an objective test which was normally a question of fact and degree, though the court would not be entitled simply to substitute their view for that of the parent. In an oft-quoted passage at page 700, Lord Hailsham L.C. says :

> It does not follow from the fact that the test is reasonableness that any court is entitled simply to substitute its own view for that of the parent. In my opinion it should be extremely careful to guard against this error. Two reasonable parents can perfectly reasonably come to opposite conclusions and on the same set of facts without forfeiting their title to be regarded as reasonable. The question in any given case is whether a parental veto comes within the band of possible reasonable decisions and not whether it is right or mistaken. Not every reasonable exercise of judgment is right, and not every mistaken exercise of judgment is unreasonable. There is a band of decisions within which no court should seek to replace the individual's judgment with his own.

The reality of practice, however, is very different. In the case of very young children placed outside the family for adoption, it is wholly exceptional for a parent to succeed in showing that he or she is not unreasonably withholding consent. Often, of course, the parent will already have argued unsuccessfully within either wardship or care proceedings that the child should return home and/or that there should be

contact. Since these issues are the basis upon which consent is most frequently withheld, it is perhaps not surprising that the courts so readily in the adoption proceedings hold that the parent's consent is being unreasonably withheld.

Court of Appeal decisions

Since 1982 there have been 27 Court of Appeal cases reported in the Family Law Reports on the issue of unreasonable withholding of consent. In none of those involving a child under five who had been placed with a view to adoption, or whose foster parents now wished to adopt and where access had been terminated, did the parent succeed in arguing that consent was not being unreasonably withheld. Of those 27 cases, 16 were decided against the parents. In eight, the parent's consent was dispensed with at first instance and the parent's appeal was dismissed. In a further eight, the court below refused to dispense with the parent's consent and the appeal was allowed.

Of the remaining 11 cases, there were six in which the court at first instance dispensed with the parent's consent and the parent's appeal against the adoption order was allowed. Three of those involved older children where the parent wished to have contact with the child who had originally been long-term fostered. One was a case in which a mother had originally lived with the prospective adopters and the child and there was a lot of continuing contact between the natural family and the child. Another was a case in which the parent had another child living with her and where there was a relationship between the children as well as with the mother.

Of the remaining five cases where the judge at first instance refused to dispense with the parent's consent and the adopters' appeal was dismissed, three involved access to older children, and one was a case in which the evidence was that rehabilitation with the mother was possible. In the final case, *Re E (Minors) Adoption: Parental Agreement* [1990] 2 FLR 397, care orders had been made on the basis that there should be continuing contact between the children and their parents. The local authority changed its plans and decided to place them for adoption, terminating parental access. The parents applied for access to the Magistrates' Court and the local authority issued a freeing application. The parents' access application was adjourned pending the outcome of the freeing application. The children were by that time five and three. The guardian *ad litem* considered that to reintroduce contact would be against their interests. The judge, while holding that adoption was in the children's interests, nevertheless found that the mother was not unreasonable in withholding

her consent on the basis of her commitment to the children and the sense of injustice which the council's decision had caused. The adopters' appeal was dismissed.

These decisions confirm that the court is more willing to uphold the parental refusal in cases where older children were placed with long-term foster parents who subsequently wished to adopt them. An influential strand in that thinking was that this was the situation with which custodianship was intended to deal, and some of the reported cases have involved the inter-relationship between the two forms of order. The most influential of these decisions is the case of *Re H, Re W* [1983] 4 FLR 614, in which Purchas L.J. at page 624 reiterated the test expounded in *Re W* above, in the following words :

> So far as the local authority's representatives are concerned, they rightly consider solely the welfare of the child in accordance with their statutory duties. Their opinion is concentrated on only one of the three interests involved. The position of the proposed adoptive parents needs no expansion and it is only necessary to remember that there is room for two reasonable attitudes which are mutually conflicting within the ambit of a reasonable parent as emphasised by Lord Hailsham in *Re W*. There is, therefore, room for the reasonable withholding of consent by the natural parent, even though those responsible for the child's welfare, who are normally professionals, hold an acceptable view that the child's welfare demands adoption.
>
> The court must therefore look at the attitude of the natural parent as one of the potentially relevant factors when assessing the attitude of the hypothetical, reasonable, natural parent. Where the natural parent presents himself or herself at the time of the hearing as someone capable of caring for the child, this is a factor which even the hypothetical, reasonable parent should take into account together with the other circumstances of the case including, of course, the ultimate welfare of the child.

In the vast majority of cases, the issue is whether or not the parent's wish to have contact with the child, or to resume care of him or her, is realistic.

Issues of contact

What remains to be seen is how such cases will be dealt with in the future, not only because of the changing attitudes which have been referred to, but because section 8 of the Children Act 1989 permits an order for contact to be made even where there is an adoption. Hitherto the courts' attitude towards attaching a condition that there should be contact to an adoption order has been that such conditions are only appropriate where they are agreed to by the adopters (see *Re C* [1989] AC 1).

The issue of contact, however, now has to be decided in accordance with

the welfare checklist provided for by section 1 of the Children Act 1989. The fact that the machinery now exists to provide properly for contact, by way of an enforceable order, notwithstanding the making of an adoption order, may make it harder for parents to withhold their consent to adoption on this basis. The Court of Appeal has recently held that the making of a contact order does not prevent a freeing order being made on the basis that the parent's consent is being unreasonably withheld: in *Re A (A Minor) Adoption: Contact Order, The Times*, 24 June 1993. The courts have yet to establish any principles for deciding when a former parent should be allowed contact with a child who has been adopted, but the only judicial pronouncement, *Re S (A Minor) Contact Order, The Times*, 8 March 1993, suggests that such orders are likely to be regarded as exceptional, and require a change of circumstances since the adoption order was made.

The hypothetical reasonable parent

As is clear from some of the passages quoted, in deciding whether or not the actual parent is being reasonable, the court looks at the attitude of the hypothetical reasonable parent. According to the case of *Re D* [1977] AC 602, this is a parent in the circumstances of the actual parent, but (hypothetically) endowed with a mind and temperament capable of making reasonable decisions. What is unclear is the extent to which the hypothetical reasonable parent has the characteristics of the actual parent in any given case. In *Re D* itself, the father in question was a practising homosexual who had had relationships with young men in their late teens and early 20s. His wife had remarried and she and her new husband wanted to adopt the boy, mainly it appeared to prevent contact between him and the father and his homosexual associates.

The House of Lords held that the hypothetical reasonable father was a practising homosexual like the actual father. Such a hypothetical reasonable father would hold that he had nothing to offer his son now or in the future and would therefore consent to the adoption, so that the actual father was unreasonably withholding his consent. The courts have not yet grappled with the situation where the characteristics of the hypothetical reasonable parent, derived from the characteristics of the actual parent, render his or her withholding of consent reasonable rather than unreasonable. For example, if the actual parents are black, is the hypothetical reasonable parent black as well? If so, is the hypothetical reasonable parent reasonably withholding consent to a transracial placement, even though the agencies involved support it in the particular case? If the actual parent is Jewish, or a devout Roman Catholic, is the hypothetical reasonable

parent entitled to object to the adoption on the basis that the child is not in a placement in which he would be brought up in that religion? Or is the hypothetical reasonable parent only endowed with the parental characteristics which make his refusal to consent to the adoption unreasonable?

Rather surprisingly, there has been no reported case in which the question of whether or not a black parent is or is not reasonable in withholding his consent to his child being adopted by a white family has been considered. In *Re N* [1990] 1 FLR 58, a Nigerian father objected to the adoption but wished to have continued contact with his child. Bush J. held that adoption was not in the child's interests in those circumstances.

Other arguments concerning reasonableness

From time to time other arguments in favour of the reasonableness of the parent's objection have been advanced, most of which have glimmered fitfully before being put out. The most recent of these is the extent to which, if at all, a parent's sense of grievance over the way in which a local authority has handled the case can make the decision not to agree to the adoption a reasonable one.

The only case in which it has been given any weight is the one quoted above, *Re E* [1990] 2 FLR 397. In a case, *Re B*, which was decided earlier, but only reported in 1990, 2 FLR 383, the Court of Appeal allowed an appeal against the judge's refusal to dispense with the parent's consent because it considered he had given too much weight to the alleged sense of grievance felt by the mother. In both decisions it has been said that the court has to look at the facts underlying the sense of grievance to see whether it is justified. If so, it is the facts which justify the refusal to consent rather than the sense of grievance itself.

Non-fault-based grounds

The *Review of Adoption Law* (DoH, 1992) at paragraphs 12.1 to 12.4, rightly points out that the tendency has been to decide that adoption is in the child's best interests and that the parent is therefore unreasonably withholding consent. It seems, however, that their proposal for non-fault-based grounds would in practice endorse the approach which they deprecate, since they would amount to no more than a decision that adoption was in the best interests of the children, and should therefore go ahead.

One of the arguments in favour of non-fault-based grounds for dispensing with parental consent, is that the fault-based grounds increase the adversarial nature of the proceedings. So long as we have adoption which can take place against the wishes of the natural parents, it seems important that their protest should be put before the court by someone whose role in the proceedings is to represent their interests and views.

An inquisitorial approach which is judge-led, while superficially attractive, presupposes a level of judicial detachment which is not always found. Any judge reading the papers is likely to form a view one way or the other about whether or not adoption is best for the child, and consequently the reasonableness of the parent's withholding of consent. If he thinks the result is a foregone conclusion, he may well pay scant attention to the views of those who disagree. That happens within the present adversarial system. In *Re B* [1992] 2 FLR 37, the Court of Appeal allowed the mother's appeal against a freeing order and directed a retrial because of the way the judge conducted the trial. Butler-Sloss L.J. said at page 38:

> it is clear, to me at least, that the judge formed a strong view on the merits of the mother's case and he intervened forcefully at a comparatively early stage of the hearing, at the stage when she was giving evidence and before she was cross-examined. He, in effect, cross-examined her himself and reduced her to tears. He made some ill-considered and unfortunate comments and has raised in the mother a justifiable sense of grievance, in that there is the appearance, at least of a denial of justice.

The risk seems much greater if the system does not permit the parties a right to advance their own case.

It is important to recognise that contested adoption cases are fought for the highest stakes. It should be recognised that what is being adjudicated on is a decision that will affect the child and his or her family, not just until his or her majority but for life. While there is scope for conciliation around the issue of contact, it is not possible to 'settle' a contested adoption case. It is about one or other party being persuaded to give in. In practice that is going to be the natural family.

Procedural changes that may reduce conflict

At the same time our procedure could be significantly improved in ways which would encourage parents to consent. Recognition by the adopting family of the value of contact for the child and a willingness to accept it, would obviously make a considerable difference to the willingness of many natural parents to consent. So, we could be sure, would greater openness in the planning and court process. At the moment any adopter can ask for

a confidential serial number in their case. Even when the identity of the adopters is known to the parents, this can result in their becoming Mr and Mrs A, and a lot of 'hole in the corner' secrecy, which is often unnecessary. Similarly, save in exceptional cases, the Schedule 2 report and the guardian *ad litem*'s report should be made available automatically to the natural parent.

Where several families are being considered by the agency as possible adopters, it seems reasonable for the parents to have an opportunity to help select the adopters for their child, and that they should be allowed to meet them if they wish. It would also help many parents to agree, if they had been regularly supplied with information about their child's progress in the foster or adoptive placement, and with photographs of the child. The fear that the parents will seek to disrupt the child's placement seems often to be exaggerated. Again, this would be likely to be minimised if the adopters met the parents and were not encouraged to fantasise about them as potential child abductors.

Conclusion

Adoption law and practice are in a period of transition. Cases are decided on the basis of the evidence presented to the court. There is an urgent need for those responsible for training adoption and child care agency staff to raise the sorts of issues addressed above and to disseminate the research findings to their staff. Only by doing so will the perceived wisdom about what is best for children in these circumstances be challenged and changed. At present, even where there is knowledge of relevant research and other viable models of practice, they seem to be regarded as of no application to the particular case with which the court is concerned.

The courts too have spent the last 20 years or more hearing from the 'experts' that adoption with no contact with the natural family was best for children and that life story books were enough. They need to be shown different models of adoption, and be convinced that they are workable and in the best interests of the child with whom they are concerned.

Reference

DOH/Welsh Office/Home Office/Lord Chancellor's Department (1993), *Adoption: The Future*, Cmnd. 2288, London: HMSO.
DoH/Welsh Office (1992), *Review of Adoption Law: Report to Ministers of an Interdepartmental Working Group: A Consultation Document*, London: DoH.

5 Contested adoptions: the winner takes all

Jill Smart and Ian Young

Introduction

This chapter looks at the effect of contested adoption proceedings on the main protagonists – the birth parents and the prospective adopters – from the perspectives of two adoption law practitioners. Its central claim is that current law and social work practice encourage 'the winner takes all' approach to children subject to adoption applications. This approach is out of step with the philosophy of the Children Act 1989 and in the vast majority of cases results in applicants for adoption orders being 'winners' and birth parents feeling like 'all-time losers'. But what about the children concerned? Their long-term best interests would be promoted if this primitive approach were abandoned and replaced by a 'no winners, no losers' philosophy. This can only be brought about by encouraging birth parents to maintain some contact with their children and prospective adopters to accept that this is in the best interests of the child. In this chapter we take an anecdotal approach, drawing on examples of adoption cases from our own practice in order to demonstrate, from the perspectives of two who are working on a daily basis with contested adoptions, how damaging and unnecessary a 'winner takes all' approach is for all parties.

The effect on birth parents

By the time that a hearing of an adoption application takes place, the contest is usually all over bar the tears, with the applicants for the adoption order as the 'winners'. Why? Because the birth parents will not usually

have had contact with their child for many months and the child will often have been placed and settled with prospective adopters, forcing courts to the conclusion that the most important decisions have already been made and that the child's best interests would not be served by making contact orders that the prospective adopters might resist.

Before getting to a contested adoption hearing the birth parents will have been involved in prolonged litigation under the Children Act 1989 or its statutory predecessors, the Children and Young Persons Act 1969 or the Child Care Act 1980, on whether they should have the care of or contact with their child. Alternatively, they may have been involved in wardship proceedings, which prior to the 1989 Act, were a means by which local authorities obtained care orders. The birth parents will therefore have already invested a great deal of time, energy and emotion in unsuccessfully resisting the orders which have resulted in their child being permanently removed from their care. They are often not eager to experience the additional stress and strain of contesting an adoption application, but usually do because the absolute finality of an adoption order means that they are unlikely to see their child again. This realisation spurs them on.

Experienced lawyers know that birth parents who have been through the process of losing their child as a result of these proceedings experience a great deal of grief, which culminates in a bereavement represented by the final act of making the adoption order. The birth parents' grief can manifest itself in feelings of anger, non-acceptance, and denial of what has happened. In some instances it results in suicide. By the time that an adoption application is made birth parents are often resigned to the fact that their child will not return to them, but this resignation does not inhibit their fierce determination to contest the making of an adoption order.

Case study 1 – Prolonged litigation

Margaret's child, Chloe, was the subject of care proceedings, which were not opposed by Margaret because the local authority's plan was for Chloe to be rehabilitated to her. A care order was made, but instead of rehabilitating Chloe to Margaret, the local authority decided against pursuing this plan and made arrangements to have Chloe adopted against Margaret's wishes. Margaret applied to discharge the care order but after a lengthy hearing she was unsuccessful, so she appealed to the Crown Court (which was the appropriate appellate court prior to the Children Act 1989). Her appeal was upheld but the local authority then decided to defeat the appellate court's decision by making Chloe a ward of court (which was possible prior to the Children Act 1989), thus preventing Margaret from removing Chloe from foster care. These wardship proceedings took a further nine months and the result was that the court gave

leave to the local authority to place Chloe with long-term foster parents with a view to adoption, and terminated Margaret's contact. The original care proceedings started in 1988 and the adoption hearing took place four years later in 1992. Throughout this time Margaret went through all the emotional reactions described above, but by the time the contested adoption hearing was reached she had accepted the inevitability of an adoption order, although she still resisted the making of the order and refused to give her consent. Margaret wanted contact with Chloe despite the making of the adoption order but the adoptive parents were not prepared to accept her ongoing contact, even though Margaret would have settled for a limited form of contact.

Case study 2 – Child parent interests come second

Anne is a teenage mother whose child, Robert, was the subject of care proceedings under the Children Act 1989. Robert was taken into the interim care of the local authority and shortly afterwards Anne herself was made the subject of care proceedings (she was 15 years old at the time) because of her unruly behaviour. Anne had exhibited behavioural problems since she was a young child, but when she was separated from Robert her behaviour hit a new low which resulted in her being placed in secure accommodation. Her grief at being parted from Robert manifested itself by her cutting her wrists and becoming involved in prostitution. She was also found in possession of drugs and said that she had been raped. While in secure accommodation she had contact with Robert and this progressed well enough for it to be increased substantially.

After completing her term in secure accommodation she went to live in a local authority children's home. Following one contact visit she ran off with Robert but was persuaded to return by a social worker. Anne claimed that this was not a serious attempt to abduct Robert, but the incident, considered in the light of her generally disruptive behaviour, caused the local authority to apply to terminate her contact. As a result Anne made a serious attempt at suicide by overdosing on paracetamol tablets.

In due course her contact was terminated by the court on the basis that her son's welfare took priority over hers, even though she herself was still a child. She appealed this to the Court of Appeal and was successful. The court took the view that her welfare, like that of her son, was important when making a decision of this kind and that it would be promoted if she continued to have contact with Robert. The court took into account the evidence that Anne would probably repeat her life-threatening acts if she did not continue to have contact with Robert.

The local authority with the guardian for Robert, successfully appealed the Court of Appeal's decision in the House of Lords. The result is that Anne is no longer entitled to contact with Robert. The plan of the local authority is that Robert should be adopted. By the time the adoption hearing takes place it is

possible that these various proceedings will have continued for three years. Anne is determined not to consent to the adoption, as she herself was adopted and has unhappy memories of her childhood. As in all these cases, the local authority has simply failed to look for a family who would accept ongoing contact by Anne. The result is bitterly contested and massively expensive proceedings, and misery for the birth mother.

Sometimes, despite the fact that the adoptive placement is unstable or unhappy, adoption orders are made in the face of opposition by birth parents. There is very real evidence that it is extremely difficult to successfully oppose adoption orders where there has been no contact between birth parents and their children for months prior to the hearing and where contact is opposed by the prospective adopters. Similarly, where birth parents are unjustly and unfairly treated by local authorities (see case study 3) adoption orders are still made, leading to further feelings of injustice and grief for birth parents.

Case study 3 – Children's views

Mary and Oliver are the birth parents of eleven children. Two are currently living with them and a third is in the care of the local authority and has some contact with Mary and Oliver. The rest of the children are the subject of adoption orders following proceedings at various times. Two of these children were placed with prospective adopters who applied for adoption orders. Mary and Oliver opposed their adoption on the grounds that the children were not happy with the applicants. The two children had been the subject of four moves to different foster homes before their final placement. They came to the applicants and were described as deeply disturbed children presenting very great problems. The previous carer had warned the applicants of those problems, which included temper tantrums in which they destroyed their toys and were violent to each other. The applicants were not the most instinctive of parents. They had business interests which required them to work long, hard hours in order to maintain their standard of living. They had high expectations of the boys' behaviour and resorted to physical chastisement when those expectations were not met. The court found that the chastisement by the applicants was reasonable and not severe.

Mary and Oliver applied for contact because they wanted to resume caring for the two children and contact was seen as a start of that process. (Had they been treated more fairly by the local authority from the outset, this polarised position might have been avoided.) They had shown that they were caring well for two children recently born to them and felt that they could provide a better home than the applicants. They also wanted contact to provide the children

with information about their culture and background, which the children were not receiving in their current placements as the applicants were from a different cultural and racial background. The court found that Mary and Oliver should not have contact even though the two boys themselves were ambivalent about the adoption – sometimes keen on it, then less than enthusiastic.

Despite this ambivalence the court dispensed with parental consent, refused the contact application and made adoption orders. These hotly contested proceedings lasted many days in the High Court and in the Court of Appeal. This case is a good example of the huge expense to the public purse of proceedings of this kind, a fact commented on by the judge throughout the hearing.

Is the position of birth parents less hopeless in contested freeing proceedings?

As can be seen above, although adoption proceedings are usually very difficult for birth parents successfully to oppose, the same is not always true in freeing for adoption proceedings where the applicants are local authorities rather than prospective adopters.

Case study 4 – Sibling relationships

Martha is the birth parent of two children, Michael and Glenn. Her background was tragic and was described by the court as unimaginably appalling. She was beaten by her mother and sexually abused by her step-father and other members of her family. She became pregnant by her step-father when she was sixteen and that child was adopted forthwith. In her later years she was admitted to a psychiatric hospital for treatment, and her second child, Michael, was born there. She did not suffer from any mental illness but her main difficulties lay in the area of her emotional relationships with others, including her children, most probably as a result of the family environment in which she grew up.

Later she had a third child, Glenn, who when he was 18 months old suffered some facial bruising and scratch marks. Martha admitted causing these but later withdrew these admissions. Glenn then suffered a fractured arm, and care proceedings were commenced resulting in the making of a care order. Contact between Martha and Michael was reduced to once a week and the local authority commenced freeing proceedings.

Michael was a remarkable boy, highly intelligent and responsive and showing a high degree of commitment and care to his mother. His clothes were shabby, reflecting some of the privations of his home but, in spite of

these privations, he obtained a place at a local grammar school and was regarded by his teachers as a most impressive boy. Michael was desperately upset at the thought of Glenn being adopted and his losing contact with him. People whose job it was to talk to Michael about it found that he could not discuss the termination of his relationship with Glenn without tears coming into his eyes. Likewise Glenn loved his elder brother very much. There was still a bond between Glenn and his mother. Glenn knew that she was someone special and more than just a friendly visitor bearing sweets. He rushed out to see her whenever she arrived.

A freeing order was made which resulted in extreme distress for Michael and Martha. Martha was advised to appeal to the Court of Appeal. The decision on appeal was that Martha was not unreasonably refusing to give her consent to the freeing order, because a reasonable parent would take into account Michael's interests and it was very clear that he would be very upset at not seeing Glenn again. It was reasonable for the objective mother to seek to keep the boys in contact with each other.

Sometimes local authorities pursue freeing proceedings even when the child is not prepared properly for the adoption, where prospective adopters have not been identified and where proceedings are taken simply to progress the child's case, without much thought to the child's individual needs.

Case study 5 – Changes in the lives of birth parents

An application by a local authority to free a child, Stuart, for adoption was lodged with an application to dispense with the consent of his mother Emma. Stuart had been in the care of the local authority and boarded out with a foster mother since 1986. In 1987 parental rights were assumed by the local authority and upheld by the court. The application for freeing was lodged in 1989.

Emma had contact with Stuart once a fortnight. She had been unable to provide a settled home for him but since 1989 had had a home of her own, and claimed that her circumstances had changed. Stuart saw Emma as a significant person in his life. The application for freeing attempted to dispense with the consent of Emma on the basis that she was withholding her consent unreasonably. There had been a substantial delay on the part of the local authority between the upholding of the resolution assuming parental rights and the lodging of the freeing application. In breach of the Boarding Out Regulations, the local authority had hardly visited the child and he had not been prepared for adoption. A guardian *ad litem* for Stuart took the view that Stuart was not ready to be adopted and that Emma was now in a position to offer Stuart a home. In the light of the adverse guardian *ad litem* report the local authority withdrew its application.

If the local authority has delayed pursuing its adoption plans and then applies for a termination of contact and a freeing order (where the child is not usually placed with the prospective adopters), the court may order that the birth parents be reassessed as possible carers for their child, if they are in a position to offer their child a home.

Case study 6 – Terminating contact

A local authority obtained a care order in respect of two young girls, Jill and Joan, in 1990 because their mother, Doreen, had left them unattended in her flat. The father of the children was violent to Doreen and she was inclined to run away from him leaving the children at times of violence. The mother's contact with Jill and Joan was erratic and, following the children's placement in care, she had written an emotional letter to the foster mother stating that she did not wish to see them any more. After a third child was born, Doreen and the new baby attended a residential assessment centre where her care of the baby was seen to be very good and she resumed contact with Jill and Joan. Doreen progressed so well that she had been able to set up her own home with the third child, and for a while had unsupervised contact with Jill and Joan.

The local authority applied to the court for leave to terminate Doreen's contact with Jill and Joan in order to place them with prospective adopters, who were not willing to accept ongoing contact between Doreen and the girls. The guardian *ad litem* felt that Doreen should have the opportunity to have her care of all three children assessed before her contact was terminated because she had been able to show sufficient progress with the third child to justify having this chance. On the other hand, the local authority had delayed implementing its adoption plans, which had allowed Doreen to mature and demonstrate that she could satisfactorily care for her third child. In view of this, following an appeal to the Court of Appeal, the local authority was refused leave to terminate Doreen's contact.

Court attitudes

For birth parents the feeling that their position is hopeless in contested adoption proceedings is often reinforced when the judge hearing the case makes it very clear from the outset that their chances of successfully opposing the application are poor and that, in effect, public money is being wasted. Occasionally, adoption proceedings are settled outside court by the birth parents giving their consent because they have been advised by their lawyers that their case is hopeless. But, for the most part, the proceedings are fought, not because parents are not resigned to the fact

that an adoption order is to be made despite their opposition, but simply because, having come so far through so many hearings, meetings and disappointments, they are not going to give up their final chance to stop their child being permanently separated from them. The stakes, to say the least, are high.

Attempts by judges, therefore, to persuade them to consent to the adoption will not dissuade them from their chosen course of action. All that is achieved is to make them feel that at the very least they have not had a fair hearing. Judges may make their feelings known in a variety of ways – for example, by complaining at the length of time that lawyers for the birth parents spend in cross-examining the witnesses for the applicants, or by interrupting them in the presentation of their case.

Sometimes judges have to be reminded that adoption cases are almost always emotional and delicate and require the sympathy and sensitivity of the court. Where judges make some ill-considered and unfortunate comments, raising in the natural parents a justifiable sense of grievance that there has perhaps been a denial of justice, then the higher courts will set aside the judge's decision and order a new hearing.

Case study 7 – Denial of justice

Two children, Peter aged 12 years and Diane aged ten years, were the subjects of proceedings for a freeing for adoption order. The children had been placed with foster parents for nine years following the passing of an assumption of parental rights resolution under section 3 of the Child Care Act 1980. The foster parents had wanted to adopt the children for a long time and the children wanted to be adopted by them. The mother had not seen the children for eight years although she had seen them at a distance from time to time but had not made herself known to them.

The judge in the County Court took the view that the mother's objections to the freeing orders were unsustainable and that she was unreasonably withholding her agreement. The judge formed a strong view as to the merits of the mother's case and he intervened forcefully at a comparatively early stage of the hearing, when the mother was giving evidence, and reduced her to tears. He also made some ill-considered and unfortunate comments which upset the mother greatly. The mother did not oppose the adoption of Peter and Diane by the foster parents, but she wanted to have contact with them. There was some evidence that Peter had for some years expressed a desire to see his mother. The Court of Appeal, in its judgment, said that adoption cases were almost always emotional and delicate and required sympathy and sensitivity in the handling by the court, and that this was even more so where the case of the birth parent appeared weak, and where it appeared from the outset that they might well be unsuccessful in the proceedings. The judge was severely criticised.

The effect of proceedings on prospective adopters

For birth parents, contested adoption proceedings come at the end of a long grieving process where the making of the inevitable adoption order is a bereavement. For prospective adopters, by contrast, the process is similar to the prospect of a difficult birth with feelings of anxiety and a wish that it may all soon be over. Prospective adopters often ask their solicitors how long the legal process will take. Entirely coincidentally, the answer is usually nine months! Prospective adopters have a great deal of support from the local authority from whom they are to receive the child. They are pointed in the direction of experienced solicitors and, in most cases, the local authority agrees to pay legal fees where legal aid is not available. In addition, it is usually possible for the solicitor to have access to local authority files on the birth family in order to draw up a Statement of Facts in dispensation of consent cases and to help the prospective adopters prepare their case.

There is an enormous contrast between the amount of co-operation afforded to the prospective adopters and that afforded to the birth parents. Furthermore, when the matter comes before the court the local authority will often be separately represented and will support the application made by the applicants. This means that applicants continue to receive support from the local authority not just through the period leading up to the final hearing, but throughout the hearing too. Often, the local authority has interest separate from that of the applicants and is only in court to defend the social workers from birth parents' claims that they have not handled the case properly.

Often the child who is the subject of the proceedings is placed with the prospective adopters. Their greatest fear is of being forced to return the child to the local authority social workers because the court has decided that the case for adoption is not made. This has been known to happen, as the case study below shows.

Case study 8 – Ambivalence by birth parents

Carmel, a young mother from Eire, came to London to live because she was pregnant and did not want her parents to find out about this. After the birth she arranged with the local authority to have the child accommodated and told the social workers that she wanted the child adopted. The child was placed with prospective adopters, who were naturally delighted. They took a long holiday shortly after this to cement their relationship with the child and decided to commence adoption proceedings on their return.

> Meanwhile, whilst the prospective adopters and the child were away, Carmel had renewed her relationship with the child's father, Dermot, who had followed her to London. Dermot wanted to see the child and he and Carmel had jointly decided to remove the child from accommodation provided by the local authority. On their return from holiday the prospective adopters were confronted by a reluctant social worker asking for the return of the child. They were naturally distraught at this request as the child had been in their care for the previous eight weeks.

Other anxieties faced by prospective adopters are the possibility that the child will not be the sort of child they had dreamed of. Sometimes the child is returned by adopters to the local authority because the child simply does not fulfil their expectations, as the case below demonstrates.

Case study 9 – Failure to share information

A child had been placed for adoption following lengthy and complex care and adoption proceedings in the High Court. Some years later the child was returned by the adoptive parents who could no longer tolerate the child's appalling behaviour. They were very concerned that the local authority had failed to tell them the whole of the background to the case and the full reasons for the child behaving as he did. They later became aware of the reasons, which were that the child's behavioural problems stemmed from the severe sexual abuse to which he had been subjected by his birth father.

The adoptive parents were concerned that the child's behaviour was unlikely to change either in the short or long term and they wished to rescind the adoption order as they had no wish for the child to have any legal connection with their family. Meanwhile, the birth mother wished to resume contact with the child. She had divorced the birth father and was living a more settled lifestyle. However, because she had not seen the child for many years it would be very difficult to reintroduce her to the child.

Sometimes, the anxieties of the prospective adopters lead them unintentionally to put pressure on local authorities, thus forcing them to make very hasty decisions regarding children's futures. For example, a local authority may have found an ideal couple to care for a child of mixed parentage in that their racial origins may exactly match that of the child. The local authority may be forced to make a decision to apply for leave to terminate the birth parents' contact with the child simply because they do not wish to lose the perfect couple, who insist that ongoing contact with the birth parents is not something which is on their agenda, and that they

are not prepared to enter into introductions with the child while that contact continues. They may also be in touch with other adoption agencies regarding children available for adoption, and since they are viewed as a scarce resource they are in a position to exert considerable influence.

Case study 10 – Issues of contact

The local authority accommodated a child with the consent of the birth mother. She had learning difficulties and found it difficult to care on her own for her child. She told the local authority that she wanted to have the child adopted, and thereafter her contact with the child was sporadic and eventually ceased. After a few months the local authority found an ideal couple, Tim and Carol, to care for the child and made plans to place him with them. However, the birth mother changed her mind about contact and indicated that she would consent to the adoption provided that she could have face-to-face contact with the child after the adoption. Tim and Carol were not prepared to agree to this form of ongoing contact. The local authority did not want to lose them, so it made an application for an interim care order and immediate leave to terminate the birth mother's contact before the final hearing, despite the fact that the mother had never done anything on contact visits to place the child at risk. The local authority refused to reconsider its plans despite advice from a guardian *ad litem* for the child that this was simply not good practice.

The mother's change of heart meant that a reassessment of her caring capabilities was necessary. The court took the view that, pending the final hearing of the case, the birth mother should be entitled to have contact, and that only where there was a severe and exceptional risk to the child should contact be terminated. Tim and Carol withdrew their interest in the child.

The anxieties of prospective adopters are very real even though they receive a great deal of support from local authorities. Sometimes local authorities make poor decisions simply to keep them happy.

Conclusion

Contested adoption proceedings give rise to extremes of emotion in both birth parents and prospective adopters because, unlike proceedings under the Children Act 1989, where legislators have done what they can to quell the heat and emotion, the current practice of making adoption orders which exclude birth parents' contact has meant that children are treated as items of property to be won or lost in the contest. 'Winner takes all' is still the ethos at the root of contested adoption proceedings.

In our experience, this approach could be changed if local authorities were to approve only those prospective adopters who were willing to accept adoption with contact by birth parents. Unless they do, there will be no change, as courts are reluctant to interfere with the status quo with which they are often faced, namely the child in placement with prospective adopters who will not entertain any form of contact.

6 The welfare of the child in contested proceedings

Gerison Lansdown

Introduction

There has been widespread concern in recent years at the way in which adoption, as a legal process, has been perceived as a service for the prospective adopters rather than as a service promoting the welfare of children. The language surrounding adoption compounds this view and commonly-used phrases such as 'available for adoption' make the child sound like a commodity for sale. Much of the debate over the countless anti-abortion bills in recent decades focused on the opportunity for unwanted babies to be produced as a source of supply for would-be parents. The growth in international adoption has developed in the context of a growing sense that people have a right to a child (Humphrey and Humphrey, 1992). The tradition of adoption which results in a total severance from birth parents, and a new name and identity for the child, is powerful testimony to the desire of adoptive parents to 'own' the child, rather than any realistic assessment of the best interests of the child.

There is now widespread concern, expressed in the Adoption Law Review (DoH, 1992), and the resulting White Paper, *Adoption: The Future* (DoH, 1993), that adoption law and practice should undergo significant reform in order better to reflect the needs of older children who form the vast majority of those placed for adoption, rather than the infants who are still the focus of current legislation. As Bill Jordan observes in chapter 2, there is also a recognition that adoption legislation should be brought in line with the Children Act 1989 in order that the breadth of child care legislation rests on a set of comparable principles.

The Children Act has a clear focus on the paramountcy of the welfare of children, and children have much more clearly prescribed and broadly-

63

based rights than they have previously enjoyed in primary legislation. Rather than proceeding, as the present adoption law does, from welfare-based ideas concerning children, this chapter maintains that the most useful starting point for examining adoption legislation and the many issues that confront us in contested situations would be to construct a principled framework which takes the rights of the child as its central focus. We have a model for achieving this in the United Nations Convention on the Rights of the Child. The Convention, which was ratified by the United Kingdom government in December 1991, provides a comprehensive framework of principles touching on every aspect of a child's life. We are now obliged under international law to comply with its stated principles and, in the light of the current Adoption Law Review, it would be timely to consider the application of the Convention principles as a basis for changes in legislation and practice in adoption. (The Adoption White Paper makes clear the government's intention to amend legislation concerning intercountry adoption by building in the principles of the Hague Convention on Intercountry Adoption – another model for such an approach.) An approach based on the UN Convention establishes the principle that children have human rights which must be respected. They are rights which are internationally recognised and which should have application to all children. Without using such a framework, decisions made about children are based on the perceived *needs* of the child without reference to their basic human *rights*.

Relevant principles

There are a number of principles in the Convention which it is essential to consider in relation to adoption law and practice, and it is useful to detail these below:

- *Article 2:* all rights apply to all children without exception and the state must protect children from discrimination.
- *Article 3:* all actions concerning children must take full account of her or his best interests.
- *Article 7:* every child has a right to a name, to acquire a nationality, and, as far as possible, to know and be cared for by his or her parents.
- *Article 8:* every child has a right to preserve his or her identity including name, nationality and family relations.
- *Article 9:* every child has a right to live with their parents unless

this is not compatible with their best interests, and, where a child is separated from a parent, he or she has the right to maintain contact.

- *Article 12:* every child has the right to express an opinion and have that opinion taken into account in any matter or procedure affecting the child.
- *Article 19:* the state must protect children from all forms of maltreatment or abuse perpetrated by parents or others responsible for their care.
- *Article 20:* the state must provide special protection for children deprived of their family environment, taking account of the child's ethnic, religious, cultural and linguistic background.
- *Article 21:* adoption procedures must ensure that the best interests of the child are the paramount consideration.
- *Article 30:* children of minority communities have a right to enjoy their own culture and to practise their own religion and language.

Paramountcy

It would be useful to begin by examining the welfare principle embodied in Articles 3 and 21. Current adoption legislation requires that courts and adoption agencies 'give first consideration' to the welfare of the child throughout childhood. The Adoption Law Review proposes that this should be changed in order to make the welfare test commensurate with that of the Children Act, in which the child's welfare is always the paramount, rather than the first, consideration.

While the White Paper, *Adoption: the Future* (DoH, 1993), does not refer specifically to the welfare test, it promises to 'define afresh' the 'balance between the rights and interests of the child, his adoptive parents and his birth parents'. This would include, 'recognition that the **child's interests, wishes and feelings** should be ascertained and given great weight and that he or she should have the right and opportunity to influence decisions directly if of an age and understanding to do so'.

The occurrence of a similar welfare test in both the Convention and the Children Act could easily lead us to see the principle of paramountcy as uncontroversial. This is far from the truth, and in the context of contested adoption proceedings it particularly warrants attention. Here we find that the concept of pursuing the best interests of the child is an extraordinarily difficult one. There are no objective measures of best interests (Ryburn, 1991). Within any family, it is likely that parents will differ widely in their interpretation of what is best for the child. We may well ask ourselves how many of us have not had major disagreements over such mundane aspects of family living as bedtimes, homework, schooling, food, discipline, boundaries, staying-out times.

How infinitely more difficult it is in the context of the permanent placement of a child and the severance of all legal ties with the birth family. How, for example, can we balance a child's immediate and long-term best interests; the child's immediate need for security and family life with a longer-term need for cultural identity; the child's need for contact with their family with the risk of losing the prospective adopters who want an exclusive involvement with the child? At worst, the welfare principle can be a tool simply to justify a desired course of action. It can and often may be used as a weapon in the armoury of professionals to override the wishes and feelings of a child or the consent of the parent, even though we know from a variety of studies that the use of compulsory powers is unlikely to serve the best interests of children (see for example Millham et al., 1986; 1989). At best, the welfare principle is employed to create a best guess in the light of all the available research and evidence in a particular case.

The welfare principle itself offers a moral mandate for the involvement of the state in the lives of children and their families. Its helpfulness however will always be limited by the ability of practitioners and their commitment to its realisation in practice, and by the inherent pitfalls and difficulties that attend any reliance on a presumption that we can judge the long-term best interests of a child. We may argue, instead, that, in order to impose some structure on the methodology of assessing the best interests of a child, there ought to be a two-tiered approach. First, and obviously, the individual circumstances of the child need to be considered in the light of all the evidence and options available. In addition, however, in making any recommendations about the future legal status of the child, there should be reference to the principles on which adoption practice should rest. In other words, if we start from the perspective that children have rights, then we have an external framework against which to assess the decision-making process.

Some of these principles will already be regarded as intrinsic to current day-to-day practice. Thus, for example, most practitioners would espouse a belief in Article 19, the right of the child to protection, and Article 7, the right both to know and as far as possible to be cared for by his or her own parents. Similarly, Article 12 and the right of the child to express her or his views, to have them taken seriously and to be heard in any judicial or administrative proceedings, and Article 9 and the right to maintain contact with parents, would find a broad acceptance in the practice beliefs of individual professionals. The problem, however, lies in the fact that where these beliefs inform practice, it is in relation to an individual assessment of the needs of the child rather than in terms of fundamental principles.

Clearly, it is not possible to avoid subjective judgments, though we can avoid the pitfall of believing that our judgments are objective (Ryburn, 1992). The determination of the welfare of children cannot be reduced to a

scientific process. The use, however, of the key principles of the Convention as a yardstick to measure every decision in adoption would begin to offer an external consistency and rigour to the decisions taken in all adoption matters, and in particular to those in the very difficult circumstances where parents and professional disagree. The remainder of this chapter will consider the sort of framework for practice that the application of the Convention's principles could offer us.

Article 12

This principle is fundamental to the Convention and is now incorporated into the Children Act 1989. It should be central to the adoption process. There is no evidence, however, that this principle finds consistent expression in practice. In the work of the Children's Rights Development Unit (Lansdown, 1992) we have often found amongst children and young people a very strong sense that they are not listened to and that their views, when ranged against those of adults, carry little weight. The Children's Legal Centre have commented recently on a number of complaints about children's wishes not being listened to when plans are being made to remove them from foster carers to an adoptive placement.

Listening to children is not straightforward and in general we probably do not do it at all well. In practice, there is still a long way to go before the principle that children have a right both to express their views and to have them at the centre of any decisions that are taken finds effective realisation.

Consultation is meaningless if the child is only involved once all realistic alternatives have been eliminated. Thus consultation with children concerning their wish to return to their original families is largely meaningless if all effective links have already been eroded or terminated. Consultation is also meaningless if the child does not fully understand the implications of a decision in both the short and the long term, and what the available options are. Serious application of the principle in all circumstances would require that from the earliest possible date in the decision-making process, the following steps are taken.

Children have adequate information appropriate to their age with which to form opinions Children cannot express informed opinions without access to all the necessary information about what choices are available and the implications of those options. This information needs to be provided in as open and fair a manner as possible. If, for example, adoption is presented as the only means of achieving security, the child is not necessarily being given a complete picture. If termination of contact with parents is presented, as it often is, as the inevitable consequence of acquiring an adoptive family, the information may reflect the preferred

outcome of the social worker rather than the only realistic set of options for the child.

Children have meaningful opportunities to express their views and explore options open to them   Listening to children will often require a considerable investment of time, with the child needing the opportunity to ask questions, to talk to important adults about the choices they face and to think through the options and their consequences. This discussion will need to be grounded in ideas and concepts that have meaning for the child emotionally, cognitively and culturally. Thus, for example, we know from the work of Brodzinsky and his colleagues (1984a) that full understanding of the meaning of adoption develops right into early adolescence, and a child's use of the term adoption should not necessarily be taken to connote understanding of all its implications. If, in contested proceedings, a child expresses a wish to be adopted, their relative understanding of the term is a vital matter for further discussion with them.

Children's views are listened to and considered with respect and seriousness   There is a danger that adults will listen to children when their views coincide with their own, but are less willing to do so when there is conflict. But a child's perspective needs to be taken seriously. That is not to say that the child's wishes must always be complied with. It is important to distinguish between consulting a child and automatic adherence to their views. What the child wants to happen may not be possible. It may be that the child lacks the understanding to comprehend the long-term implications of particular courses of action. But the child's views must nevertheless be given due weight and should fully inform any decision which is being made. As a matter of course the child should be told how their views will be considered and the status of their opinions. If we follow the path of children's rights then they must also be told the outcome of any decisions and, if that decision is contrary to the child's wishes, the reasons must be fully explained.

Children are provided with access to independent advocacy   The Adoption Review recommends that children aged 12 and over should be given party status automatically in adoption proceedings and that younger children should be able to be a party where it is considered appropriate. This is certainly an improvement over the current position where the child is only a party if the hearing takes place in the High Court. However, it falls far short of the provisions in the Children Act which give children automatic party status in all proceedings in all courts. This inconsistency is more glaring when we consider the greater implications for adoption orders compared with, for example, care orders. Though the views of

children are represented in contested cases by a guardian *ad litem* or the official solicitor, their duties do not include the duty of advocacy on behalf of the child, but only the representation of the child's perceived best interests. Only automatic party status would ensure that children were represented in all cases, as required by the principle in Article 12 that it is the right of the child 'to be heard in all judicial proceedings affecting' them.

Consent to adoption   The Adoption White Paper (DoH, 1993) proposes that 'all children aged twelve or more must agree before an adoption order is made unless incapable of giving such agreement; and that they and other children in suitable cases should be eligible for party status in adoption proceedings' (para 4.3). This approach is consistent with that which operates in Scotland and is clearly a recognition that the view of the child is central to an application to adopt. This focus is welcome but there are some concerns about its application as a universal requirement for older children, and the setting of an age for competence also has problems.

The requirement to give consent could be experienced as a pressure imposing an undue responsibility on some children. It may be felt that they are being actively required to reject their parents in order to agree to the adoption and this may make some children reluctant to consent to an adoption that they might otherwise want. One part of a solution to the dilemma that this poses is to acknowledge, as June Thoburn points out in chapter 8, that there are other perfectly acceptable forms of permanent family placement than adoption. These are alternatives which do not, by virtue of their less severe legal effects, involve children in the same conflict of choice. Another choice is routinely to place the possibility of continuing contact with original families in the range of options available to children and young people in adoption. This is something that rarely happens where there are contested cases, even though we know that the considerable body of research now available points to the importance of the maintenance of links (Ryburn, 1994).

There is also a difficulty inherent in arbitrarily choosing any particular age limit, such as 12, since many children under that age are fully capable of understanding many of the issues involved and taking a view on the proposed adoption. There must also reasonably be a concern that children under 12 years will not be adequately consulted if such a cut-off point is introduced. The Convention steers clear of introducing any age limits for participation, preferring instead to rely on the assessment of the 'age and maturity of the child'.

We should also acknowledge that acceptance of the principle of consent and the introduction of an age limit at which consent is required does not necessarily mean that there will be an improvement in practice. It can be argued that this would be better achieved by requiring guardians *ad litem* to

produce detailed evidence to the court of the measures taken to ascertain the wishes and feelings of the child. A more useful measure may well be the introduction of a right of veto for the child to any proposed adoption. This would ensure that no adoption could go ahead if the child was unhappy with it, but would avoid the necessity of the requirement for formal agreement in every case.

The other danger attendant on the giving of formal consent is that critical decisions with regard to a child's future are often made much earlier than the point at which consent to an adoption is required. By that stage the decision can be merely a formality. Involving a child effectively in decisions for the long-term future needs to happen from the very earliest stages of planning. The full and routine involvement of children in decision-making has been the plea of young people themselves for nearly two decades (Page and Clarke, 1977), yet the consistent application of this principle as a fundamental right still requires in many cases a considerable shift in approach and attitude.

Articles 7, 8 and 9

The rights espoused in these Articles – to be cared for wherever possible by parents, to preservation of identity including nationality and parental and family links – are perhaps those most at risk in the adoption process. Our ratification of the Convention highlights the conflict between a rights-based approach to work with children and much current practice in contested adoptions.

Adoption is a permanent and irrevocable process which severs all legal ties between a child and her or his birth family. It should only be used, therefore, where there is no possibility whatever of care for the child by their own parents or any member of the wider family at any stage in the future. There is a tendency, as the Adoption Law Review notes, to assume that creating security for children rests on a hierarchy of orders with adoption at the pinnacle. Compliance with the principles embodied in Articles 8 and 9, however, will necessitate a radically different approach to adoption.

Two implications ensue from a recognition of these rights. First, it is necessary to question more closely in an individual case whether the pursuit of adoption, with its effect of achieving total severance, is consistent with the promotion of the child's rights to an identity, to know their parents and to maintain contact as far as is possible, and whether, therefore, in their best interests. Second, where adoption is considered the best available option, then the presumption should always be that, as far as is possible, there should be continued and extensive contact with members of the birth family.

The Adoption Law Review rightly points out that adoption is too often

regarded as the only way of securing permanence for children, and, in consequence, the White Paper (DoH, 1993) proposes that the court must satisfy itself that 'the likely benefit of adoption is so significantly better when compared with other options as to justify an adoption order' (para 5.4). The prevailing view amongst many practitioners and prospective adopters that adoption is the most desirable route to security for children is not, as June Thoburn indicates in chapter 8, supported by research. The predominance of such a view raises a real risk that other orders, such as the proposed inter vivos guardianship order, will not be sufficiently used as an alternative to adoption, just as custodianship was largely ignored as an alternative permanent placement order (Bullard et al., 1990).

The greatest advantage of an order such as guardianship is that it would bestow parental responsibility on the guardian, and provide security and permanence for the child without severing entirely the legal links with the birth family. The particularly difficult identity problems in contested proceedings, which Murray Ryburn refers to in chapter 14, would often be wholly or partly obviated by these sorts of order, and their widespread use would be the necessary corollary to a children's rights-based approach centred on the Convention principles. Since alternative forms of order do not sever all legal links with the birth family, they may well be easier for families to accept, as was the case with custodianship before it was repealed by the Children Act 1989 (Bullard et al., 1990).

The maintenance of some legal links would be likely both to make it easier to fulfil the requirements of Articles 8 and 9 in terms of identity and contact with original family, and to reduce the need for contested proceedings. Any diminution of the need for contested proceedings would clearly be of benefit to the children who are caught up in the conflict of those contests and would be consistent with the paramountcy principle of both Article 21 and the Children Act. Reduced conflict over the process itself would also be likely to enhance the possibilities of continued contact with the family after the order has been made. We should also note that formal legal adoption is not part of the culture of many minority communities living in this country (Fratter, 1988). A rights-based approach to these children in terms of Articles 8 and 9 and the emphases on ethnicity and culture in Article 20, should probably lead us to eschew entirely the idea of adoption and complete legal severance in contested cases. Adoption in these circumstances creates difficulties both in recruiting families and, where it occurs, gives children a legal status that may leave them feeling alienated in their own culture.

Forms of permanent placement other than adoption have the great advantage that they focus on the responsibility of the person caring for the child rather than on the 'ownership' of the child. In this way they remove the presumption, which research by Triseliotis (1973) and many others has

still not dispelled, that it is possible to cut out a child's history and family background and provide a new beginning for a child. Guardianship orders would help to direct practice to a recognition that permanence is not about replacing birth parents, but about providing long-term care and security for a child. By so doing, the law would be improving its capacity to comply with Articles 8 and 9 and the child's right to a service which facilitated an understanding of their past and their relationships with their birth family.

Article 8's emphasis on the fundamental right of a child to knowledge of their family has been acknowledged in the Adoption Law Review, to the extent that it recommends that adoption agencies should have a responsibility to advise adoptive parents of the necessity of explaining the fact of the adoption to the child. It further recommends that adoptive parents should be provided with a 'package' of information about the background of a child in their care, which is to be given to the child at an appropriate age.

The Review also recommended that adoptive parents should be contacted when the child is 16 to remind them of their responsibility to tell the child. (The White Paper, 1993, while reaffirming the importance of adopted children being made aware of their adopted status, refers only to a 'suitable age' [paras 2.6; 4.18].) This would seem to be far too late for such a reminder. Probably the only way to ensure compliance with Article 8 would be to include a requirement in adoption law to inform the child. To do so would heighten the significance of telling as an essential task in identity-building. Its assertion in primary legislation as a fundamental right of all children would give an unequivocal message to practitioners and adopters about its crucial importance. Any follow-up by agencies should also take place at a much earlier age, given the evidence that even where children are told of their adoptive status they do not necessarily make sense of this and that it should be part of a continuing account (Brodzinsky et al., 1984b). The Children's Legal Centre (1993) argues that it should happen no later than the child's seventh birthday.

The Review recommends that decision-making in adoption should be founded on the same principles as the Children Act. This means that courts will consider the welfare of the child, the need to avoid delays in decision-making, and a welfare checklist which includes the wishes of the child, the emotional, physical and educational needs of the child, the age, sex, background and other relevant factors, any harm the child has suffered or is at risk of suffering, and the capacity of relevant adults to meet the child's needs. In addition, it is proposed that the courts should also consider the effect in a child's adult life of an adoption order, and the implications of an order on the child's relationships with the birth family. However, no reference is made in this checklist to the need to consider the child's race, culture, religion and language when decisions are being made.

Nor is there any requirement to consider the implications of adoption on the child's nationality and immigration status. These matters are of critical significance to the child and it is therefore essential that courts be required to take account of them in their decision-making. Compliance with Articles 8, 20 and 30 would necessitate that these issues were at the heart of court decisions, in a way that they currently are not.

Article 30 contains a requirement that children of minority communities have the right to enjoy their own culture and to practise their own language and religion. This is a requirement which our current practice largely ignores. Charles and her colleagues (1992) report that under one-quarter of the 246 black children in their study were placed in families where at least one parent was black, and this broad finding has nothing to say about other aspects of language, culture and religion. The Children Act acknowledges the importance to children of having the opportunity to be brought up by a family who can sustain their links with their language, culture and religion, and this approach is fully consistent with Article 30. Since formal legal adoption, and especially adoption against family wishes, are alien concepts to black communities in Britain, recruitment of adopters is often difficult. Rather than explore alternative forms of permanent placement in contested proceedings, which have the potential to meet the core conditions of Article 30, many agencies practise transracial adoption and defend it on the grounds that black families cannot be recruited.

Though the evidence from the study of Charles and colleagues (1992) is that the practice of transracial placement is widespread, there is very little research in this country on the experience of children in transracial adoptions. Accurate information is also needed, for planning purposes, concerning the ethnicity, language and religion of children who are placed and the adoptive parents with whom they are placed. There are, however, no nationally collected statistics available on the ethnicity of children placed for adoption nor on the ethnicity of the adopters. The only information that is collected relates to the gender and age of the child placed and the marital status of the parents. This lack of access to information means that it is difficult for agencies to assess the levels of need that exist for permanent families of different racial origins. In consequence, they are unable to comply adequately with Article 30 in ensuring that full account is taken of a child's race and culture in making placements.

Article 2

Finally in relation to contested adoptions, we should consider the principle of Article 2 that *all* the rights in the Convention must apply equally to *all* children irrespective of race, language, nationality, religion, colour,

disability or gender. It also states that children must not be discriminated against on the basis of their parents' status. This means that all the Convention rights already outlined should apply to all children and not only those who have the fortune to be able to live at home without any need for statutory intervention. We know that there is a high correlation between, for example, poverty and the likelihood of being accommodated or in the care of the local authority and that care or wardship is the route into compulsory adoption. Research in 1989 by Bebbington and Miles showed that in families where there was a single parent, with mixed-race children, three or more children in the family, dependence on state benefit, living in privately rented accommodation with one or more people per room, the chances of a child being admitted to care is 1 in 10. If this is contrasted with a white family with two parents, in owner-occupied accommodation, in employment, with two or fewer children and more rooms in their dwelling than people the chances change to 1 in 7 000.

In the light of the fact that poverty is the clearest determinant of whether children will be adopted against parental wishes, Articles cannot be espoused without a fundamental reassessment of attitudes to family poverty. The equal and rigorous application of all rights to all children in relation to adoption can otherwise not be achieved. The extreme consequences of adoption sit uneasily with the knowledge that, had parents not been prevented by poverty from full participation in family and social life, their children may never have been seen as needing adoption.

Conclusion

Whilst some of the rights of the child in the context of contested adoption may be implicit in the practice of some workers, significant progress is needed before a rights perspective to adoption which complies with the standards embodied in the United Nations Convention is developed. The child needs to be central to the process, not the adoptive parents or the exigencies of practice in an under-resourced social services economy. Adoption services will often have to recognise a broader framework for decision-making than that of the needs of the individual child as they are perceived by the practitioner involved. Without a principled perspective there will always be a danger that the rights of the child can be subjugated to personal prejudice, an unwillingness to try to resolve conflict, a failure to listen at the appropriate time to the wishes of the child or pressure from adoptive parents.

Invoking the principles contained in the Convention clearly does not avoid the complexity of the decision-making involved. Inevitably, the

application of one right may be in conflict with another. The rights framework of the United Nations Convention does, however, provide a model with which to approach the manner by which those decisions are made, and against which to test and evaluate the extent to which the child is central to the decision-making process. If Britain's ratification of the Convention is to mean anything in reality for children and young people, then some quite fundamental changes in adoption law and practice will be necessary.

References

Bebbington, A. and Miles, J. (1989), 'The Background of Children who Enter Local Authority Care', *The British Journal of Social Work*, 19(4), 349–68.

Brodzinsky, D., Schechter, D., Braff, A. and Singer, L. (1984a), 'Psychological and Academic Adjustment in Adopted Children', *Journal of Consulting and Clinical Psychology*, 52(4), 582–90.

Brodzinsky, D., Singer, L. and Braff, A. (1984b), 'Children's Understanding of Adoption', *Child Development*, 55, 869–78.

Bullard, E., Mallos, E. and Parker, R. (1990), *Custodianship Research Project: A Report to the Department of Health*, Bristol: Socio-Legal Centre for Family Studies, University of Bristol.

Charles, M., Rashid, S. and Thoburn, J. (1992), 'Research on Permanent Family Placement of Black Children and those from Minority Ethnic Groups', *Adoption and Fostering*, 16(2), 3–4, and 16(3), 13–18.

Children's Legal Centre (1993), *Review of Adoption Law: Report to Minister of an Interdepartmental Working Group – Response of the Children's Legal Centre.*

Department of Health/Welsh Office (1992), *Review of Adoption Law: Report to Ministers of an Interdepartmental Working Group: A Consultation Document*, London: DoH.

Department of Health/Welsh Office/Home Office/Lord Chancellor's Department (1993), *Adoption: The Future*, Cmnd. 2288, London: HMSO.

Fratter, J. (1988), 'Black Children with Black Families', in Argent, H. [ed.], *Keeping the Doors Open: A Review of Post Adoption Services*, London: BAAF.

Humphrey, M. and Humphrey, H. [eds] (1992), *Inter-Country Adoption: Practical Experiences*, Routledge: London.

Lansdown, G. (1992), 'UN Convention: Setting New Targets', *Adoption and Fostering*, 16(3), 34–7.

Millham, S., Bullock, R., Hosie, K. and Haak, M. (1986), *Lost in Care: The Problems of Maintaining Links between Children in Care and their Families*, Aldershot: Gower.

Millham, S., Bullock, R., Hosie, K. and Little, M. (1989), *Access Disputes in Child-Care*, Aldershot: Gower.

Page, R. and Clarke, G. (1977), *Who Cares?*, London: National Children's Bureau.

Ryburn, M. (1991) 'The Myth of Assessment', *Adoption and Fostering*, 15(1), 20–27.

Ryburn, M. (1992), 'The Myth of Assessment Revisited', *Adoption and Fostering*, 16 (3), 3.

Ryburn, M. (1994), *Open Adoption: Research, Theory and Practice*, Aldershot: Avebury.

Triseliotis, J. (1973), *In Search of Origins*, London: Routledge and Kegan Paul.

7 Contested proceedings: what the research tells us

Lydia Lambert

Introduction

This would be a very short chapter indeed if we were to rely strictly on the statement in the Adoption Law Review's summary of research (Thoburn, 1990) that 'there have been no studies which specifically looked at adoptions which were achieved against parental wishes'. However, the emphasis was on the word 'specifically', and the Review itself went on to refer to various recent studies which are relevant to the issue of contested adoption. Compared with many other important issues in adoption, such as openness, adoption allowances, and the progress and development of adopted children, there were in fact few studies of direct relevance before the completion of the *Pathways to Adoption* study, which sets the context for both contested and uncontested proceedings (Murch et al., 1991). I shall come back to this study later, but first it may be useful to look at some of the possible reasons why there has not been a specific study of contested proceedings.

Trends towards more contests

The government's *Review of Adoption Law* (DoH, 1992) points out that 'it is, and should continue to be, a basic principle of adoption law that adoption should normally only be possible with the agreement of each parent or guardian of the child'. A very similar statement can be found in the Houghton Report (HMSO, 1972) 20 years earlier and both continue 'and that it should be open to a court to dispense with parental agreement on

certain specified grounds'. Similarly, the Adoption White Paper, *Adoption: The Future* (DoH, 1993), while stressing that the court must satisfy itself that 'the likely benefit of adoption is so significantly better when compared with other options as to justify an adoption order', goes on to say, 'When the court is satisfied that adoption is likely to offer a significantly better advantage to the child . . . it will continue to have a power to override a refusal of consent by the birth parents' (paras 5.4, 5.5).

Rather like the question asked in the marriage service or ceremony about whether there is any impediment or reason why two persons should not be lawfully married, the power to dispense with parental agreement is there as a safeguard. It is there – but everyone hopes it will not be necessary to use it. Just as there is an audible sigh of relief when no-one shouts out some awful secret from the bride or groom's past, so do adopters, social workers and others breathe more easily when an adoption application is accompanied by the parents' signed agreement. For more than 40 years it was indeed the norm – on paper at least – that adoption was accomplished at the request of the parents. In their *Survey of Adoption in Great Britain*, Grey and Blunden (1971) reported that in 98 per cent of applications by non-relatives the mother's consent was attached to the application.

At that time the majority of the children involved in these applications were babies or toddlers. Practitioners were keenly aware that many of the mothers had only come to the decision for adoption after much anguish (Pochin, 1969). This has been confirmed by recent research at the Post-Adoption Centre (Howe and Hinings, 1989) and in Scotland (Bouchier et al., 1991) and by earlier studies in Australia (Winkler and van Keppel, 1984) and the USA (Pannor et al., 1978; Watson, 1986) which showed that most relinquishing mothers feel that they have no alternative choice and are effectively forced to part with their children. Thus the split between contested and uncontested applications is to some extent artificial and we are only slowly coming to appreciate the long-term effects of these decisions. In other words, contested proceedings are like icebergs as they reveal the dangers hidden below the surface in the majority of adoptions. Nevertheless, there are some obvious legal and practical differences between the two types of proceedings.

One of the Houghton Committee's concerns in the 1970s was how to lessen some of the procedural difficulties mothers experienced when they had decided to give their consent. Two studies commissioned by the Committee had found that many mothers considered the consent process too long-drawn-out and repetitive (Triseliotis and Hall, 1971; Raynor, 1971). Changes were recommended partly to help these mothers but also to make the process more secure for the children and their prospective adopters. These recommendations led directly to the introduction of the relinquishment procedures within freeing for adoption in the Children Act

1975 and they were expected to form the bulk of applications (Rowe, 1984). However, by the time these sections of the Act were implemented in 1984 through the Adoption Act 1976 (England and Wales) or 1978 (Scotland), many other changes in adoption practice had taken place. Instead of being used mainly as a shorter route in *uncontested* proceedings, freeing has become synonymous with contested adoption in people's minds. This is because the other purpose for which freeing was proposed has become the dominant factor, that is, the sanctioning of adoptions of children in care without parental consent.

The move in the direction of adoption becoming what Hoggett (1984) has called 'another weapon in the child care armoury of the state' did not happen overnight. McWhinnie (1967) and later Teague (1989) have documented the history of the development and number of grounds for dispensing with parental consent, and it is noticeable that these increased and became more like the ones used today around the same time as the establishment of Children's Departments in the late 1940s. In the process, the grounds for dispensing with consent to adoption also became more like those used for Parental Rights Resolutions. Initially, these measures were used sparingly and there were relatively few adoptions of children in care during the 1950s and 60s as the emphasis was on short-term and preventive work. Towards the end of this period, however, there was a growing realisation that a sizeable number of children were staying on in care, some of whom would benefit from adoption but whose parents had refused their permission.

Freeing for adoption

In support of their proposal for freeing for adoption to be used as a means of testing whether parental consent could be dispensed with before making an adoption placement, the Houghton Committee referred to research being carried out by Tizard on children aged four-and-a-half who had been admitted to residential nurseries in the first six months of life and had remained there because their mothers would not agree to adoption (Tizard, 1977). The Committee had mentioned earlier the then forthcoming study by the Association of British Adoption Agencies (now BAAF), which was published as *Children Who Wait* (Rowe and Lambert, 1973). This research covered nearly 3 000 children aged under 11 in 28 local authorities and five large voluntary societies. It found that social workers considered that 22 per cent of the children needed substitute families ranging from foster homes for an indeterminate period through to adoption.

The study explored information relating to consent to adoption and also

the assumption of parental rights but stressed that the data were based on social work reports rather than on first-hand evidence. Not surprisingly, there was more suggestion of probable opposition to adoption than to fostering, but one-third of the parents of children needing families did not appear to be opposed to either type of placement. Half the children needing placement had either been admitted on care orders or else parental rights had been assumed later, and there appeared to be possible grounds for assumption of parental rights for two-fifths of the remainder. The study emphasised that the majority of children waiting for families were of school age and had problems of health, development or behaviour. The researchers thought that the Houghton Committee's proposals for freeing would have important implications, especially for older children needing adoption, as prospective adopters would be 'unable or unwilling to make the necessary commitment . . . without the security of knowing that adoption can follow if the placement goes well'. It was also argued that the children needed to know how they stood in relation to their birth parents before being able to commit themselves to a new family.

These concerns were indeed found to be important considerations in the applications for freeing studied in Scotland between 1986 and 1989. The research project had been mounted at a time when it was still expected that freeing would be more widely used as a procedure for early relinquishment than for dispensing with parental agreement (Lambert et al., 1989; 1990). Thus it was not set up as a study of contested adoptions, although that is what it largely became. Two forces in particular had been at work during the nine-year interval since the Children Act 1975. On the one hand, the decline had continued in the number of babies offered for adoption following the Abortion Act 1967 and the change in attitudes towards single parents brought about partly by the increasing incidence of divorce. On the other hand, most local authorities had by 1984 taken on board the findings of the *Children Who Wait* study and other work from what has been dubbed the Permanence Movement (for example, Goldstein et al., 1973). Determined efforts had been made to place children in substitute families if there was no prospect of them returning home (McKay, 1980) and in the process agencies had built up a lot of experience in finding homes for children with 'special needs' (Thoburn et al., 1986; Hill et al., 1989). Therefore the cases where freeing was actually used turned out to be situations that were even more uncertain than had been anticipated originally and where parents were also more directly involved.

The Scottish study concentrated on 39 cases which were explored in depth through interviews with social workers and information from case files, supplemented by discussions with members of the legal profession and key personnel involved in decision-making about children in care in the local authorities. Seventeen of the adoptive parents were interviewed

and we also attempted to speak with the birth parents, but agencies were reluctant to facilitate this contact and we only succeeded in two cases. The Bristol researchers who conducted the Pathways study were also initially prevented from interviewing birth parents, but for different reasons (Lowe et al., 1991). However, they have subsequently been enabled to undertake a consumer study of birth parent's views of the adoption process and the law relating to it which will fill some important gaps in our understanding. The Pathways study itself was conducted between 1988 and 1991 and comprised a court record survey of a weighted sample of 1 268 cases from five areas and a practitioner survey of the perspectives of social workers and solicitors involved in some of these cases. In the Scottish research an additional undertaking was a census across the country of one year's applications for freeing orders. Some comparisons were also made with a small sample of cases involving applications for adoption via the traditional route and another small sample of applications for parental rights resolutions.

The link with parental rights resolutions and termination of access

In England and Wales these resolutions were removed by the introduction of the Children Act 1989, but they can still interact with adoption at the moment in Scotland. An influential Scottish judgment in 1982 (*Lothian Regional Council* v. *H*, 1982 SLT (Sh. Ct.) 65) limited their use as a prelude to adoption but they are sometimes resorted to as a solution to legal difficulties involving children subject to the Children's Hearings system. This is a complex area which has been discussed by the Scottish Reviews of Child Care and Adoption Law. As already observed, the boundaries between the two procedures were narrowed by the similarity between some of the grounds for parental rights and those for dispensing with agreement to adoption, in particular the 'persistent failure without reasonable cause to discharge the parental duties in relation to the child'. This was found to be the most frequent ground put forward in the freeing applications studied in detail, although it was often combined with 'unreasonably withholding agreement to adoption'. When preparing cases and deciding which route to take to achieve adoption, it was not surprising that local authority legal departments made use of a ground which could apply to more than one type of application. However, past experience with contested resolutions meant that it was rigorously examined in court.

During the 1980s, an important aspect of applications for parental rights

resolutions was the link with applications to terminate parental access, which were often made at the same time (Millham et al., 1989). They caused much distress and few can have been sorry when they disappeared in that form with the introduction of the Children Act 1989, which emphasises continuing parental responsibility and a presumption of contact between parents and children. Contact orders made under section 8 of the Act can now provide *for* contact as well as restricting it and applications can be made by other family members, such as grandparents. However, there is considerable uncertainty about using these orders in adoption applications. The few birth parents interviewed in the freeing research indicated that they would have been more likely to agree to adoption if they could have maintained some links with their children, but practitioners who favour a more 'open' type of adoption usually prefer this to be an informal arrangement (Fratter, 1991). Many of the adoptive parents we saw were wary about enforced contact, although those who had previously fostered the child were more likely to consider continuing some links. Similar reactions were found by Thoburn and her colleagues (1986) in their study of permanence in child care. One of the especial difficulties about making access arrangements if using the freeing process has been that there is no provision in the current legislation for this to be considered at the stage when the parents are still parties to the proceedings. It is also difficult for other family members to intervene.

Delays and other procedural problems

While such factors may be important considerations with regard to the long-term well-being of individual children, research on both sides of the border has shown that the most immediate problem in all types of contested adoption has been the length of time taken first to prepare cases in the agencies and then to reach a final conclusion in court. For example, the Pathways study found that a contested freeing case took on average about six months from the date of the panel recommendation and the date when the application was lodged in court, and then about ten months from this date to the date of the order. A contested adoption application generally took even longer at the agency stage and then about eight months at the court stage. Both types of contested proceedings took almost twice as long as uncontested applications in court. There are two stages before the adoption order is granted in freeing applications and the proceedings could be lengthened still further in some of the more heavily contested cases by appeals, which had to be heard first before the adoption application could proceed. In many freeing cases there is also likely to be

an interval of several months between applications if the child has not already been introduced to or placed with prospective adopters.

In Scotland, interviews with adopters revealed very mixed feelings about taking on a child in the middle of a contested freeing application. Understandably, adopters much preferred the security of knowing that, as one of them said: 'the legal aspect has been cleared up and you know exactly where you are going'. Such a viewpoint would be echoed by most adopters, but it is necessary to bear in mind that children involved in contested proceedings are often older and, consequently, they have experienced difficulties at home and then an unsettled period in care, probably punctuated by at least one attempt at restoration to their families. Helping them to settle into yet another new home is not likely to be an easy task, even without anxieties about the legal situation.

The Pathways to Adoption study uncovered some interesting variations in the ages of children involved in contested proceedings. Some of the differences appeared to relate to agency policies and others to changing practice in the use of freeing and also in placing children with disabilities. Overall, the study found that children in contested freeing cases were on average two years younger than children in contested adoption cases. However, the fact that patterns appeared to be changing within the fieldwork period (1986–8) indicates the experimental nature of much of the work at this time. This was corroborated by some follow-up work during 1988 in the Scottish project which showed that disillusionment with freeing was leading some practitioners to revert to using contested adoption instead.

Defining a contested case

Whichever type of proceedings is used there has, in fact, been considerable difficulty in defining a 'contested' case. To many people this phrase conjures up images of courtrooms full of lawyers and witnesses battling it out, and it seems rather odd to include cases where no-one turns up to challenge the proceedings so that the judge, or magistrates, simply dispenses with the agreement and grants the order. However, it is impossible to be sure in advance that a parent will not exercise her or his right to contest the application. There has been a growing recognition, too, that many birth parents feel unable to 'sign away' their children and yet have no intention of disrupting the proceedings. An interesting development under the freeing process has been the attendance at hearings of some birth parents, not in order to contest them but to 'see that justice has been done' and, thereby, come to terms with their loss.

In the Scottish research we found that there seemed to be a continuum between reluctant choice and open conflict and we used four groupings to describe these positions:

- Freed by choice.
- Freed by acceptance.
- Freed without consent.
- Contested freeing.

The groups were by no means hard and fast and some parents moved between them during the long wait for the cases to be decided. For example, parents who originally requested adoption changed their minds and contested the proceedings, while others eventually signed their agreement or came to accept the situation although their agreement was formally dispensed with. Some parents put up an initial fight but did not appeal against the orders once granted. By contrast all the cases in the 'contested' group were hotly challenged and disputed on both sides and several went to appeal. Three parents in this group successfully regained their children and only four out of 11 children had been placed for adoption by the end of the research.

The Pathways study also experienced difficulty over the definition of a contested case and the researchers eventually devised a threefold classification of agency placements that were contested as having one or more of the following conditions:

- Applications made without birth mother's and/or birth father's agreement.
- Applications made to dispense with birth mother's and/or birth father's agreement.
- Contested final hearing.

Using these criteria, the Bristol researchers found that 26 per cent of the agency adoption applications and 75 per cent of freeing applications were contested. When they examined the eventual outcome of these applications, 95 per cent of the contested adoptions resulted in an order being granted, compared with 84 per cent of the contested freeing applications. Interestingly, they found no difference in the outcomes between contested and uncontested freeing applications as 84 per cent of the latter also resulted in a final order. In Scotland, there were very similar results from a census of all freeing applications in 1987–8, as orders were granted in 87 per cent of the cases that had been decided and there had been a request to dispense with parental agreement in 76 per cent of them. However, more Scottish than English applications were refused rather than set aside for other reasons.

Making judgments

Although the Pathways study is justified in overall terms in concluding that the findings suggested that 'contesting an application appears to have little effect on the outcome of the case', the Scottish study argued that freeing did provide a somewhat better chance for birth parents to succeed in challenging the application. Nevertheless, it also demonstrated that this result was only achieved after long drawn-out battles which were damaging to all the parties. When we examined these cases in more detail we found that being able to show positive qualities or some capacity to modify problematic aspects could influence the outcome (Hill et al., 1992). In such cases judges were reluctant to take what one called the 'Draconian' step of dispensing with parental agreement, and social workers had sometimes appeared to have acted prematurely or else had not been sufficiently explicit about why adoption was considered to be in the child's best interests. This was particularly relevant where parents favoured long-term fostering as an alternative to adoption, as judges were not necessarily familiar with the arguments for permanency.

In addition, freeing was still a new procedure at the time when the research was carried out and judges were faced with several unfamiliar aspects. For example, on the one hand, there was a new requirement to ascertain that placement for adoption was likely before dispensing with parental agreement. On the other hand, judges were unable to balance the 'reasonableness' of a parent's claim against the claims of prospective adopters as they were not parties in freeing applications, although in fact they did appear to be considered if the child was already living with them. One consequence of this situation has been to sharpen the debate about what weight to place on the welfare of the child and this seems to have moved closer to being considered paramount in some recent judgments.

Practitioners' perspectives

Little reference has been made so far to the information collected by both the Bristol and the Scottish researchers about the views of the social work and legal practitioners. This is partly because the reports made extensive use of extracts from the interviews, which are better read as a narrative. In this way they aim to show some aspects of the difficult process of reaching professional decisions about the children involved and whether to apply for adoption, if necessary against the parents' wishes. The interviews revealed that these decisions were hardly ever taken until after social

workers had worked for many months or even years to try and alleviate the problems which had brought people into contact with the social services or social work department.

Even when child care reviews were starting to recommend consideration of long-term placement or adoption, social workers often continued their efforts at rehabilitation. This was partly because they knew that the court would need to be satisfied that such work had been carried out or at least attempted, but also, in freeing applications, because uncertainty about the outcome meant that it was important for children to maintain some contact with their families in case the orders were refused and other plans became necessary. Working with parents who were angry and upset at the way things were turning out was not easy, especially when attempts at restoration broke down. The formal procedures laid down within agencies and by legislation and regulations required the collection and substantiation of evidence and the preparation of a series of reports, which were very time-consuming tasks. In both studies the majority of social workers involved in these cases were generic or basic grade social workers and these reports had to be fitted in along with a range of other duties. Usually the reports would then be checked by supervisors and perhaps 'quietly re-written' before being submitted to the Adoption Panel or the Court.

As the agency is a party to freeing applications, extra care has to be taken with these forms and the statement of the grounds for dispensing with consent. This has required close liaison with solicitors in the agency's legal department from an earlier stage than is necessary in contested adoptions and the researchers found that this had accounted for some delays in processing applications when freeing was first implemented. However, once agencies became aware of the need for better links between the social work and legal departments, new guidelines were drawn up and time limits sometimes imposed.

In preparing a contested application the most important factor for the social workers involved in these complex cases was the ability to obtain knowledgeable legal advice to assist in the decision-making process. Lawyers, for their part, valued a clear statement of the facts and the reasons for taking the course of action, which enabled them to finalise the application to the court. They then held overall responsibility for presenting the agency's case in court and calling witnesses. Both studies narrate how many things could go wrong before the hearings could take place and add to the difficulties. Undoubtedly, though, the actual hearings themselves, if contested, were the most devastating experience for all concerned, especially if they were spread over several days or months. The Scottish study also showed that even after the final hearing there was often another agonising wait for the written judgment to be delivered before decisions could be taken about appeals.

Proposals for reducing conflict

Cumulatively, the various difficulties experienced with the freeing procedure led the Adoption Law Review in England and Wales to recommend its abolition (DoH, 1992), although the Scottish Review proposed to retain it (Scottish Office, 1993). Both Reviews have recommended that parental agreement to the adoption *placement* should be obtained as a way of resolving some disputes at an earlier stage in the proceedings. There are a number of problems with this proposal, which the government acknowledges 'met with mixed reactions' during consultation in England and Wales (*Adoption: The Future*, DoH, 1993 (paras 4.8–4.13)). The White Paper recommends: 'Where the adoption application is from a family with whom the child has already lived for a considerable period, the Government believes it is unnecessary to involve the court until the final adoption order is made', and promises further discussion on the subject of placement orders before new legislation is framed. Whatever the eventual decision, there is clearly a strong desire to reduce the amount of conflict, but it seems unlikely to eliminate it altogether.

Even if proposals to include birth parents and other members of the family more positively in the legal process and to allow continuing contact in some cases are enacted, there are still going to be situations where birth parents change their minds or are opposed throughout to the adoption plan. Although agencies are much more aware of the importance of prevention and restoration wherever possible, some children will continue to need alternative families against their parents' wishes. These may be foster rather than adoptive families but, unless we take extreme measures and bar them from adoption, contested situations will still arise. The research findings indicate that measures to improve the procedures are urgently needed (Ryburn, 1992). Nor should we forget that the majority of adoptions made with parental consent have involved much heartache and a reluctant decision to part with the child.

Future research

As the research and data detailed in this chapter show, there is already a lot of information about contested proceedings and time could usefully be spent on a more thoroughgoing examination of the data. This could perhaps provide the basis for further work if the recommendations of the Adoption Law Review result in major changes to the stage at which the issue of parental agreement to adoption is considered. There must be doubts, however, about whether the focus of such a study should be specifically on contested proceedings or whether there would be greater

benefit from locating them within the wider context of the full range of applications, in much the same way as the Pathways study has done.

One group which has not been covered in any detail in this chapter is birth fathers, but their views are likely to become more important in future when making plans for children (Cole and Donley, 1990). This will be relevant in respect of open adoption and if there is a trend towards long-term fostering, rather than adoption in contested cases. At this moment we also do not know what effect the new Child Support Agency may have on adoption. Quite soon we will need to think seriously about whether it would be right to try to obtain a spectrum of views from adopted people who were the subjects of contested cases in the 1970s and 1980s. Post-adoption workers and counsellors are already seeing some of them, but it would be beneficial to mount as broadly based a study as possible. This might include examining what happened to the children who returned to their families after a long contest. We also need to know more about situations where grandparents (as described in chapter 13), or other relatives, have tried to intervene in the proceedings. In any of these possible investigations, the aim should be to learn more about what these experiences have meant to the people involved, in order to assist practitioners and to identify the things that can and should be put right in the future.

References

Bouchier, P., Lambert, L. and Triseliotis, J. (1991), *Parting with a Child for Adoption*, London: BAAF.

Cole, E. and Donley, K. (1990), 'History, Values and Placement Policy Issues', in Brodzinsky, D. and Schechter, M. [eds], *The Psychology of Adoption*, Oxford: Oxford University Press.

Department of Health/Welsh Office (1992), *Review of Adoption Law: Report to Ministers of an Interdepartmental Working Group: A Consultation Document*, London: DoH.

Department of Health/Welsh Office/Home Office/Lord Chancellor's Department (1993), *Adoption: The Future*, Cmnd. 2288, London: HMSO.

Fratter, J. (1991), 'Adoptive Parents and Open Adoption in the UK', in Mullender, A. [ed.], *Open Adoption: The Philosophy and Practice*, London: BAAF.

Goldstein, J., Freud, A. and Solnit, A. (1973), *Beyond the Best Interests of the Child*, New York: Free Press.

Grey, E. and Blunden, R. (1971), *A Survey of Adoption in Great Britain*, London: HMSO.

Hill, M., Lambert, L. and Triseliotis, J. (1989), *Achieving Adoption with Love and Money*, London: National Children's Bureau.

Hill, M., Lambert, L., Triseliotis, J. and Buist, M. (1992), 'Making Judgements about

Parenting: The Example of Freeing for Adoption', *British Journal of Social Work*, **22** 373–89.
HMSO (1972), *Report of the Departmental Committee on the Adoption of Children*, (Houghton Report), Cmnd. 5107, London: HMSO.
Hoggett, B. (1984), 'Adoption Law: An Overview', in Bean, P. [ed.], *Adoption*, London: Tavistock.
Howe, D. and Hinings, D. (1989), *The Post-Adoption Centre: The First Three Years*, Norwich: University of East Anglia.
Lambert, L., Buist, M., Triseliotis, J. and Hill, M. (1989), *Freeing Children for Adoption*, Final Report to SWSG, Edinburgh.
Lambert, L., Buist, M., Triseliotis, J. and Hill, M. (1990), *Freeing Children for Adoption*, London: BAAF.
Lowe, N. with Borkowski, M., Copner, R. and Murch, M. (1991), *Report of the Research into the Use and Practice of the Freeing for Adoption Provisions*, Bristol: Socio-Legal Centre for Family Studies, University of Bristol.
McKay, M. (1980), 'Planning for Permanent Placement', *Adoption and Fostering*, **4** (1), 19–21.
McWhinnie, A. (1967), *Adopted Children: How They Grow Up*, London: Routledge and Kegan Paul.
Millham, S., Bullock, R., Hosie, K. and Little, M. (1989), *Access Disputes in Child-Care*, Aldershot: Gower.
Murch, M., Lowe, N., Borkowski, M., Copner, R. and Griew, K. (1991), *Pathways to Adoption*, Final Report, Bristol: Socio-Legal Centre for Family Studies, University of Bristol.
Pannor, R., Baran, A. and Sorosky, A. (1978), 'Birth Parents Who Relinquished Babies for Adoption Revisited', *Family Process*, **17**(3), 329–37.
Pochin, J. (1969), *Without a Wedding Ring*, London: Constable.
Raynor, L. (1971), *Giving up a Baby for Adoption*, London: ABAA.
Rowe, J. (1984), 'Freeing for Adoption; an Historical Perspective', *Adoption and Fostering*, **8**(2), 10–11.
Rowe, J. and Lambert, L. (1973), *Children Who Wait*, London: ABAA.
Ryburn, M. (1992), 'Contested Adoption Proceedings', *Adoption and Fostering*, **16**(4), 29–38.
Scottish Office (1993), *The Future of Adoption Law in Scotland: A Consultation Paper*, Edinburgh: Social Work Services Group.
Teague, A. (1989), *Social Change, Social Work and the Adoption of Children*, Aldershot: Gower.
Thoburn, J. (1990), *Review of Research Relating to Adoption*, London: Dept of Health/ Welsh Office, (also Appendix C (DoH, 1992), in *Review of Adoption Law, A Consultation Document*, London: HMSO).
Thoburn, J., Murdoch, A. and O'Brien, A. (1986), *Permanence in Child Care*, Oxford: Blackwell.
Tizard, B. (1977), *Adoption: A Second Chance*, London: Open Books.
Triseliotis, J. and Hall, E. (1971), 'Giving Consent to Adoption', *Social Work Today*, **2**(17), 21–4.
Watson, K. (1986), 'Birth Families: Living with the Adoption Decision', *Public Welfare*, **44**(2), Spring, 24–8.
Winkler, R. and van Keppel, M. (1984), *Relinquishing Mothers in Adoption*, Melbourne: Institute for Family Studies.

8 Uses and abuses of research findings in contested cases

June Thoburn

Introduction

This chapter is concerned with the place research findings play in court decisions concerning children separated from their families, and with how far they ought reasonably to be relied on in individual cases. It outlines a framework for using research in child care cases, which would include contested adoption cases, and considers how far current practice achieves this model.

The use of research findings in court

Section 1(5) of the Children Act 1989 requires that the court 'shall not make the order or any of the orders unless it considers that doing so would be better for the child than making no order at all'. This means that in all the proceedings prior to an adoption or freeing hearing, including consideration of contact or applications for discharge of an order, it is necessary to balance the evidence about the likely impact on the child of all the alternatives. This is a very important point because, as Elizabeth Lawson has indicated in chapter 4, by the time consideration is being given to adoption the 'die is often cast'. If the recommendations of the Adoption Law Review are accepted, adoption hearings will be brought into line with Children Act hearings, and each alternative will have to be weighed in the light of the child's identified needs at all stages of the placement and court process.

It is for this reason that research findings are used increasingly to inform social workers, legal practitioners and the courts of what is known about the likely impact of one course of action rather than another, not only on the welfare of the child, but also on the other parties to the proceedings. They are especially likely to be called on if the parent is a young person under 18 or a particularly vulnerable adult.

The researcher or professional who gives expert evidence, or the guardian *ad litem* or social worker reviewing the options available to the court, must also consider whether the research cited in support of alternative courses of action is in general terms relevant to this type of case. Having heard the expert witnesses cross-examined on the research, the court must decide in the light of the evidence whether it is relevant to *the particular case*.

It is important to note here that one would expect the expert evidence of an academic researcher to be different in nature from that of a practitioner. Practitioners acting as experts, such as psychologists or psychiatrists, usually rely on their practice wisdom, often supplemented by usually brief contact with the child and/or parents or carers. They will often refer to research, but unless they are actively engaged in research themselves (as some of the best professional witnesses are) their account of research findings may be dated and/or limited to only one of the available options. Academic researchers rarely see the parties but are usually more up to date on a wider range of research findings on placement outcomes.

There are, then, three stages when looking at research findings:

- What is the research evidence about *all* the alternatives which might be considered for this particular child?
- How relevant and comprehensive is the research being cited to *this set of circumstances*?
- How relevant are these findings to *this particular child* with this particular parent and with this particular history. Additionally, if we are talking about adoption, how relevant are they to these particular adopters or these particular foster carers who wish to become the child's permanent carers?

It is possible to consider the extent to which this framework can usefully be applied in contested proceedings by relating it to three frequent and very specific questions which currently exercise the courts. These questions have been selected because many court decisions hinge on the answers to them, and because in the past they have tended to turn on statements of belief or even 'common sense' rather than on evidence. In looking at them it is possible to draw some conclusions about the appropriate use of research findings.

- *Statement 1*: Children in care because the court has found that they have been abused, cannot return home to parents if those parents do not admit that they were at least partially responsible for the abuse. This statement appears to be in line with the first of the factors highlighted in what has come to be known as the Orange Book (DoH, 1988, p.76) about the circumstances in which children can be safely returned home. In that guidance it is listed as one point amongst several, but not infrequently it is picked out as *the* key issue in the sense that it has been asserted that, if there is no acceptance of responsibility, all other considerations are irrelevant and the child cannot return home.
- *Statement 2*: Children placed with substitute families are more likely to experience placement breakdown if they have continued contact with birth parents, but this does not apply if they have continued contact with siblings placed elsewhere. It may be that this view is expounded less often in the light of recent research, but it still occurs frequently and much of the practice informed by the permanence philosophy of the 1980s was based on it.
- *Statement 3*: Children placed permanently for adoption are more likely to have a satisfactory outcome than children placed permanently with foster parents. This statement still lies behind many placement decisions and many of the decisions about contact which are currently appearing for adjudication.

Researchers and other experts are almost invariably asked to comment on statements such as these when they appear in reports.

The importance of citing research on each available option

These three assertions will now be considered in the light of the three stages of research interpretation introduced at the beginning of the chapter.

First, research ought to be cited about *all* the options which might possibly be considered as relevant to the particular child. This is where we return to the chapter title – the uses and abuses of research. One abuse of research can be related to the first 'statement' – 'you can't send children safely home if the parents don't accept responsibility for the abuse'. In a considerable number of cases only one alternative is explored and exposed to critical analysis in the light of research findings. It is not uncommon to read in social workers' reports that 'research indicates if the parents don't admit abuse the risks of re-abuse are too high for the child to be returned

home, and therefore the child should be adopted' – end of story. The implication of this statement is that if the child is adopted he or she will live happily ever after. However, the argument is seldom put that there are risks attached to adoption as well.

It is the duty of expert witnesses to produce evidence which points in each direction for each option, as indeed should social workers and guardians *ad litem*. All those who are giving evidence must give *all* the evidence, even if it doesn't support the conclusion which they are advocating. We all know how difficult it is to include evidence which supports the opposite of what we think will be best for the child, but the role of those charged with treating the child's welfare as paramount must be to seek to ensure that *all* relevant evidence, including relevant research findings, is available to the court. If, for instance, evidence is being presented about the pros and cons of fostering and adoption, it is important to present what research says about both options – and then, if one option is preferred, to explain how fine the balance is and the reasons why some research findings are stressed and others given less weight in the particular case. Just leaving 'inconvenient' findings out of the report should not be an option for social workers, guardians *ad litem*, or expert witnesses.

The relevance of research to particular situations

The second question identified earlier was the relevance of particular research studies to the particular set of circumstances. There are some crucial questions that we should address in seeking to answer this:

- Who carried out the research, and were they appropriately qualified to do so?
- Where was the fieldwork for the research conducted?
- When was the study undertaken?
- What was the size of the sample?
- How were the sample cases identified and how representative are they of the total population being studied?
- What research methods were used and were they appropriate tools for exploring the question to be examined?
- What variables were being measured?
- What outcome measures were used?
- Were the methods used in the analysis appropriate and did the data reported support the conclusions drawn?

The key point is that it is essential to get hold of the actual research article or book in order to use it in an ethical way in court, or if it is known

that another expert will be using it and there will be a requirement to comment on their evidence. The questions posed above are key ones to consider in relation to any research study – an area of preparatory work which is not always thoroughly undertaken by witnesses. The Department of Health research summaries, *Social Work Decisions in Child Care* (1985) and *Patterns and Outcomes in Child Placement* (1991) have been extremely useful in helping child care professionals become more research-literate. These summaries are not enough, however, when it comes to the crucial decisions about the lives of individual children.

Who undertook the research? Was the research carried out by an independent person? Was the research internal to the agency whose practice was being evaluated, but written up with an element of independence (for example by the research section or audit section of the agency)? Was it the result of practitioners evaluating their own work? Was the person who did the research skilled enough to undertake that particular study? Useful research may be done in all these ways, but it may have an impact on the credibility of that study for court purposes. For instance, it is important for practitioners to evaluate their own practice, but the court may consider that a degree of bias in interpretation may have crept in.

One such study which is fairly influential is *Dangerous Families* (Dale et al., 1986). This study is often quoted with reference to the first of the three statements detailed above: can the child go home if the parents do not admit that they were implicated in the abuse? It is an interesting study with many pointers for practice but its problem for evidential purposes is that it only evaluated the style of practice favoured by those particular workers, and was carried out by the workers themselves without an independent element. None of the children whose case studies are reported in the book and whose parents did not admit that they were implicated in the abuse went home, so it can only tell us about what may happen when parents *do* accept responsibility. It is no basis for decision-making about children who might go home when the parents *don't* accept responsibility. The researchers put forward arguments as to *why* they take the stance they do, and the book could legitimately be called upon in evidence given by practitioners explaining why they adhere to a particular model of practice, but the book should not be cited as *research* evidence on this particular issue of non-admission and return home.

Where was the research conducted? A lot of the research currently used is American. That is largely because more research funds are available there, particularly for longitudinal research involving large numbers of children. Are American studies relevant to particular cases here? American studies on transracial adoption, for example, often include children

adopted from overseas as well as black children born in America who were adopted by white parents. Also, adoption in America is very different from adoption in Britain, most notably because much of it is arranged privately. Much intercountry adoption outcomes research concerns children from overseas adopted in the Scandinavian countries or Holland, so one has to ask to what extent these cultures are more or less welcoming to people from minority ethnic groups and cultures.

When was the study undertaken?   This is particularly relevant to the question of foster care and adoption as viable permanence options, largely because the hypothesis that adoption is more successful than fostering is based on a set of studies of practice in the 1970s. This was before practitioners had grasped the importance of not letting children drift in unplanned care. Foster care practice has changed dramatically and there are now far fewer cases where children are drifting in indeterminate long-term foster care because of lack of planning. As the Department of Health publication *Patterns and Outcomes* puts it (DoH, 1991, p.64) '*Child Care Now* found little evidence of placements drifting on too long . . . The problem now seems to be that of the quality rather than the quantity of planning.' Most recent studies of long-term foster placements, especially those of Kelly and McCauley in Northern Ireland (in preparation), Aldgate (1990) in Oxfordshire, and recent studies in the United States by Fein and her colleagues (1990), show that this problem of drift once a child is placed in permanent foster care is not now so much of an issue. Indeed the breakdown rates for children in planned foster care are now similar to the breakdown rates for similar children placed with adoptive families. It is vital, therefore, to ask, when evaluating the usefulness of research, *when* was the study being cited undertaken; what was practice like at the time those particular placements were made; and is the study still relevant to current practice?

Size of sample   The issues raised here are perhaps best illustrated with reference to the question of the relationship between breakdown and placement for either adoption or fostering. Two different studies can provide valuable insights here (Thoburn et al., 1986; Thoburn, 1990, and Fratter et al., 1991). The first was a small qualitative study of 29 children, 21 of whom were placed with permanent new families. It was a study in which a great deal was learned about the children, their birth families and their new families. It was not, however, possible from such a small study to learn anything about the relative breakdown rates of placements for adoption or fostering. From the other study, however, which involved 1 165 children placed for adoption or permanent fostering, very different sorts of conclusions could be drawn.

Table 8.1 Outcome by continued contact

Age	Contact	Still in placement No.	%	Disrupted No.	%	Total No.	%
All ages	None	663	81	151	19	814	100
	With parents	132	68	61	32	193	100
	With siblings/ relatives	121	77	37	23	158	100
	Total	916	79	249	21	1165	100
χ^2 = 16.278	DF = 1	p = < .001					
5–8	None	225	84	42	16	267	100
	With parents	41	84	8	16	49	100
	With siblings/ relatives	41	73	15	27	56	100
	Total	307	82	65	18	372	100
χ^2 = 3.975	DF = D	p = < .137	Not significant				
9 or over	None	148	60	98	40	246	100
	With parents	80	61	51	39	131	100
	With siblings/ relatives	66	75	22	25	88	100
	Total	294	63	171	37	465	100
χ^2 = 6.502	DF = 2	p = < .05					

The children in this study comprised a total cohort of those placed over a five-year period by the major UK voluntary organisations. With a sample of this size it was possible to analyse the results in such a way as to explore differences in breakdown rates between adoption and fostering. Twenty-two per cent of the placements in this study broke down. The proportion breaking down was closely related, however, to age at placement, with the proportion of children experiencing breakdown going up with the age of the child at placement. Fewer than ten per cent of those who were aged five or under at placement experienced breakdown, compared with almost 50 per cent of those who were aged 12 when placed (see Table 8.1).

The bar chart on the top left of Figure 8.1 (see overleaf) seems to support the third proposition above, that placements are more likely to break down if the child is in foster care than adoption. It shows that 27 per cent of placements broke down when the child was in permanent foster care and

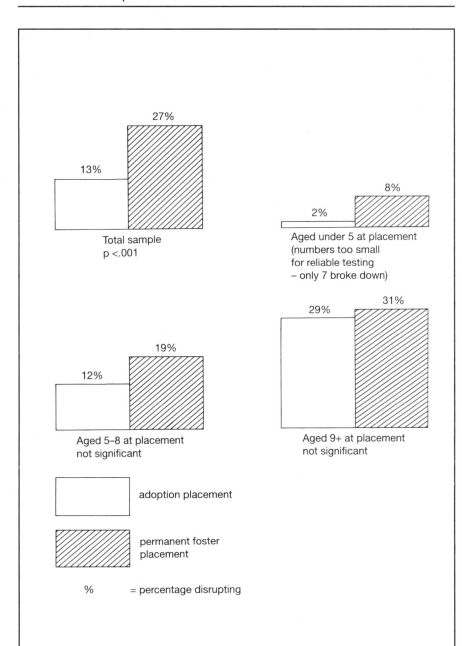

Figure 8.1 Outcome by placement for adoption or permanent foster placement and age at placement (those 'fostered with a view to adoption' omitted)

only 13 per cent when the child was placed for adoption. As has been noted already, however, the age of the child at placement is a key factor in explaining breakdown, and the difference between adoption and fostering in the top left-hand chart is completely explained away if we hold constant the age of the children when placed. More children are placed for adoption when younger and more children are placed in permanent foster care when they are older and more likely to be behaviourally disturbed. When, by using 'logit' analysis, the age at placement as well as other key variables were controlled, no difference was found in breakdown rates between those who were fostered and those who were adopted.[1] If we looked at all the five-year-olds, all the six-year-olds and so on, we would find the same placement breakdown rate whether or not they were fostered or adopted.

The critical point about size of sample is that it is not possible to control for the different variables in studies based on small numbers of cases, and cross-tabulations can therefore give a false impression of causation. This is a particular problem when looking at the question, 'can the child go safely home if the parent doesn't accept responsibility?'. In any one research study the numbers going home where the parents do not admit that they were at least partially responsible for the injury or neglect are very few, and the proportion of that small number who are re-abused is even smaller. Thus it is particularly difficult to find reliable research findings on this question because of the small numbers involved. Another problem with research studies which might help us with this question is that there is a tendency to combine different types of abuse in the same studies. Once we differentiate the sexually abused older children from physically abused infants, numbers in each group are likely to be too small for quantitative analysis.

What research methods were used?   Key questions to consider here are: was there a control or comparison group and were the methods used appropriate for exploring the questions posed? Often the sample size dictates the methods to be used. With large numbers the most frequent methodology is survey methodology, although there are one or two notable exceptions, such as the National Child Development Study, which used health visitors to complete detailed interviews and standardised developmental scales on 1 600 children born in 1958. These included adopted and fostered children, and children being brought up in two- and one-parent families, who have been followed-up into young adulthood

---

1   See Statistical Appendix in Fratter et al. (1991) for an explanation of logit analysis. The slight apparent difference in the bar chart is explained by the breadth of the age groups, with the younger ones in the five- to eight-year-old group more likely to be adopted than fostered, and the older ones more likely to be fostered.

(Seglow et al., 1972). Most often a survey is used for large numbers and this is not as suitable a method as qualitative analysis for finding out *why* a particular result occurs. A question which arose from the survey of 1 165 placements (Fratter et al., 1991) was why a larger percentage of children of mixed-race parentage experienced breakdown than either white children or children both of whose parents were black. A further study is planned of children of mixed-race parentage. The issue in this case is one which can only be explored through detailed interviews with a smaller number of the young people and their new parents.

Similarly, if we go back to the issue of whether foster care or adoption placements are most stable, the large-scale survey (Fratter et al., 1991) could only indicate that there was no difference in breakdown rates. Aldgate and her colleagues (1990), on the other hand, in considering the merits of foster care, looked at a sample of those in long-term foster care and used a comparison group of children from similar backgrounds who were not in care but who were receiving a social work service. They discovered, by using standardised tests of behaviour and academic achievement, that the well-being of children in foster care was on average higher, and they were doing better at school, than similar children who had not gone into care.

What variables are being measured?   When considering the placement of children, there are many variables which may have an impact on outcome. There are variables about the children and their early history: how old were they when placed? Did they appear to be behaviourally disturbed? Had they been abused or neglected? Had they experienced a range of different placements? There are also variables about the new family and the placement, such as the age of the parents, whether they have other children, and whether the members of the birth family continue to visit after the placement. There are variables about the nature of the social work practice at the various stages of the placement, and with the different parties. Finally, there are variables about which legal routes to placement were used, and the agency and the court processes.

Many of these variables overlap, as, for example, was noted earlier with the question of age at placement overlapping with the likelihood of the placement being an adoptive or foster placement. Figure 8.2 shows a similar pattern for the variable about whether the child had continued contact with birth parents and other family members after placement. Again it is possible to see that age at placement is masking the effect of contact. In fact, when the logit analysis was used, it was found that fewer placements broke down when the child had continued contact with parents after placement. (See statistical analysis appendix, Fratter et al.,

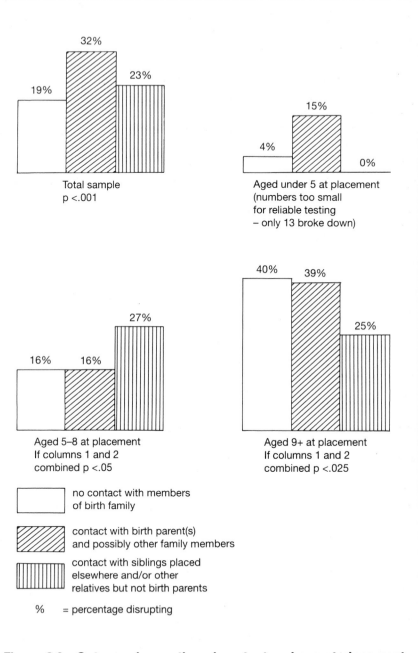

Figure 8.2   Outcome by continued contact and age at placement

1991.) Interestingly, this study contradicted the view that, at least as far as five- to eight-year-olds were concerned, contact with siblings placed elsewhere was either a neutral or a beneficial factor. More placements of children in this age group broke down if they were separated from a sibling with whom they were having continued contact. Again, the frustration of the survey methodology was that it was not possible to find out more about why this was so.

What outcome measures are used?　The smaller the study, the more possible it is to use a range of outcome measures from a variety of different perspectives. The larger the study, the more likely will it be that only crude outcome measures such as breakdown rates are considered, since detailed interviewing of large numbers is beyond the scope of most British researchers and their funders. One way round this is to collect general information on a large group, and supplement this with more detailed information on smaller numbers, a methodology very satisfactorily used by Millham and his colleagues (1986) when considering the links between children in care and their parents. In small-scale studies we can ask all sorts of questions about well-being, progress, or satisfaction with the placement or the social work or other practice.

It is interesting to note that the most negative outcome measure for the small study of 21 children placed with permanent new families was that the birth children of the adoptive parents were least satisfied with the placement. If the birth parents' views had also been considered, it is likely that an even lower satisfaction rate would have been found.

Were the methods used in the analysis appropriate? Did the data reported support the conclusions drawn?　This question would lead us into a fuller discussion of research methodology than there is space for here. The recently-produced guide on evaluative research by Cheetham and her colleagues (1992) is useful background reading. Some of the points already made have shown how surveys or small qualitative studies can be misinterpreted.

Conclusion

We can return now to the three statements. First, there are research findings on contentious issues which point generally towards one direction but must be scrutinised in each case to see whether the research

populations are sufficiently similar to the particular case under consideration. Such an examination can usefully be carried out by re-framing statements as questions. 'Can children go safely back home if there is no acceptance of responsibility for the harm which has occurred?' is one such question. Research, which is mainly American, suggests that there *is* a greater risk of re-abuse in these cases (see Browne et al., 1988 for a review of these studies). This is more clearly demonstrated, however, with cases of sexual abuse than physical abuse, and oddly enough it is much more conclusive about older children than infants. Recent British studies summarised by Bullock and his colleagues (1993) suggest that abused children who return home when under the age of two are least likely to be re-abused or returned to care and amongst these (although not specifically identified as a separate variable in the studies) were children whose parents did not accept responsibility for the injury.

Then there is the second group where the research is evenly balanced, such as that on the respective viability of foster and adoptive placements. Recent studies suggest that, when other variables are held constant, there are no advantages either way, at least as far as placement stability is concerned. Smaller-scale studies on satisfaction or well-being are contradictory. Some, such as those of Triseliotis and Russell (1984) and Hill et al. (1989), report that children speak very positively of the beneficial effects on them of being adopted, whereas the young people interviewed in the 1986 study referred to above (Thoburn et al.) who were permanently fostered did not feel strongly one way or the other so long as they knew that their placement with the foster family was secure. Some of the young people interviewed by Bullard and Mallos (1990) in a study of custodianship said they very much preferred to have a legal status which conveyed a sense of permanence but did not require them to change their name and sever their links with the past. Thus it is vital to read the research very carefully if it is cited as being relevant to this question of whether foster care or adoption is to be preferred, and to look for clues within the study about how one option rather than the other might be beneficial in the particular case before the court.

Finally, there is the third group of statements or questions, such as the one on the respective merits of continued contact or otherwise with members of the birth family after placement. There will be some cases where continued face-to-face contact is not appropriate and it may be necessary in a particular case to terminate contact and say why the weight of evidence should be overruled. However, the research findings point overwhelmingly in one direction – towards continued contact being in the interests of most children, in that it appears to be associated with greater stability of placement as well as other positive outcomes.

References

Aldgate, J. (1990), 'Foster Children at School: Success or Failure', *Adoption and Fostering*, **7**(2), 38–49.

Browne, K., Davies, C. and Stratton, P. [eds] (1988), *Early Prediction and Prevention of Child Abuse*, Chichester: Wiley.

Bullard E., Mallos, E. and Parker R. (1990), *Custodianship Research Project: A Report to the Department of Health*, Bristol: Socio-Legal Centre for Family Studies, University of Bristol.

Bullock, R., Little, M. and Millham, S. (1993), *Going Home*, Aldershot: Dartmouth.

Cheetham, J., Fuller, R., MacIvor, G. and Petch, A. (1992), *Evaluating Social Work Effectiveness*, Milton Keynes: Open University Press.

Dale, P. with Davies, M., Morrison, T. and Waters, J. (1986), *Dangerous Families: Assessment and Treatment of Child Abuse*, London: Tavistock.

Department of Health and Social Security (1985), *Social Work Decisions in Child Care: Recent Research Findings and Their Implications*, London: HMSO.

Department of Health (1988), *Protecting Children: A Guide for Social Workers Undertaking a Comprehensive Assessment*, London: HMSO.

Department of Health (1991), *Patterns and Outcomes in Child Placement*, London: HMSO.

Fein, E., Maluccio, A. and Kluger, M. (1990), *No More Partings: An Examination of Long Term Foster Family Care*, New York: Child Welfare League of America.

Fratter, J., Rowe, J., Sapsford, D. and Thoburn, J. (1991), *Permanent Family Placement: A Decade of Experience*, London: BAAF.

Hill, M., Lambert, L. and Triseliotis, J. (1989), *Achieving Adoption with Love and Money*, London: National Children's Bureau.

Kelly, G. and McCauley, C. (in preparation), *A Study of Long Term Foster Placements in Northern Ireland*, London: BAAF.

Millham, S., Bullock, R., Hosie, K. and Haak, M. (1986), *Lost in Care: The Problems of Maintaining Links between Children in Care and their Families*, Aldershot: Gower.

Seglow, J., Pringle, M. and Wedge, P. (1972), *Growing up Adopted*, London: NFER.

Thoburn, J. (1990), *Success and Failure in Permanent Family Placement*, Aldershot: Avebury.

Thoburn, J., Murdoch, A. and O'Brien, A. (1986), *Permanence in Child Care*, Oxford: Blackwell.

Triseliotis, J. and Russell, J. (1984), *Hard to Place: the Outcome of Adoption and Residential Care*, Aldershot: Gower.

9 Issues of attachment, separation and identity in contested adoptions

Nick Banks

Introduction

In order to consider the particular issues of attachment and separation that originate in contested adoptions, it is necessary to set them in the general context of attachment theory and research. This chapter first discusses the concept of attachment and the relevant psychological literature. It then considers the possible effects of separation or disrupted attachment on children of various ages, before looking at the assessment of strength of attachment and the effects of separation anxiety. The effects of discord during contested adoption proceedings are then explored, and the confusion that frequently occurs in contested adoptions between strength of attachment and the normal and adaptive behaviours associated with poorly managed separations is examined. The chapter concludes with a discussion of the issues that contested adoptions raise in relation to identity formation, in particular for black children in transracial placements.

Historical development of the concept of attachment and its emotional expression

Attachment is a theoretical construct jointly developed by John Bowlby and Mary Ainsworth in the 1930s (Bowlby, 1952; Ainsworth, 1940). Typically for the time, the mother was seen as of primary importance and therefore attachment theory focused exclusively, until fairly recently, on the child's emotional bond to the mother and the social, emotional and

cognitive effects of breaking the maternal attachment through the experience of separation, deprivation and bereavement.

Attachment theory postulates that there is a primary attachment figure who provides a secure base from which an infant can explore and discover its world. The theory sees the security or insecurity of attachment as being a significant contributor to a child's emotional difficulties. Central to attachment theory is the idea that children have a basic need to develop a secure dependence on parents before they will successfully be able to explore unfamiliar situations.

The formation and importance of attachment

At approximately seven months the infant develops an attachment to a specific person. This age can only be approximate as studies have shown that there is a wide range from three-and-a-half months to fifteen months of age (Rutter, 1975). We are uncertain as to exactly which factors influence the development of attachment but it appears clear that feeding and care-taking are *not* the only essential features, and indeed may be *less* significant than some other factors. It also appears reasonably clear that attachments are not formed simply by spending a lot of time with a child. The intensity and satisfaction of interaction probably have more effect than duration alone.

Bowlby (1952) argued that in order to develop appropriate mental health the infant and young child should experience a warm, intimate and continuous relationship with his or her mother in which both find satisfaction and enjoyment. However, although the mother may well occupy a central and important place in a child's life, later studies (Rutter, 1975) have suggested that, although the main attachment is usually to the mother, in a third of the cases the main attachment was to the father and it has been found to be the brother or sister, or even non-family members.

Whether or not lack of continuity in itself has a harmful effect appears to depend on the reasons for disruption of the relationship (Rutter, 1972), the quality of the relationship prior to separation (Vernon et al., 1965), previous separation experiences (Ainsworth, 1962; Stacey et al., 1970), the duration of the separation (Heinicke and Westheimer, 1966), the quality and familiarity of the substitute care situation (Robertson and Bowlby, 1952), the age at separation (Cooper, 1980; Rowe et al., 1984), and the individual temperament of the child (Stacey et al., 1970; Berger and Passingham, 1972).

Significance of separation

The significance of separation from attachment figures was documented as early as 1952 by Robertson and Bowlby, who identified three phases of separation response. These were:

- Initial protest, brought about by separation anxiety.
- Despair, related to grief and mourning.
- Denial or detachment, related to psychological defence mechanisms such as repression of painful experience.

Bowlby discussed the possibility that a child who showed little or no separation anxiety may give a false impression of coping. Pardeck and Pardeck (1988) have noted that denial may show itself where adopted children continue to hold on to a view that they will return to their biological parents. Children may not be able to express themselves in ways that are understood to those who wish to be close to them, as these care-givers are themselves deeply involved and unable to be objective (Harper, 1990).

It is worth looking further at how the particular stage of denial may present itself where assessments of the child's and parents' functioning and interaction are being made for presentation in court. (See also chapter 3 and chapter 5.) Bowlby (1979) has noted that it is not uncommon to observe distress in children at the time of separation from their parents. It has also been observed that following this distress it is not uncommon, upon reunion, for the child's immediate relationship with his or her parents to be upset (Heinicke and Westheimer, 1966). The significance of this is that negative statements which are both inaccurate and based on assessments at a superficial level may be made about a child's attachment to those providing care.

While it is clear that emotional upset to relationships is likely to result from a brief separation of two-year-old infants from their mothers, we are a long way from demonstrating beyond doubt that long or regular separations are a causal factor in personality disorders with this age group. However, there is evidence that long separations are linked to a form of personality disorder. This has implications for the initial planning of separation and placement decisions in contested adoptions.

The long-term effects of disrupted attachment

Bowlby's work suggests that many children's and adults' reduced capacity to establish emotional bonds can be traced to early disruptions in attachments. Whilst disrupted attachments are clearly not the only form of environmental or emotional disturbance that can be linked to psychiatric difficulties, it can be argued that the breaking of emotional bonds is one that is particularly significant and well-documented (Bowlby, 1979).

The psychiatric disturbance that has been most clearly linked with the early disruption of affectional bonds in childhood is what is clinically described as psychopathic or sociopathic personality type. Typically the

individual who would be labelled as such is persistently involved in petty crimes, acts of neglect and abuse within a family setting and self-injurious acts, such as chemical substance misuse, addiction and suicide.

In such cases the ability to initiate and sustain emotional bonds is lowered and in some extreme cases almost absent. Of particular relevance to contested adoption is Rutter's finding (1971) that separation is only associated with antisocial behaviour disorder when the separation is allied to 'family stress or discord'. Rutter (1972) has further argued 'that it is distortion of relationships rather than bond disruption as such which causes the damage' (p.108). However, this finding was deduced retrospectively. What we do not have is research on individuals who have experienced similar separation traumas but have been much less affected than those with severe difficulties. These are clearly the extreme effects of breaking attachments through separation from one or other of a child's parents.

Shorter-term separations and effects at different ages

We could speculate that if children were to be placed and remain in large anonymous and insensitive institutions then we would expect to see serious consequences, and indeed this tends to be the case. What we need to ask is: what are the expected outcomes on the child's well-being and what are the effects of separation at particular ages, when children are separated for shorter periods of time from those they are attached to, or when they are placed with a substitute family pending adoption?

Separation and behaviour

It has been suggested (Bowlby, 1979) that the most intense and disturbing effects of separation are fear of being abandoned, yearning for the lost figure and anger at not being able to find this lost figure. These responses are linked with an urge to search for the lost attachment figure and a tendency to direct anger towards those who appear to be responsible for the loss, or to be blocking or sabotaging reunion or the recovery of the lost attachment figure.

It is important to consider whether parental separation does cause specific behaviour when children are placed in substitute care. It has been shown in a study of 139 children, some of whom we can expect to have been the subjects of contested adoption proceedings (Rowe et al., 1984),

that 60 per cent of the children who were less than a year old at the start of placement did not present with behavioural difficulties in the care of substitute parents. However, 54 per cent of those who were twelve months to four years of age at the start of the placement did present with three or more difficult behaviours, such as sleeping difficulties, demanding attention, eating difficulties, lack of concentration and temper tantrums or withdrawal. In comparison, only 43 per cent of the children in the sample who were over five years of age had three or more difficult behaviours. The authors concluded that 'it seems clear that it was those aged one to four who were perceived by foster parents as being the most upset and difficult to handle at this stage' (p.72).

The authors of this study further speculated that, as many of those children in the one to four years age group had a number of upsetting experiences in addition to being separated from parents, these factors, together with the developmental needs of the child acting in conflict with their actual experiences, combined to produce greater behavioural and emotional difficulties. Also of interest was that, though the one to four age group demonstrated more behavioural and emotional difficulties, we know there is greater risk of failure of placement with older children which tends to increase into adolescence. It may be that substitute families are more able to accept difficulties with younger children and/or young children who have been in their care since an early age.

What is clear from the study of Rowe and her colleagues is that those responsible for placing children should be aware that younger children aged one to four years, often perceived as being unlikely to have problems, may in fact present with more difficulties. In contested adoptions placements of children of this age are often portrayed as relatively trouble-free, and possible difficulties are not as thoroughly examined as they should be.

Taking the whole group of children in the study of Rowe et al., it appears likely that it is the separation from the birth parents which results in emotional and behavioural difficulties, and not something to do with a child's experience of living with the birth parents which results in an inability to form attachments.

The study went on to suggest that those children who experience several upheavals, presumably increasing the existence of what Bowlby (see above) termed separation anxiety, are those most likely to have behaviour problems. Of children who had experienced one or two changes of care-giver, 17 per cent presented with three or more problems. Of those with three to four changes of care-giver, 42 per cent presented with three or more problems. With five to ten changes of care-giver, 51 per cent of children presented with three or more problems; and with eleven or more changes of care-giver, up to 75 per cent presented with three or more problems.

What we appear to be seeing is a pattern which allows us to say with a fair degree of certainty that children whose experience is that of disrupted attachment, in whatever form, are likely to show behavioural difficulties that test the capacity of the carers to continue to care or to 'prove' their attachment. This experience of disruption can stem principally from separation from their biological families, which the children perceive as a rejection by adults who are not able (for whatever reason) to be consistent nurturing figures. It may be exacerbated by only limited care being provided by the substitute family, so that emotional needs may remain unmet or only partly met.

We should at this point add a cautionary note, since we cannot be entirely certain yet from the research findings that behavioural difficulties in new placements stem entirely from attachment disruption. Rutter (1972) noted that it may well be the upset and tension before the break, rather than the actual break itself, which led to the child developing antisocial behaviour. He quotes a study which found that parental separation resulted in less antisocial behaviour than unbroken but 'quarrelsome and neglecting homes' (McCord and McCord, 1959).

Where plans are made for permanent substitute families it is essential to consider new carers' abilities to cope with the likely emotional demands made on them by the child. They should be prepared in advance so that they have realistic expectations of the behaviour of children who have suffered disrupted attachments. It is vital that they can recognise that difficult behaviours might very well be no reflection on the quality of the relationships they are developing themselves with children, but rather a traumatic grief reaction in which the causal factors leading to behavioural difficulties are both loss of secure relationships and physical parental separation.

Difficulties in forming attachment compared with difficulties of separation anxiety

It is important to make a clear distinction between difficulties in forming attachment and difficulties resulting from separation anxiety. Often in contested adoptions the evidence of the local authority focuses to some degree, as a reason for ending contact and considering adoption, on the child's reactions to contact with parents. What is in fact a normal behavioural display of separation anxiety is often misinterpreted by social services as a display of outright rejection by the child of the parents. Individual children demonstrate individual reactions. For some children reactions find expression in emotional and physical withdrawal, while for others they may show themselves in behavioural difficulties. The two case studies below serve to demonstrate these differences.

Sarita was a four-year-old Hindu girl whose father had been accused of neglect. While he was attempting to attend to the stock control needs of his shop, Sarita began to demand his attention by first crying and then pulling tins and jars from the shelf. He had allegedly locked her in a store cupboard to enable him to continue stock-taking uninterrupted. Shoppers had informed social services of Sarita's crying and she had been taken into local authority care. When her parents were eventually allowed to visit her in a foster placement four days later, Sarita appeared to withdraw and ignore her parents. This continued for several visits and was observed and recorded by the supervising social worker as 'showing a marked rejection of her parents due to a likely history of mistreatment. Being placed in a secure environment where her emotional needs are being met allows Sarita to leave her insecure past behind. I would recommend that the Department proceed with the idea of securing a permanent substitute family with a view to later adoption.'

The supervising social worker appears unaware of the symptoms a four-year-old may show on separation from her parents. When Sarita was removed from the family, social services came unannounced and took the child from the parents without any prior preparation. It does not take much imagination to consider how traumatic this would have been for a four-year-old child. There are many other situations where poor practice is much less apparent but where there is still the same confusion between the presenting symptoms of a normal reaction to a badly managed separation, and an inability to form an attachment or a lack of attachment to parents.

In some instances grief reactions evolve into behavioural displays of anger.

Michael was a seven-year-old boy who had been placed in care with a view to long-term fostering or adoption, following his mother's assessed inability to meet his emotional and physical care needs. Michael's mother had been warned by social services that she should not leave him unattended while she went out to socialise or conduct her business of prostitution. Neighbours had reported that Michael had at times been left alone from Friday night to Monday morning while his mother was working in London for the higher rates of pay than can be obtained in Birmingham.

On one occasion Michael had gone to a neighbour's house to ask for food after being left alone for some 48 hours. On returning home his mother had beaten him for disclosing their secret. The bruises were apparent when Michael changed for P.E. in school two days later. Michael's teacher telephoned social services who placed him initially in a residential institution for four days and then with a foster family. Michael was intensely upset about being separated from his mother, crying and refusing to talk or eat for several days. He was also violent towards residential care staff, kicking out whenever he was approached to see if he needed anything.

The foster parents he was placed with were experienced carers who had acted as substitute parents for over fifteen years. They were able to tolerate Michael's behaviour for only two weeks before the placement broke down. When being dropped off at school he had used offensive language, both to a foster parent and teacher, and had become violent and destructive at school, tearing up other children's work and attacking children if they protested. At the foster home Michael broke several door-panels and threw cups and plates through two windows. On two occasions, he had opened his bedroom window, which was at the front of the house, and thrown objects at passers-by. When challenged about this he ran away. He was found by the police and claimed he was looking for his mother.

After he had been separated from her for five weeks while in institutional and foster care, social services agreed to let him see his mother. He appeared detached and uninterested in her at the first meeting. His mother's attempts to speak to and cuddle him were both ignored and resisted. At the end of the visit his mother seemed so frustrated and angry about his refusal to acknowledge her that she left saying he could 'bloody well stay with the social workers for all I care'. A second foster placement broke down and Michael was temporarily returned to a children's home while, after further preparation, another foster placement was sought.

Many if not all of these difficulties might have been avoided if social services had been aware that, despite the apparent poor treatment of Michael by his mother, an involuntary separation from his primary attachment figure would be likely to result in intense fear and anxiety.

The effects of sudden loss of contact, whether in the early stages or later, as part of adoption plans formulated against parental wishes, are often not taken into consideration or are misinterpreted. The grieving shown by children may be of considerable duration, and when it is assumed to have disappeared may show itself in a disguised form. Children are expressing a lack of trust that there are attachment figures available who can make them feel safe and secure. Even attachment figures who treat children with less care and concern than is considered desirable can elicit strong emotional feelings if separation is threatened or enforced. In Michael's case only continuing contact with his mother was likely to ease the trauma of separation.

Are the symptoms of separation remediable?

Is a grief reaction an inevitable outcome of separation from an attachment figure? One small-scale intensive study carried out by two of Bowlby's colleagues, Robertson and Robertson (1971) is particularly illuminating.

They attempted to assess whether acute upset was a normal reaction to separation, independent of circumstances, and how this upset could be reduced. To do this the Robertsons involved themselves in the foster care of four children aged between one-and-a-half to two-and-a-half years whose mothers were hospitalised for periods of one to four weeks. They used a control group of nine children who were taken care of in their own homes by a relative. To eliminate aspects of the separation which might interfere with the ability of the children to settle and could be additional sources of stress, for example unfamiliar environment and new routines, strange care-givers, and so on, the Robertsons spent time getting to know the children four weeks or so before the expected separation date. The Robertsons kept the image of the mother to the forefront of the agenda by talking about her regularly and referring to her picture. Fathers visited as often as they wished.

While some distress was noted, such as some aggression, sadness and over-activity, this did not amount to the generally observed pattern of acute panic and bewilderment described by other researchers. The children were able to return to their mothers and resume their relationship. They presented with little of the insecurity that is generally observed.

The Robertsons were cautious in suggesting that the difficulties associated with early separation could be eliminated, and recognised that they were able to operate under ideal conditions, which provided them with preparatory control prior to separation. However, what this small study does provide is a model which could be adapted to minimise the traumatic experience of young children who experience separation. Separation in the context of a planned-for period of hospitalisation is very different from a young child's coming into involuntary care as a result of the permanent loss of parent or family conflict. There are likely to be a number of other factors preceding any contested adoption which will influence how children both perceive and react to the experience of separation. In these more complex situations we could reasonably expect, especially where all original family contact has been ended, that there will be many more difficulties attendant on the separation and that they will be much more difficult to resolve. The principal practice guideline, however, is the same as for the management of any other separation – the maintenance of the greatest possible degree of continuity between past and present life.

Assessment of attachment and separation anxiety

The ways in which secure attachments can be assessed cannot be considered in detail in this chapter. Every assessment should take account

of the particular age, gender, ethnicity and background experience of the child in question. As Murray Ryburn indicates in chapter 14, the abilities of workers properly to undertake comprehensive assessments will determine whether they are able to serve the best interests of children in contested situations.

Ainsworth (1962), in considering the effect of the quality of care-giving and its influence on the intensity of the attachment, classified three types of attachment behaviour:

- Securely attached infants who cried little in the presence of a stranger and seemed content to explore in the presence of mother.
- Insecurely attached infants who tended to cry frequently in the presence of a stranger even when held by their mother and who showed inhibited exploration.
- Unattached infants who showed no responsive behaviour to the mother.

Main and Solomon (1986) have recently added to Ainsworth's two categories of insecure attachment a third category, that of *disorganised attachment*, to fit those children who show some of the evidence of attachment, but do not display these signs in any apparently consistent and organised way.

Ainsworth discovered that secure attachment was significantly correlated with maternal sensitivity and responsiveness to the infant's needs. Essentially, testing for a secure attachment involves assessing the child's emotional bonding to a care-giver by observing their behaviour when a potentially threatening situation is encountered. In other words, does the young child turn to the care-giver for reassurance or comfort when a stranger (psychologist) enters the room and offers to take the child out? Does the child demonstrate that the care-giver is seen as a secure base from which the sincerity or friendliness of the strange person can be tested? Is there a preference for the care-giver over the stranger? If the care-giver leaves the room how does the young child respond? Does the child show indifference and interact freely with the assessor, or are they reserved and inhibited with the assessor, frequently checking out and seeking assurance that the preferred individual will soon return?

This is over-simplified and clearly other observations need to centre on the direct interaction of the care-giver and child, noting the amount of reciprocity, sensitivity and synchronicity, and enjoyment of each other's presence. Attachments should essentially be a two-way process between care-giver and child and need to be observed over several sessions. Clearly, the skill and sensitivity of the assessor are of paramount importance, and it is all too easy, as Murray Ryburn discusses in chapter

14, for assessors who already hold definite views about a child and its family to participate in a spurious assessment process, in which they see what they expect to see and ignore other possibilities.

As will be discussed later, multiple attachments to other care-givers can and do naturally occur. These tend to be hierarchical in nature, with some evidence (Schaffer and Emerson, 1964) that each of the people to whom an infant is attached may serve a different function. Therefore, the person whom an infant prefers may depend on the particular situation.

Assessing reactions to separation when children enter substitute care

Where young children are placed in substitute care pending adoption proceedings, the following are some of the important points that need to be taken into consideration in assessing reactions to separation. These do not represent a hierarchy and need to be considered as a whole. It cannot be emphasised too strongly that the background of a child's life must be the context for assessment, so that the effects of factors such as poverty and deprivation are not confused with aspects of attachment.

- What is the child's change of emotional state since separation? Do they cry more easily, more frequently and without apparent reason? Do they constantly ask about their parents or siblings? Do they rarely ask for and resist discussion about their parents and siblings?
- How have their sleep patterns changed? Do they sleep more or less frequently? Do they sleep more during the day, less at night, earlier or later in the morning?
- Do they wake up in the night more frequently than when living with birth parents? Whom do they ask for? Are they easily comforted and by whom?
- Do they have frequent accidents with bowel and bladder control; more than when living with their birth parents?
- How has their feeding pattern changed? Do they eat more or less than before and more or less of particular foods?
- How has their social interaction with familiar children and adults changed? Do they show more reserve or more demanding and clinging behaviour? Do they demonstrate verbal or physical anger? Are they less responsive to the attention given to them by their parents? Do they seem to 'look through' familiar children and adults as though they were not there? Are they apathetic? Are they passive? Do these changes fluctuate?
- Does their play show distinct qualitative and quantitative changes?

Do they 'play' in stereotyped ways, repeating movements and scenarios over and over as though stuck in a particular pattern? Do they play more or less with favourite toys and comfort objects (has 'teddy' been rejected or has 'teddy' taken on an even greater significance for the child)?

- Do they engage more in self-comforting behaviours at the expense of play with toys or social interaction, for example thumb- or clothes-sucking, hair-twirling? Do they sit and day-dream more?
- Do they show more anxious or worried behaviour, such as constant nose- or skin-picking, or tearing off wallpaper or destruction of their own or others' artwork or construction activities?

The above may be some indicators of separation anxiety where children show changes in behaviour, but other symptoms may also be displayed.

Multiple attachments

The early research (see for example Bowlby, 1952) could lead us to believe that all substitute placements stemming from separation are doomed to failure from the outset. This is clearly not the case. This view arose from seeing attachment as a dyadic relationship with exclusive membership of mother and child, the disruption of which would lead inevitably to catastrophic consequences for the child. The role of the father and other care-givers has until relatively recently been ignored.

More recent research has acknowledged that multiple attachments can exist and indeed are likely to form. It has been argued by some (Rutter, 1975) that 'most children have multiple attachments of varying intensity and that there tends to be a persisting hierarchy among these with some continuing to be stronger than others' (p. 66). The formation of multiple attachments is seen as giving an advantage to a child who will have alternatives to turn to at times of separation or difficulty. It appears that the beginnings of social competence in the child do not stem simply from the existence of a mother–child relationship but from the quality of the relationship between care-givers and child.

If this is the case, then the single most important early experience is missing for children who are in situations of contested adoption and where original family links are severed. What does seem to be clear is that there is no reason to end past attachments to enable new ones to form, and that the continuation of past attachments can support the identity needs of the child.

Identity issues in separation

For conceptual purposes psychologists have distinguished between personal and social identity. Erikson saw the achievement of a satisfactory personal identity as a key developmental task:

> The young person in order to experience wholeness, must feel a progressive continuity between that which he has come to be during the long years of childhood and that which he promises to be in the anticipated future: between that which he conceives himself to be and that which he perceives others to see in him and to expect of him (1968, p.87).

Social identity as a concept was developed in the 1970s (Israel and Tajfel, 1972) to explain in-group and out-group relations and social processes. Social identity has been defined as 'the individual's knowledge that he/she belongs to certain social groups together with some emotional and value significance to him/her of the group membership' (Tajfel, 1972, p. 31). Thus, social identity is self-conception as a group member. Individuals become psychologically connected to their group through their self-definitions as members of the group.

Ethnic identity

Difficulties may arise more for the black child placed in substitute care in a white family, pending adoption, than for the white child placed in a white family. This is because of the likely confusions for such a child in separating the position of white family members from the white society to which they belong. This is a society which black children experience as racist, where all cultures and ethnic groups are not valued equally and discrimination based on cultural and ethnic differences is rife. There is a possibility that placing black children with white families when they are young may sabotage later attempts in placement with black families. The evidence of research suggests (see for example Aboud 1987; Davey, 1983) that children who have been transracially placed for a long time often internalise a view of themselves as white or believe that white is preferable and superior. In these circumstances, by the time a review of the long-term foster placement has occurred, the likelihood of successful cultural reintegration and emotional identification with a black family would have been jeopardised.

A recent contested adoption case reported in *The Birmingham Post* (28 November 1992) of a five-year-old Sikh girl who was transracially placed from birth illustrates some of the issues.

The girl was reported to have been placed with a white foster family when she was six days old. Her unmarried Sikh mother returned to India shortly after her birth. When the girl was two years and eight months old social services attempted to remove her from her foster placement when the foster family sought to adopt her. A two-year court battle followed which resulted in a decision permitting the white couple to adopt the child.

This was clearly a situation where, by initially placing the child with a white family, insufficient attention was paid to considering her long-term psychological needs. By attempting to remove her at age two years and eight months it is likely that even further damage could have been done, as the research on outcomes for those who suffer disruptive attachments in their early years indicates. Both the initial placement and later attempts to remove the girl were not located within an appropriate framework of child development.

Attachment to this particular family for this girl is likely to involve the taking on of the family's values, beliefs and ways of construing the world. Unless steps are taken to provide the girl with information and a positive encounter with her own culture, ethnic mis-identification may occur. In this process compensation for the reality of not being white leads to an internalisation of all things perceived as white, without analysis or selectivity.

Mis-identification in terms of ethnicity is in fact separation or distancing one from oneself. A denial by carers of the need, early in a child's life, for accurate ethnic identification may lead to intense anxiety, confusion and later anger when racial slurs are encountered. We know from a number of studies, including the British study of Gill and Jackson (1983), that the majority of white adopters of black children do not take an active role in exploring the child's ethnic background. It was an area that was ignored as it was not seen as a matter of concern by the parents. Furthermore, many of the families in this study who had previously lived in multi-racial areas had chosen to move out of these shortly after adoption, further limiting the child's contact and experience with their ethnic group. In terms of attitudes towards their ethnic group the vast majority of the children said that they would not like to live in the same way as African-Caribbean or South Asian people, one child explaining, 'I wouldn't fit in with the way they live; I wouldn't be able to fit in . . . I wouldn't be known' (p.79), and another child saying, 'well, most Black families seem to be quite disorganised, really. I wouldn't like to have a disorganised family or anything like that, but I don't really know how they live' (p.79).

Given the evidence from this study and other studies (see for example Andujo, 1988), it is not surprising that black practitioners and pressure groups wanting to act in the best interests of the child have been active in

attempting to establish same-race placement policy procedures. How effective this has been, however, is doubtful. A recently published survey in 1992 (Charles, Rashid and Thoburn) discovered, when looking at the major voluntary adoption agencies, that out of a cohort of 241 black children, 68 per cent were placed transracially, and, when the placement of very young children was considered separately, the percentage rose to 84 per cent.

The Rowe and Thoburn study (Fratter et al.,1991) found that one of the factors likely to be associated with the maintenance of contact was where black children with two black birth parents were placed transracially. They found on the other hand that 'those of mixed parentage are . . . more like white children and are less likely to have continued contact with birth parents' (p. 41). Acknowledgement of difference (Kirk, 1964) is perhaps aided in transracial placements, and adopters may thereby be helped to recognise more clearly the fact that their child has a different birth heritage. In the case of transracial placements that are contested, however, we could speculate that if negative views are held of original families, these are likely to lead to the generalisation of negative racial stereotypes that could militate against children's achievement of positive and accurate ethnic identification.

For the white child issues of identity are also important. Research has shown that an awareness of origins is important in developing a sense of personal identity (Triseliotis, 1973; Raynor, 1980) and that it aids children in feeling sufficiently secure to come fully to terms with their status as adopted people. It seems that being provided with adequate information about birth parents, or contact with them, offers a high degree of protection against feeling stigmatised when others highlight their 'difference' or the 'failure' of their birth families. Insecurity about origins in long-term care appeared in the study of Rowe and her colleagues (1984) to peak at age 14–16 with 58 per cent of children indicating difficulty. Later this dropped at age 17 to 35 per cent. The available evidence suggests that a warm supportive environment is no substitute for having good information about one's origins (Rowe et al., 1984). Ryburn (1992) notes that adoption could sometimes be kept a secret from those who were adopted, and the discovery in adulthood of adoptive status could be a shattering event. Rockel and Ryburn (1988) have described how lack of information about the reasons for adoption can cause adoptees to seek out their birth parents in adulthood in a way that seems a search for self. Where there have been contested adoptions, background information, as Murray Ryburn suggests in chapter 12, may be subject to significant bias, and there may be a lack of willingness on the part of birth families to provide it themselves.

Conclusion

We do not know enough from existing research to understand fully the implications of breaking and re-forming attachments and of the long-term psychological effects of separation during different developmental stages. Nor can we be confident about the impact of family characteristics upon the formation of personal and social identity. In relation to contested adoptions, all too often conclusions about a child's depth of attachment to his or her family of origin, or assessments of the effects of separation, may be based on views of practitioners that are not sustained by the available research.

References

Aboud, F. (1987), 'The Development of Ethnic Self Identification and Attitudes', in Phinney, J. and Rotheram, M. [eds], *Children's Ethnic Socialisation: Pluralism and Development*, Newbury Park, CA: Sage.

Ainsworth, M. (1940), *An Evaluation of Adjustment Based on the Concept of Security*, Child Development Series, Toronto: University of Toronto Press.

Ainsworth, M. (1962), 'The Effects of Maternal Deprivation: A Review of the Findings and Controversy in the Context of Research Strategy', in *Deprivation of Maternal Care: A Reassessment of its Effects*, Geneva: World Health Organisation.

Andujo, E. (1988), 'Ethnic Identity of Transethnically Adopted Hispanic Adolescents', *Social Work*, **33**, 531–5.

Berger, M. and Passingham, R. (1972), 'Early Experience and Other Environmental Factors: an Overview', in Eysenck, H. [ed.], *Handbook of Abnormal Psychology*, 2nd edition, London: Pitman.

Bowlby, J. (1952), *Maternal Care and Mental Health*, Geneva: World Health Organisation.

Bowlby, J. (1979), *The Making and Breaking of Affectional Bonds*, London: Tavistock Routledge.

Charles, M., Rashid, S. and Thoburn, J. (1992), 'Research on Permanent Family Placement of Black Children and those from Minority Ethnic Groups', *Adoption and Fostering*, **16**(2), 3–4.

Cooper, C. (1980), 'Paediatric Perspectives', in Adcock, M. and White, R. [eds], *Terminating Parental Contact*, London: BAAF.

Craft, M., Stephenson, J. and Grainger, C. (1984), 'The Relationship Between Severity of Personality Disorder and Certain Adverse Childhood Influences', *British Journal of Psychiatry*, **110**, 392–492.

Davey, A. (1983), *Learning to be Prejudiced: Growing up in Multi-Ethnic Britain*, London: Edward Arnold.

Earle, A. and Earle, D. (1961), 'Early Maternal Deprivation and Later Psychiatric Illness', *American Journal of Ortho-Psychiatry*, **31**, 181–6.

Erikson, E. (1968), *Identity: Youth and Crisis*, New York: Norton.

Fratter, J., Rowe, J., Sapsford, D. and Thoburn, J. (1991), *Permanent Family Placement: A Decade of Experience*, London: BAAF.

Gill, O. and Jackson, B. (1983), *Adoption and Race: Black, Asian and Mixed Race Children in White Families*, London: Batsford.

Greer, S., Gunn, J. and Coller, K. (1966), 'Aetiological Factors in Attempted Suicide', *British Medical Journal*, **2**, 1352–5.

Harper, J. (1990), 'Children's Communication of Anxiety Through Metaphor in Fostering and Adoption', *Adoption and Fostering*, **14**(3), 33–7.

Heinicke, C. and Westheimer, I. (1966), *Brief Separations*, New York: International Universities Press.

Israel, J. and Tajfel, H. [eds] (1972), *The Context of Social Psychology: A Critical Assessment*, London: Academic Press.

Kirk, D. (1964), *Shared Fate: A Theory of Adoption and Mental Heath*, New York: Free Press.

Main, M. and Solomon, J. (1986), 'Discovery of an Insecure Disorganized/ Disoriented Attachment Pattern: Procedures, Findings and Implications for the Classification of Behaviour', in Yogman, M. and Brazelton, T. [eds], *Affective Development in Infancy*, Norwood, NJ: Ablex.

McCord, W. and McCord, J. (1959), *The Origins of Crime: A New Evaluation of the Cambridge-Sommerville Youth Study*, New York: Columbia University Press.

Pardeck, J. and Pardeck, J. (1988), 'Helping Children to Adjust to Adoption Through the Biblio Therapeutic Approach', *Adoption and Fostering*, **12**(3), 11–16.

Raynor, L. (1980), *The Adopted Child Comes of Age*, London: Allen and Unwin.

Robertson, J. and Bowlby, J. (1952), *Responses of Young Children to Separation From Their Mothers*, Paris: Courier of the International Children's Centre, **2**, 131–40.

Robertson, J. and Robertson, J. (1971), 'Young Children in Brief Separation', *Psychoanalytic Study of the Child*, **26**, 264–315.

Rockel, J. and Ryburn, M. (1988), *Adoption Today: Change and Choice in New Zealand*, Auckland: Heinemann/Reed.

Rowe, J., Cain, H., Hundleby, M. and Keane, A. (1984), *Long Term Foster Care*, London: Batsford/BAAF.

Rutter, M. (1971), 'Parent Child Separation: Psychological Effects on the Children', *Journal of Child Psychology and Psychiatry*, **11**, 259–83.

Rutter, M. (1972), *Maternal Deprivation Reassessed*, Harmondsworth: Penguin.

Rutter, M. (1975), *Helping Troubled Children*, Harmondsworth: Penguin.

Ryburn, M. (1992), *Adoption in the 1990s: Identity and Openness*, Birmingham: Leamington Press.

Ryburn, M. (1994), *Open Adoption: Research, Theory and Practice*, Aldershot: Avebury.

Schaffer, H. and Emerson, P. (1964), 'Patterns of Response to Physical Contact in Early Human Development', *Journal of Child Psychology and Psychiatry*, **5**, 1–13.

Stacey, M., Dearden, R., Pill, R. and Robinson, D. (1970), *Hospitals, Children and Their Families, The Report of a Pilot Study*, London: Routledge and Kegan Paul.

Tajfel, H. (1972), 'Experiments in a Vacuum', in Israel, J. and Tajfel, H. [eds] *The Context of Social Psychology: A Critical Assessment*, London: Academic Press.

Triseliotis, J. (1973), *In Search of Origins*, London: Routledge and Kegan Paul.

Vernon, D., Foley, J., Sipowicz, R. and Schulman, J. (1965), *The Psychological Responses of Children to Illness*, New York: C.C. Thomas.

10 The role of the guardian *ad litem* in contested adoptions

Phil King

Introduction

Adoption means different things to different people – the child, the new family, the birth family, the local authority, the courts, and the general public. The guardian *ad litem* must start with an understanding of the cognitive, emotional and cultural meanings that adoption has for the key individuals involved. Moving children, with all their past social, emotional, ethnic and cultural influences, into new permanent families is a complex and delicate task. Does the legislation help the child who has to make this profound step, or does it get in the way? If the adoption is contested, how does this affect a child's interests – the very thing which the guardian is charged to safeguard.

This chapter examines the role of the guardian *ad litem* in contested proceedings by focusing on a particular study.

Lisa, a white English child, was one year old when she was placed with foster carers. Kerry was only fourteen-and-a-half years old when her daughter was born and she lived with her own mother and stepfather. Lisa's father was not named but there were strong suspicions that he was Kerry's stepfather.

Kerry had been sexually abused by her birth father and had spent time in care herself. Her mother and stepfather had five children. These children were all received into care after Lisa as a result of neglect – they later disclosed sexual abuse. The parents became hostile and unable to work with social services – Kerry took her parents' side, but gradually started to co-operate with social workers who offered her help not only as a young parent but also as

an individual. She came to trust her social workers and that trust was reciprocated with sensitive services which continued when she and Lisa moved to a residential family centre.

Lisa was now two years old. The attachment between mother and child began to grow in this nurturing environment. Kerry started to mature and her parenting skills increased. This was planned as a long stay, with mother and child eventually moving to their own accommodation. Tragically, the placement ended after a year when it was found that Kerry had sexually abused both Lisa and another child. Kerry returned to her own parents, and Lisa was placed, in an emergency, with foster carers. It took some time for contact to be arranged on neutral ground, a confusing and disruptive time for Lisa. Contact was unsuccessful and was terminated; the mother had resumed her hostile attitude.

Lisa was three-and-a-half years old when she last saw her mother. She moved on to prospective adopters a year later. She then disclosed that her previous foster carers had been sexually abusing her. The prospective adopters handled this badly, and consequently Lisa suffered emotional abuse. Lisa, by then a very damaged child, was placed with specialist foster carers who, with much love and care, started the long process of helping her to heal.

Kerry was never informed of this disruption. There was effectively no communication and her situation was not reassessed at this point.

A strong attachment developed between the foster carers and Lisa. Despite the plan for her to move to prospective adopters, it became clear that this should be her permanent home. She was now seven-and-a-half years old, and had been placed for three years. The panel approved the match, and Lisa, who clearly wanted to stay with her carers, did not have to face another disruption. The local authority applied to free her for adoption without consent on the grounds that the mother was withholding this unreasonably. The parties were poles apart. The local authority had worked hard at reunification and it had failed. The mother felt badly let down, believing she had not been provided with a proper chance. Social services did not want contact but offered an exchange of information when they saw that Kerry would provide information about herself for Lisa's life story book.

The mother broke down in tears giving evidence. In her heart she knew that Lisa should stay with her carers. She opposed because she did not want Lisa to think she had been given away, she wanted some form of contact and she grieved for a lost opportunity at reunification. She did genuinely want what was best for her child now, but as she said: 'if only I could hear it from my daughter myself, I would believe this is what she wants.'

Lisa got the permanent home she desperately needed with the people she loved. The mother would have agreed to this in a different framework; she would have 'acted reasonably' through some negotiated agreement. Future contact is yet to be considered.

Duties of the guardian *ad litem*

A guardian *ad litem* is appointed when an application is made for adoption or freeing and it appears that a parent is unwilling to agree, or when there are special circumstances. The guardian's role, as defined in the Adoption Rules 1984 and Magistrates Courts (Adoption) Rules 1984, is imprecise. For example, she or he has a duty to investigate 'so far as he considers necessary' the information in the various reports and statements, as well as any other matters which she or he considers relevant. A full reading of the duties indicates that the role is very poorly defined, placing too much reliance on information supplied by just one party to the proceedings, and on the discretion of the individual guardian. This is in sharp contrast to the very proactive, expansive and well-defined role of the guardian in proceedings under the Children Act 1989. The *Manual of Practice Guidance for Guardians ad Litem and Reporting Officers* (DoH, 1992) is helpful in that it suggests a 'Children Act' approach to these applications, but what is required is a legislative framework of clearly defined duties. A checklist of all the main issues to be covered would encourage some consistency in approach whilst maintaining flexibility.

While the Adoption Law Review Consultation Document (DoH, 1992) goes some way towards this by introducing a 'welfare checklist' similar to that in Children Act proceedings, the White Paper (DoH, 1993) does not refer specifically to the welfare checklist.

In Lisa's case it would be all too easy to look at the basic facts and regard the matter very much as a *fait accompli*, paying little or no attention to the issues other than her pressing need for a permanent home. For example, with regard to contact Lisa had different needs at the time of the adoption to those at the time of termination of contact. Once she had the security of a permanent home, her needs with regard to contact may be different. Was there sufficient openness to allow this to be re-examined?

In adoption proceedings the child is usually represented only by a guardian. The court does have the power to make the guardian a respondent in his or her own right but this is representation for the guardian alone, not the child. In specified proceedings under the Children Act 1989, a solicitor is invariably appointed to represent the child, either through the guardian or on direct instructions from a 'competent' child. This combination of solicitor/guardian representation is much admired and the team approach on behalf of the child maximises thorough presentation of the child's rights and interests (King and Young, 1992). It is my belief that children should have automatic party status in adoption proceedings, and that a solicitor should always be appointed. The task of reaching a conclusion on such a fundamental issue is too onerous for the guardian

alone. This is a matter which the Adoption Law Review does not fully address.

Child-focused enquiries

The guardian's enquiries should always be child-focused, but with a sensitivity to the needs and perspectives of others. I find it useful to imagine what the child would ask of a guardian now, in several years' time and as an adult. Looking back, would the child be satisfied with all of the efforts that had been made? Can basic questions that the child has, or may have, be answered?

The guardian must provide the court with this sort of information so that the judgment of the court can reflect the child's perspective. It is my belief that children should have a copy of the judgment made about them in any court case to refer to whenever there is a need.

Fortunately, in Lisa's case the judge made a careful and sensitive judgment which covered all the significant events in her life, both good and bad. It gave a balanced view and honestly looked at shortcomings on all sides. The reasoning was clear and will be helpful to Lisa in later life. Judges, therefore, need to be aware that the child may see a copy of their judgment.

Evidence to the court

As the parties to the proceedings in contested adoptions are usually pushed into polarised positions by the legal process, the information supplied to the courts often reflects this. The local authority frequently offers a catalogue of the parents' every actual or suspected disaster in the form of a statement of facts, and the information in the Schedule 2 reports is also carefully chosen. This selectivity is to do with a pressure to win the case, and this and its wider implications are further discussed by Murray Ryburn in chapter 14. The parents' affidavit in response (assuming that they have received edited versions of reports through order of the court) is often similarly one-sided, especially when this may be the first information they have received for some time. The battle of information begins with affidavits flying back in reply. No one's case is helped, least of all the child's. The authors of Schedule 2 reports should remember that in time a child may read this record and that it will remain on the adoption file for 75 years. Great care must be taken with the use of words and the accuracy of information, as this will give the adopted adult an impression of their origins and the reasons for the adoption.

The guardian has a crucial task in analysing the information supplied and adding to it in a way which gives a fair and balanced picture, thus

providing the middle ground. This can be a time-consuming task when there is such selectivity by the other parties, but the child has a right to this balance. The report should be written so that all parties can see it. It can be tempting for guardians to discriminate in their use of information if it is at odds with their recommendations, but experience in other proceedings shows that an evenly balanced picture carries greater weight.

In Lisa's case the local authority made little reference to the positive period in the family centre, or the abuse by foster carers and the trauma of the breakdown with adopters. Indeed, the mother learnt of this for the first time from the guardian. This failure to communicate, all too common in these cases, only fuels the contest. Honesty, although painful at times and provoking strong reaction, ultimately oils the wheels of partnership and negotiation. Kerry's response, equally, missed important information about her own failure to seize opportunities, and she denigrated the once excellent partnership she enjoyed with social workers.

Children's interests

The guardian is charged with safeguarding the interests of the child during the court proceedings. The recent White Paper, *Adoption: The Future* (DoH, 1993), states: 'A guardian *ad litem* (GAL) will be appointed in many adoption cases to watch over the interests of the child. Their function will be modelled on their role in care cases under the Children Act' (para 4.4). This is a mammoth and complex task of examining and balancing the needs of the child through careful investigation. The needs of the child do not exist in a vacuum apart from the interests of others. All the parties to the proceedings have their views on how these needs are best met. Consideration has to be given to the effect of the proposed plans on the child's changing needs. The task of looking at the child's needs towards adulthood is difficult but vital and the Adoption Law Review recognises this. The 'welfare test', which it is proposed will be included in the consideration of the decision about adoption, must also refer to 'the likely effect on the child's adult life of any change in his legal status'. The two main studies of adopted adults' experiences show that for many adopted people a lack of sense of identity carried through into adult life with significant effects (Triseliotis, 1973; Haines and Timms, 1985).

One cannot examine a child's interests without a full consideration of their rights. In 1991 the United Kingdom agreed to be bound by the United Nations Convention on the Rights of the Child, and it is vital that this also acts as a checklist in determining a court decision about a child. In chapter 6, Gerison Lansdown looks at how a children's rights framework can contribute to the decision-making process.

In Lisa's case, her overriding need was for a permanent home. The

recognition of this need had to be made clear to her, given the history, but should not have prevented an examination of her other needs and rights. She lacked full information about her birth family for a variety of reasons, but supplementing this had to be delayed until she had the bedrock of stability from which to take on board more information.

Wishes and feelings of the child

Providing an accurate voice for children and ensuring that their perspective is clearly understood, is fundamental to the role of the guardian *ad litem*. Unlike Children Act proceedings, the guardian in adoption has no direct duty to have regard to the wishes and feelings of the child, only insofar as this is referred to in Schedule 2 reports. In practice, a guardian would include an examination of this in his or her report, and the Adoption Law Review proposes the same approach as in other proceedings.

A child will have expressed views to a range of people, but the guardian must give the child an opportunity to talk afresh. This is a skilled task at the best of times, especially given the time-limited nature of the guardian's involvement, and is even more difficult when the issue is adoption.

A child will have been given information about adoption and the reasons for it. What sort of explanations have been given? Have all the possibilities been explored? Will the child worry that a wish to have more information about or to see the birth family will be seen as a threat to their current home? What sort of information does the child have about their birth family – how honest is it? Does the child really understand the concept of adoption other than meaning, 'I'm staying here'? If, like Lisa, the younger child may have been in placement for some time, with no contact with the birth family for a long period, they will have difficulty grasping all the past and future implications.

Lisa expressed a very strong wish to stay with her beloved carers who had helped her through painful times. She felt loved and valued there and wanted adoption which for her meant a 'forever' home – especially important in this case, as the original plan had been to move her on. Lisa had carers who knew and valued the importance of her life story work and planned to develop the information available to her. On one occasion she spontaneously mentioned to the guardian that her mother could not look after her. She was not able to talk about this any further, but clearly she wanted to begin the conversation and saw the guardian as some live link. However, what she needed first was to know that she would be adopted; she could then begin her journey of discovery and fortunately she had carers who would help her.

It is unrealistic to expect a child to express views about something that is

in the past, on which the door may have been long closed. It would, however, be helpful to provide opportunities at each crucial stage for a child to express their views. This could be when care proceedings are current and the plan is to return home; when it has been decided that reunification is no longer to be pursued; on application for a placement order, as suggested in the Adoption Law Review; and then on an adoption application. This would have meaning for children both emotionally and cognitively.

What is being contested?

The guardian must identify clearly what is in dispute. Often there has been a period of poor communication between the parties so the possibilities of misunderstanding are considerable. Combine this with the fact that the first clear communication from the authority to the parent may be through the application and the statement of facts, and the conflict may become disproportionate.

Kerry's reasons for contesting were given earlier; she could not accept hearing the child's wishes from elsewhere, although she did take some comfort from information about Lisa's present happiness and evidence giving her wishes.

In another case of two sisters aged two and four years, all evidence was that the parents would hotly contest the application. Numerous attempts at reunification had failed. The parents' first response was to contest: they were angry that no more attempts would be made to return the children. They had received no counselling. The guardian began to sift through the information with them – they were grieving. They began to realise that they wanted to agree and after consulting their solicitor, a negotiated settlement was arrived at which included contact.

Planning and delay

The guardian has to look at all the plans and the process of making them. The group decision-making of conferences can be poor but, once made, decisions can often be difficult to change. Early involvement of the guardian is clearly important. In my opinion she or he must comment on the validity of plans made and, as in Children Act proceedings, seek to effect change where appropriate. Whilst this is accepted as a part of the guardian's role by the courts, local authorities are not always comfortable with criticism of their planning processes and of the conclusions they reach.

In Britain, permanency planning became synonymous with placing children in permanent substitute homes, most frequently through adoption.

It is now recognised that it must include intensive work towards reunification with the birth family as the first preferred option. Sadly, recent research has indicated that, although there is little evidence of children drifting in care, which was a serious concern in the past (Rowe and Lambert, 1973), rigid plans for permanency are being pursued which largely exclude the birth family (Rowe, Hundleby and Garnett, 1989). It is also sad that the resources, expertise and post-placement support which exist in homefinding services cannot be extended to reunification work. Children need to know that everything possible has been done to reunite them with their families before permanent placement elsewhere. Where this cannot happen, the key ingredient in making plans must be flexibility. The difficulty for guardians is that there is quite often a delay in the making of the application so plans are already well advanced, if not set, by the time of their involvement. It may well be impossible to shift the course slightly, never mind change it. Lost opportunities and sighs of 'if only' are probably familiar to most guardians, but frequently they have arrived too late. As suggested in Discussion Paper 3 (DoH, 1991), the court can act as a rubber stamp. Those feelings of opportunities lost are very uncomfortable for the guardian acting in such profound proceedings as adoption.

It will be interesting to see if the Children Act has had an effect on delays in adoption applications. Experience suggests that as parents can now make applications for contact and/or discharge of a care order if they are dissatisfied with the position (contact is often reduced when reunification is declared no longer possible), their early application encourages an equally early application for a freeing order. All of the issues are heard together, which makes sense not only in human terms, especially for the child, but also in economic terms as well. Another case example will illustrate.

There had been massive delays in planning for four white English children – the Bartletts – who could not return home. The two eldest had been grossly sexually abused and were placed separately to their younger siblings. It was only the parents' application for contact which led to the involvement of guardian and solicitor, who brought pressure to bear on the authority to make their proposed applications. The foster carer wished to adopt the younger siblings against the wishes of the authority and the grandparents were considered as carers as well. A further child was born during the proceedings and her case consolidated. In the end there were a total of 21 applications before the court, a mammoth task, but a clear determination for each individual child was made. The issue of contact was live throughout for each plan before the court.

However, there is still the problem of children being freed for adoption and not yet placed with a family. How can a guardian give full advice, for example, on contact, in a situation when a child is in limbo? The Adoption Law Review (DoH, 1992) and the Adoption White Paper (DoH, 1993) suggest the earlier involvement of the courts, and this and the problems of placement orders are discussed by Mary Ryan in chapter 3.

Assessments

Courts seem to be increasingly looking towards guidelines on the conduct of assessments (DoH, 1988) to gauge the adequacy of information put before them and the guardian's views on this. There will be assessments on the needs of children and the capacity of the parents, amongst others. Assessments are not carried out in isolation and the services provided have to be considered as a whole. Assessments are not static and the situation may have changed by the time an application is made. One of the main findings in *Patterns and Outcomes in Child Placement* (DoH, 1991, p.76) was that:

> much more weight ought to be given to detailed observation and carefully collected evidence . . . the consequences of relying on personal values making false assumptions or ignoring or distorting evidence can be very serious indeed . . . all the professionals involved in child care decisions would benefit from rigorous training in collection and use of evidence.

In the case of the Bartletts, for example, the authority wanted to place all the children together. The two younger siblings, aged two- and three-and-a-half years, had been with their carer for 18 months at the time of the final hearing. The first adoption panel had approved the plan nine months into placement and, on meeting nine months later prior to the final hearing, declared on the basis of information supplied that the needs of the children were unchanged! A rigid policy of keeping siblings together was adhered to despite the fact that these siblings had been separated in care with no contact between them for a period of 11 months. There were no assessments of the nature of the children's attachments and their individual needs. In Lisa's case there was no reassessment of the mother's situation, despite a breakdown in the prospective adoptive placement. This case illustrates how the birth family can be the one source of continuity.

The complex task of assessing attachments following past disruption is referred to in the previous chapter by Nick Banks, and he highlights how there can be confusion between strength of attachment and normal reaction to separation. It is vital that any assessment gives full consideration to the placement with members of the wider family – experience has

shown that this can be too easily neglected. *Patterns and Outcomes* acknowledges the research on the positive aspects of placement within the wider family by stating, 'the stability of placements especially for long-term cases makes it worth trying hard to seek out relatives and overcome obstacles'. An effect of the Children Act seems to be that placing with relatives is being used to a significant and much greater extent than was evident before (Hunt, Thomas and Macleod, 1993).

Partnership and negotiation

One of the key principles of the Children Act 1989 is that an authority should work in partnership with the parents and the child, if of sufficient understanding, as long as this does not jeopardise the child's welfare. In times of stress people become more rigid and power issues escalate. The adversarial nature of adoption proceedings encourages and reinforces this and undermines, if not kills, any existing partnership. I would argue that it is possible for there to be continuing partnership when there is a point of conflict. The participants need to show qualities of flexibility, common sense, mutual respect, some trust and good communication skills. Openness is crucial and parents who are involved in this way will be given a proper opportunity to make more considered decisions rather than to respond to a one-sided account of all their failings. There should be a legal framework which encourages this where the child's interests remain central. The Act provides a framework for partnership and a greater scope for negotiated solutions. However, there are possible implications for children's and parents' rights in moving major decisions out of a court forum – 'Negotiating agreements in the "shadow of the law" may not always be preferable to adjudication in its, admittedly uncomfortable, full glare' (Hunt, Thomas and Macleod, 1993). Partnership does not necessarily exclude court proceedings.

In line with this, the importance of negotiation within public law proceedings is becoming more recognised. This is not plea bargaining where a child's interests are put in jeopardy, but a serious attempt by key parties to find some negotiated settlement. We know that children are badly served by contested divorce, and much mediation and conciliation work now takes place to find negotiated solutions to avoid the great human and financial costs involved in divorce. A lot can be learnt from this. Sadly, early indications show little evidence of greater family participation in public law proceedings or decision-making. According to Hunt et al., 'children have virtually disappeared from proceedings; parents remain confused and uninvolved, detached and usually silent observers'. It is, of

course, important that courts are fully satisfied with negotiated settlements rather than rubber stamping them.

There will be times, however, when a negotiated settlement proves impossible because a court is needed to adjudicate on one or several issues. Once this is determined there should still be the possibility for parties to negotiate again, based on the finding of the court. Partnership and negotiation should take place whenever courts have to make decisions about children, and the courts should encourage negotiation and mediation meetings to take place, as in private law proceedings.

Anti-discriminatory practice

A guardian must ensure that all children, irrespective of race, culture, gender, age, religion, class, sexual orientation and disability are afforded the same services, opportunities, respect and value, whatever the plan. Any discrimination must be challenged, using the powers of the court if appropriate. These issues will affect not only the adoptive placement offered, but also the chances of an appropriate placement. For example, some agencies still have difficulty recruiting adopters from minority ethnic groups, for many reasons, one of which may be that adoption is a white European concept.

The following case example shows how adoption was inappropriate for a African-Caribbean child, because the legal effect of the order and its exclusive nature were not in keeping with the culture of the foster carer and the mother.

Leroy was born to a very young mother who had been in care herself. An attempt at supported independent living broke down and the mother and child returned to an African-Caribbean foster carer who had cared for the mother and helped her greatly in the past. The mother soon decided to move on leaving Leroy with the foster carer. He remained there between the ages of six months and two years. In that time concerted efforts were made to reunite mother and child, supported by the foster carer, who arranged with the mother excellent opportunities for contact. The attempt failed. The mother strongly opposed adoption. The foster carer, who had an aunt/grandmother-type relationship with the mother, was uncomfortable with the idea of adoption. She felt wholly secure with a residence order which allowed a continuing role for the mother, with residence and main responsibility clearly defined. A residence order was made by the court.

Cross-cultural factors have an immense influence on assessments and decision-making. One of the most disturbing messages from *Patterns and Outcomes* was about the disproportionate number of children of mixed ethnicity in public care. With this in mind, guardian *ad litem*/Reporting Officers panels need to address the shortage of guardians from minority ethnic backgrounds.

Legal status and permanence

Leroy's situation serves as a reminder that adoption is not the only way to secure permanence. It is not the order in itself that makes a child's situation stable and secure, but rather the child's and family's feelings of security with each other. It is their sense of permanence which is important, as noted in the research studies which have informed the Adoption Law Review and the White Paper. At times the view that the making of an adoption order in itself will create such a fundamental state of relationships would seem to prevail. Understandably some children and families do want adoption as an official seal on the security they strive for. This will be right for some families, but the view that adoption is the only alternative way of securing a stable permanent home limits choice. The whole range of options must be considered equally, so that choice is influenced by the individual needs of the child. As June Thoburn states in chapter 8, information and research need to be cited on *all* of the options in the balancing exercise. The guardian is in a central position to do this.

Although custodianship had been little used, it was, in theory, appropriate to many families, particularly for children living with relatives, where to change family relationships legally would have been inappropriate. The proposals for inter vivos guardianship or guardianship orders in the Adoption White Paper (DoH, 1993) must be welcomed.

Contact

The importance of openness and of children maintaining links with their families has been demonstrated by research (Ryburn, 1994; Millham et al., 1986). (See also chapter 8 on the uses and abuses of research.) This has been reinforced by the Children Act 1989 and the Adoption Law Review, although the Adoption White Paper states clearly that once an adoption order is made 'the more important objective is to support the new family relationship'.

Adoption proceedings are family proceedings, as defined by the Children Act 1989, so the whole menu of orders is available: contact orders can be made with adoption orders. It seems that, given the strong emphasis in the Children Act, contact issues are now more actively considered in adoption proceedings. For example, in Lisa's case, contact had ceased many years before, but the hearing still looked at the issue. On hearing the mother's up-to-date situation, the authority offered to act as a post-box to send her regular information on Lisa. The door was therefore left open for contact to be activated as Lisa's needs dictated.

Contact can take many forms, and the guardian should firstly explore the purpose and the pros and cons to help determine what form may be most appropriate. The starting point should be a presumption of contact in some form. This exploration should be done in the framework of the child's current needs, age and understanding, and likely future needs. For example, identity issues are likely to increase in adolescence, and will have implications for contact.

Contact not only enhances identity formation (Ryburn, 1994), but facilitates attachments to the new family and helps in separation work by facilitating the grief process (Fahlberg, 1994) – in other words, letting go. (An excellent account of this in fiction is found in *Second Best* by David Cook (1991).) All of this requires a range of flexible and imaginative post-adoption services. Sadly, it seems that these are few and far between (Rickford, 1993).

Some of the contest in adoption is often about contact. Although the existence of contact orders has encouraged its active consideration, it is argued that the orders in themselves will be of little use to enforce contact. A child will not be able to have positive relationships with adults who are forced together or who may be hostile to one another. However, if people come together for an agreed positive common purpose, want to make it work, and have a regard for one another's importance to the child, then the child will be able to maintain positive attachments to them. Good negotiated agreements about contact are therefore required. Courts should be there to encourage and endorse – not to enforce. The guardian can have a key role here. As noted earlier, this is not plea bargaining; it is simply a question of those individuals coming together to work out the best arrangements for the child. As a consequence, a child must be placed with adopters before any arrangements can be agreed. Additionally, one cannot on the one hand give adopters full legal parental responsibility and then regulate it without their agreement. For adopters to see the advantages to the child, and themselves, of contact with the birth family, the recruitment and selection of people must highlight this.

It is interesting how foster carers who become adopters have a very positive attitude to contact. They have been selected and trained with

contact in mind. In the case of the Bartletts, the foster carer and mother had never met until the final hearing. However, after they heard one another's evidence, the mother, who had been very hostile to this placement, said if the children were to be freed she wanted them to stay with that carer, and both suggested the possibility of postal contact. The foster carer benefited from meeting the mother, albeit in court, and got a more rounded picture. She could make her own judgment and thus talk to the children about the mother with more meaning.

If the recommendation is for no contact, the guardian needs to examine clearly and be satisfied by the reasons for this. The skill and sensitivity needed in observing and assessing contact is discussed by Nick Banks in chapter 9. It seems that the very act of contesting an adoption is often viewed as potentially disruptive to the placement, so contact is resisted. The guardian needs to assess whether this really is the case. However, it is often better for matters of contact to be properly assessed after the stress of the contest, when all parties may be able to act more flexibly.

Children may say that they do not want any contact, or the adults may think contact may be too upsetting for them. Again this needs to be examined in detail. The difficulties for the guardian in eliciting the views of the child have been discussed earlier, but what a child should not be denied is the right to experience and show their painful feelings. Children need to grieve a loss, and if they are helped in so doing, this will strengthen attachments within the new family (Fahlberg, 1994).

The guardian should also advise the court on other people the child may benefit from having contact with, such as extended family members. Flexibility is the key in considering and making contact arrangements, as children's needs and wishes change.

Children Act 1989

It is clear, as Bill Jordan has pointed out in chapter 2, that the existing adoption legislation is not in harmony with the Children Act 1989. This chapter has made some references to the effect the Children Act has had on adoption. The role of the guardian in Children Act proceedings has expanded massively and become more proactive. This needs to be the case throughout the whole planning process for a child, not just the earlier stages. The Children Act should, I believe, guide all decisions for a child to live permanently elsewhere, including adoption. For example, the lack of automatic timed review of care orders under the Children Act seems to me to be a serious omission. When a care order is made, a date could be set to review reunification plans, with the option for an earlier hearing if needed.

If plans have been successfully achieved, appropriate orders could be made for the child to remain at home. If unsuccessful, authority to proceed to securing an alternative permanent family (as suggested by Mary Ryan in chapter 3) could be determined at this stage, as well as considering important issues such as contact.

Conclusion

Hopefully, future adoption legislation will steer parties away from an adversarial process, and allow two families who share a common link – the child – to arrive at flexible arrangements that can meet and respond to the wishes and changing needs of that child. Openness and partnership must be encouraged to allow all involved to negotiate secure permanent arrangements for children who can no longer live with their birth families. To protect the rights and interests of children such arrangements should be scrutinised and endorsed by the courts, which should be involved at an earlier stage, and at all key stages thereafter, when decisions are to be made. This would allow the guardian to play a more meaningful role in safeguarding the interests of children and in giving them a voice when such profound decisions are being made.

References

Adoption Agencies Regulations (1983), SI 1983/1964, London: HMSO.
Adoption Rules 1984, SI 1984/265, London: HMSO.
Cook, D. (1991), *Second Best*, London: Faber and Faber.
DoH (1988), *Protecting Children: A Guide for Social Workers Undertaking a Comprehensive Assessment*, London: HMSO.
DoH (1991), *Patterns and Outcomes in Child Placement: Messages from Current Research and Their Implications*, London: HMSO.
DoH/Welsh Office (1991), *Inter-Departmental Review of Adoption Law: The Adoption Process, Discussion Paper 3*, London: DoH.
DoH (1992), *Manual of Practice Guidance for Guardians ad Litem and Reporting Officers*, London: HMSO.
DoH/Welsh Office (1992), *Review of Adoption Law: Report to Ministers of an Inter-Departmental Working Group*, London: DoH/Welsh Office.
DoH/Welsh Office/Home Office/Lord Chancellor's Department (1993), *Adoption: The Future*, Cmnd. 2288, London: HMSO.
Fahlberg, V. (1994), *A Child's Journey Through Placement*, London: BAAF.
Family Proceedings Rules 1991, SI 1991/1247, London: HMSO.
Family Proceedings Courts (Children Act 1989) Rules 1991, SI 1991/1395, London: HMSO.

Haines, E. and Timms, N. (1985), *Adoption, Identity and Social Policy*, Aldershot: Gower.

Hunt, J., Thomas, C. and Macleod, A. (1993), *Statutory Intervention in Child Protection: the Impact of Children Act 1989*, University of Bristol: Socio-Legal Centre for Legal Studies.

King, P. and Young, I. (1992), *The Child as Client*, Bristol: Jordan's Family Law.

Magistrates Courts (Adoption) Rules 1984, SI 1984/611, London: HMSO.

Millham, S., Bullock, R., Hosie, K. and Haak, M. (1986), *Lost in Care: The Problems of Maintaining Links between Children in Care and their Families*, Aldershot: Gower.

Rickford, F. (1993), 'Havoc in the Home', *Community Care*, 30 September.

Rowe, J. and Lambert, L. (1973), *Children Who Wait*, London: ABAA.

Rowe, J., Hundleby, M. and Garnett, L. (1989), *Child Care Now: A Survey of Placement Patterns*, London: BAAF.

Ryburn, M. (1994), *Open Adoption: Research, Theory and Practice*, Aldershot: Avebury.

Triseliotis, J. (1973), *In Search of Origins*, London: Routledge and Kegan Paul.

11 Adoptive parents and contested adoptions

Murray Ryburn

Introduction

This chapter is based on a summary of a research project aimed at understanding and assessing the effects of contested adoptions on adoptive parenting and at considering issues in post-adoption contact following contested adoptions. It is based on a sample of 74 placements made following adoption proceedings hearings that were contested to the point of the final hearing.[1]

The chapter is divided into five sections. In the first the research project itself is outlined. The second section briefly looks at the level of post-adoption contact revealed in the study. The third considers the adversarial decision-making process and its effects on the availability and exchange of information. The fourth section considers the effects of contested adoptions on adoptive parents, and their immediate and extended families, while the final section considers the effects of contested adoptions on adoptive parents.

The research project

Initial conjectures

Three conjectures shaped the research project. The first was that, because of the contested nature of all the adoptions in this study, the goodwill

1 For reasons of length there is only a brief description of the sample and the methodology employed in this study; for further detail see Ryburn, M. (1994), in preparation.

likely to be necessary for post-adoption contact to work effectively would be largely absent and that levels of contact would be very low. Where the research examined the extent of post-adoption contact following contested proceedings will only, for reasons of space, be touched on in this chapter.[2] The second conjecture was that an adversarial process which had been followed through to the end would polarise attitudes and contribute to appreciably negative views of birth parents. Where there was some form of continuing post-adoption contact, it was thought this might ameliorate adopters' views of birth parents by providing an alternative source of information that broadened the field of vision beyond the court contest itself. It was also thought that, in the absence of post-adoption contact, adopters would be more likely to feel hampered by a lack of sufficient available information to meet their children's changing needs.

The third conjecture was that the adversarial process would be likely to be a negative and stressful one for all prospective adopters, and that this would be likely to impose an additional burden of difficulty in the already challenging task of parenting by adoption.

The sample

In September 1993, with the help and support of the national adoptive parents' organisation, PPIAS (Parent to Parent Information and Adoption Service), to which nearly all UK adoption agencies belong, a postal questionnaire was sent to 140 adoptive parents who had experienced contested adoption proceedings. Eighty-five of the 140 questionnaires were returned within the requested three-week time-scale, giving a 61 per cent response rate. Ultimately, only 67 questionnaire responses were used in the study, as for a variety of reasons 18 did not fit all the criteria for inclusion. The 67 questionnaires yielded a sample of 74 placements where adoptions had been contested up to the point of the final hearing. There were eight instances (11 per cent of the total) where children had been living with their adopters *throughout* contested freeing hearings, and they were included. For ease of expression the term 'contested adoptions' is used throughout to include these children as well.

Method of enquiry

The questionnaire gathered quantitative and qualitative data through the use of open questions. Responses comprised a mixture of factual infor-

2   Any readers who wish for further detail of this part of the study should see Ryburn (1994), in preparation.

mation, which provided the quantitative data, and affective and interpretative comments. The qualitative analysis involved the collation of the latter in relation to each question, as well as for each cluster of related questions. Common themes and insights were then also identified. Where appropriate, statistical significance was tested, and where there were questions concerning attitudes, the numbers of positive and negative statements were aggregated for defined groups within the sample and then compared with the mean to see if they were indicative of differences in approach.

One of the problems with any self-report research is a tendency for respondents to attribute a greater measure of consistency to their actions and feelings over time than might have been perceived had contemporaneous observation been possible (Festinger, 1957). Time-sequencing questions were employed as an attempt to convey the idea that consistency over time was not particularly sought for, or regarded as desirable, and to convey the belief that most respondents would have different attitudes and feelings at different points in the process of contested proceedings.

Contact, information, attitudes and the adversarial process

Levels of contact following contested adoptions

The initial supposition that there would be low levels of post-adoption contact where there had been contested proceedings was not supported, to a surprising degree, as Table 11.1 indicates. Forty-two per cent (31) of the 74 included in the study had had some form of continuing contact with one or more birth parents, and in most cases with other relatives such as grandparents and siblings (a figure which excludes those who have sibling

Table 11.1   Nature of post-adoption contact

	N	%
Want no contact	17	23
Unsure of contact	3	4
Want contact	14	19
Letter contact – birth parent/s and sometimes other relatives	21	28
Direct contact – birth parent/s and sometimes other relatives	10	14
Direct contact – siblings	9	12
	74	

contact by virtue of living in the same family). In 14 per cent of cases (10) this was direct contact involving at least one birth parent and in nine instances other relatives, ranging from the other parent, siblings or cousins to great-great-grandparents. In frequency this contact varied from annual visits to frequent 'exchanges' of visits at birth and adoptive families' houses.

For those with letter contact, this ranged in one instance from separate letters on a regular basis to a grandmother, the mother, the father and a half-brother, to contact with the birth mother only. The frequency of letter contact varied between annual letters and exchanges of photographs to letters and photographs six or more times a year. Most exchanged letters using the agency as a 'post-box', but in two instances adopters and birth families wrote directly to each other. In relation to a further 19 per cent (14) of cases in the sample where there was no form of contact, adopters indicated that they would like to establish birth parent contact. There were nine instances (12 per cent) where adopters helped children to maintain contact with brothers or sisters who were placed in other adoptive families. Here the frequency of contact ranged from an annual visit to visits 'four or five times a year'. Only in relation to 17 (23 per cent) of the total of 74 cases did adopters say that they wanted no contact with the birth family, and even here, seven adopters acknowledged nonetheless that there would have been advantages in meetings.

The level of contact described by adopters in this survey is remarkable given that all these adoptions were contested, and that a measure of goodwill is thought to be necessary for contact to work. Even in the 23 per cent (17) of cases where adopters did not want contact there were seven instances where adopters believed that there could have been important advantages in meeting. Two, in addition, commented with a measure of regret that the issue of contact had never properly been explored with them by the placing agency.

Given the general tendency to move from more limited to more open contact (see for example McRoy, 1991; Iwanek, 1987), and that an appreciable number of adopters without contact seek it, it is likely that a higher proportion of adoptive families in this sample will establish some contact so that it becomes very much the rule rather than the exception.

For adopters to have sustained or initiated contact in the bitterness of the circumstances in which many of these adoptions took place – especially given that some children had suffered appreciable harm at the hands of a birth relative – is a remarkable achievement. It is also evidence of the advantages, even in these circumstances, that were seen to accrue from contact. We must also note that in the 31 cases of continuing birth family contact it had been sustained in the main since placement, which was an average time of 4.6 years.

Information, attitudes and the adversarial process

Attitudes of adoptive parents to birth families

Adoptive parents were asked to describe their feelings towards the birth family before, during and after the court case. This was in an endeavour to see if there was a significant change in attitude, and to try to gauge the effect of the court contest itself.

In 48 responses (65 per cent) there was an indication of changing feelings over time. In the remainder the response was written as a single statement or a repeated statement. Where changing feelings were expressed over time, there was a clear tendency (expressed in 36–75 per cent of the 48 instances) for the most negative expressions of feeling, usually anger, to relate to the time of the court case. In eight of the remaining 12 cases where changing feelings were recorded over time, the time of the court hearing was identified as the period where the strongest feelings of sympathy for birth parents were present, and these expressions of feeling were usually contained in statements such as 'the deepest sympathy for the ordeal she was going through'.

Whether or not changing feelings were recorded by respondents over time, or whether more strongly negative or positive feelings were expressed at the time of the court hearing, appeared to be independent of the different dimensions of contact. It is possible to conclude that the court hearing itself acts as a catalyst in polarising feelings more strongly and, in general, it seems to contribute to many more strongly expressed negative than positive feelings. An amelioration of negative feelings over time was generally reported, but it is a matter of concern that the court process itself appears to contribute significantly to the genesis of the most negative expressions of feelings.

As one of a number of analyses it was decided to amalgamate the three questions to assess the distribution of positive and negative expressions of feelings in relation to the different dimensions of contact. The frequency of different words and phrases in each case was therefore recorded as 'positive', for example sympathy, or 'negative', for example anger, with repetitions of the same word/phrase ignored. There were considerable differences between the proportions of those with or wanting contact and those unsure or not wanting contact using positive and negative adjectives in relation to birth parents.

Those not wanting/unsure of contact and those with only sibling contact express a similar pattern of feeling towards birth parents. (See Table 11.2.) Those wishing for or having contact appear to articulate appreciably stronger feelings, both of sympathy and anger, but positive feelings

Table 11.2   Proportion of instances where positive and negative adjectives used to describe feelings towards birth parents

	Sympathy	Anger	N
Want no/unsure of contact	55%	30%	20
Want/have contact with birth families	91%	51%	45
Sibling contact	55%	33%	9

significantly outweigh negative feelings. A larger sample would be helpful in testing this more thoroughly, but it does seem consistent with one of the findings in the post-placement contact findings of this research (see Ryburn, 1994, in preparation), which was that those who have or want contact express more views in total in relation to its advantages and disadvantages.

Creation and reduction of conflict

In attempting to understand the effects of contested proceedings from the perspective of adopters it seemed important to consider whether in their view there were actions that reduced or increased conflict, or strategies that might have reduced it. Respondents were asked separate questions as to whether in their view birth parents, adopters, social workers and agencies, or the legal system played a role in either increasing or reducing conflict. They were also asked for their ideas about any strategies that might have reduced conflict. Responses were compared with the different dimensions of contact.

In just over half of cases it was felt that the agency had acted in general to reduce conflict:

They did all they could. They were sensitive, caring and professional.

They were excellent. The adoption society placed a worker with both parties and they were very supportive to us.

In about one-third of cases the agency was seen as having exacerbated tensions, and the most commonly identified themes were muddle, delay, lack of clear planning and information-sharing, and an apparent inability to recognise where mediation would have been useful. No relationship was established between adopters' views about the role of social workers and their agencies and the different dimensions of contact:

Not enough information about what was happening between the natural family and the social worker – this produced anxiety.

The social worker who took over the case placed one mother against the other causing tremendous stress.

Things were left to drift . . . this prolonged a very painful process for all involved.

Where the legal system was concerned these proportions were almost exactly reversed and a majority of respondents perceived various aspects of the legal system as having operated to increase tensions and hostilities.[3] Those with some form of continuing contact were significantly more likely to regard the legal and court system as generating avoidable conflict ($\chi^2 = 13.1$):

The proceedings were far too long and too protracted.

It was very much 'us against them' with the children as the prize.

The judge could not understand the idea of continuing access, and raised a lot of issues in court which were unnecessary. We almost lost the case just because she did not think it was a 'real' adoption if we still allowed access.

The solicitor was in it for the battle rather than the child.

The adversarial system leaves so much unfinished business.

The third of respondents who felt that the legal system had reduced conflict mentioned particularly the important role of the guardian, or curator, *ad litem*, while other comments tended also to mention particularly good personnel:

The court were very supportive (or at least the court clerk was) and so was the judge on the second hearing.

They were efficient in keeping confidentiality and got on with the job quickly and with no fuss.

The GAL was very supportive to both us, and we think to the father, in explaining and in his report.

Adoptive parents were asked to comment, if they could, on strategies the legal system might have taken to reduce conflict. There were 21 suggestions made (coming from 28 per cent of the sample), the most radical being for the total overhaul of the court system:

3 It is interesting to note that where the issue of delay was concerned that the respondents in Lambert and her colleagues' study (1990) expressed greater dissatisfaction with social workers than they did with the courts, pp. 145–6.

The English adversarial system is flawed enough in sorting out rights and wrongs in matters like theft and fraud. Where the issues are 'what is right for a child' I would advocate scrapping the whole process in favour of a round table investigative procedure with as many sessions as it might take to reach a negotiated agreement . . .

So far as the legal system was concerned, suggestions appeared to be independent of the different dimensions of contact. Neither those with nor those without contact commented in significantly different ways on strategies to reduce conflict involving birth parents. Greater reliability on the part of birth parents was the most mentioned strategy.

Those with contact were significantly more likely to make suggestions for strategies that they themselves might have taken in order to reduce conflict ($\chi^2 = 4.39$), and in over 80 per cent of instances these strategies centred on the instigation of contact or on earlier contact. Typical of suggestions were the following:

It might have reduced conflict if I'd thought more about contact initially or about the parent's wishes, rather than accepting that all contact should cease.

Write to birth mother assuring her of her child's happiness and welfare. Social Services anti the idea.

Those with contact also were much more likely to perceive an unfulfilled role for the agency in reducing conflict ($\chi^2 = 13.1$) and, once more, this very clearly centred on issues of contact.

It is possible to conclude that those with contact are more likely to regard the court and legal system as generating avoidable conflict in contested adoptions, and they are more likely to view both the agency and themselves as having a more crucial role when it comes to reducing conflict. As a group they expressed a broader perspective on the reasons for the conflict surrounding their adoptions, and they were generally united in suggesting contact and greater openness as the single strategy which could, given the adversarial system, lead to a reduction in conflict.

Discussion with children about adoption

Ready access for children to information about their families of origin has long been recognised as an important factor in adoption (see, for example, McWhinnie, 1967; Triseliotis, 1973). Kirk's research (1964) indicated that the ability of adopters successfully to manage discussion about adoption with their children in ways that acknowledged the importance of their original families might be a factor in successful parenting. There has, however, been very little research in relation to how often adoptees raise issues about adoption in their adoptive families, the circumstances in

which they do so, and the types of question that are important to them. Kaye and Warren's research (1988) lends broad support to the fact that the ability freely to discuss matters of adoption is associated in general with better adjustment by adoptees. It also indicated that in families where adoptees were experiencing more problems (measured on a wide range of factors including schooling, health, and uptake of counselling services) adopters seemed to feel less comfortable in talking about adoption.

Although no measure is available of what is likely to be a normal amount and range of family discussion about adoption for children of different ages placed for varying lengths of time, the questionnaire sought broadly to quantify the amount of discussion about adoption, the subject matter covered, the effect of contested proceedings on the availability of information, and any key periods in the lives of adoptees when such discussion was to the fore. (For a full discussion of these issues, see Ryburn, 1994, in preparation.)

The study found that those with no contact were more likely to report lower levels of interest on the part of their children in discussing adoption than those in the direct contact group ($\chi^2 = 6.46$). Where there was contact there was a discernible difference in the reported information requests of children, and these requests tended to be more diffuse, wide-ranging and to focus less exclusively on requests for information in relation to children's birth mothers. Thus all of the eight responses that specifically detailed requests for information in relation to birth fathers came from the group which maintained some form of birth family contact. Most of the requests for information about other relatives also came from the contact group:

She was finding it difficult at the age of 11 that no one knows anything about her father.

Where are my brother and sister? Do you think we will ever meet? Will I ever be able to find them? Are they OK?

There may well be a relationship between limited requests for information and lack of contact, but it is likely to be a reflexive relationship in which each operates in recursive fashion to reinforce the other. Sachdev (1991) in a retrospective study involving 107 randomly selected adoptees (where there had been no birth family contact) found that two-thirds reported inhibition in asking questions during childhood about adoption, and that this related to fears of being perceived as disloyal. Such inhibition was hinted at by one respondent who said that her son spoke about adoption:

A little, usually at night (when it's dark and you can't see his face) or on long car journeys (again when you can't look at him because of driving).

This adopter maintained contact for her child with birth siblings. In general, we might expect less inhibition where contact exists, since adopters have thereby signalled that questions and discussions about adoption are permissible, whilst contact with birth parents in particular seems likely to convey a message to children that to raise questions about them does not amount to disloyalty.

Less than half of the respondents expressed satisfaction with the level of information that they had available to answer their children's questions. In two instances respondents reported being turned down by their agencies when they requested further information. In three other instances respondents perceived the placing agency as not very co-operative:

> *We asked the Social Services Department for further information when he was 13/14. This was refused.*

> *I have asked the London local authority to give us news and to take it* [contact] *from there. They think it is inadvisable but have also lost touch as she has moved away.*

It is a matter of concern that more than half of the responses indicated the lack of sufficient information to respond adequately to children's questions. The contested nature of these adoptions has probably almost inevitably been a factor in restricting the available information, as seven adopters specifically noted.

There was no significant difference when satisfaction level was compared with the nature of contact. There was, however, another important difference. Those with direct contact who still expressed dissatisfaction made comments relating to the quality of information. This was summed up in two responses from adopters with letter contact, one stating 'we lack anecdotal facts' and the other that 'the "feelings" information is missing'. There seemed, as a possible consequence of continuing contact, a greater acknowledgement of the range and depth of information that could be useful to children in understanding and coming to terms with their lives in their families of origin.

Half of those responding to questions about whether they felt that the contested nature of their adoptions had affected the availability of information felt that it had. Many felt that they had more information as a consequence of access to reports and court records. A smaller group commented, as noted above, that it limited disclosure of information from birth families. A third of the total sample believed that with the information available it was difficult to find positive things to tell their adopted children about their birth families. For 14 per cent of respondents the contested nature of the adoption had the benefit, they thought, of offering some form of tangible evidence to their children that their birth parents had cared for them and did not want to lose them.

There were 56 (76 per cent) with life story books. In 49 instances (66 per cent) respondents reported that they had had agency help in making them, but only 11 (15 per cent) had agency help in updating them. This latter finding is indicative of a general failure on the part of agencies to recognise, as the recent White Paper (DoH, 1993, p. 8, para 4.25) seems to accept, that the regular updating of life-story information is a necessary part of effective post-adoption services for all parties. It perhaps also reflects, in the case of those in this study, the hostility that some adopters reported on the part of birth families, which would make this task impossible even if there were the will and resources to undertake it.

No significant relationship was established between the dimensions of contact and responses given in relation to questions about life story books.

The stress of adversarial decision-making

Effects of the contest on parents, family and other children

The final set of questions asked respondents to describe in general the effects of contested proceedings on themselves and any other children. In this case the sample size is 67 as there were 67 different families involved. No differences were distinguished in relation to the different dimensions of contact.

In relation to the effects on themselves, 55 (82 per cent) used stress-related adjectives including 'a nightmare', 'sheer hell'; three described marital problems; three experienced physical illness as a result of the stress; one underwent divorce; one was 'more determined' and one talked of financial pressure.

There were 34 families with other children in the family. Nine (26 per cent) said there was no effect on the other children as they were too young or not involved; 20 (59 per cent) used stress-related adjectives; two described physical illness induced by stress; and three talked of jealousy and antagonism stemming from the attention that it was necessary to give to the children who were the subject of the court hearings.

If the other children in the family were adopted, the stress generally related to their feeling insecure about their own adoptions. Two respondents commented on how difficult it was for their own birth children to understand how a child's future home with the family could hang on the outcome of a court case.

The families who had adopted following contested freeing for adoption reported slightly less stress, which is perhaps explicable in that they were not in direct conflict with the birth parents. They too, however, were not

immune from the effects of stress, and commented in particular on the feeling of powerlessness which derived from the lack of a clear role in court proceedings, which is something noted also by Lambert and her colleagues (1990, p. 136).

The stress that a contested adoption places on adopters is predictable, but the strength of this feeling and the measure of common agreement about its harrowing and harmful effects, not only on adopters, but on others in their families, are possibly not and are extremely worrying. The following comments are typical:

Nobody understands the agony that prospective adopters go through:

1st   To be approved
2nd   To get children in competition
3rd   To get children placed in your home
4th   To jump all the legal hurdles
5th   To get the child to settle and other family to accept them
6th   All the above with the knowledge that they may be removed.

I doubt if the emotional drain ever leaves the adoptive parents. It was an extremely stressful time for us both. Even writing this is not easy.

It was traumatic . . . We worried all the time, couldn't sleep and I ended up on anti-depressants. It was very stressful for both boys. . . . Our youngest son was having problems at school anyway and all this extra worry didn't help – he ended up ill.

Mentally and emotionally exhausting because we could identify and feel for the natural parents.

In the initial years I think the contested adoption put a pressure on us to prove that we were a 'better' family and I set an impossible standard for myself.

It had a terrible effect. We felt sad about the circumstances but, above all, our faith in the legal system was nil (almost). It made us insecure, angry, determined and very anxious. It would be impossible to explain how awful it was to feel impotent, powerless, disregarded but also the injustice to the child's needs was breathtaking.

It put a tremendous strain on my marriage and family. My son was having major problems with his nerves and my husband became frustrated and violent. The court case took two years. My husband and I divorced three years ago.

It was devastating, akin to learning your child has a terminal illness, not knowing whether they are going to live or die. Five months of sheer hell. I can remember crying myself to sleep on many occasions. Affected our marriage. Also experienced much guilt and anxiety about whether we were doing the right thing in not returning him to his birth mother. All three children were aware that N might leave our family. Eldest child, aged nine, developed physical symptoms, e.g. problems with eyes. Three-year-old suffered most because of our anxiety and I believe the effects have been long lasting.

Respondents were asked finally about the effects of the contested proceedings on their family networks. Twenty-seven described their wider families as largely unaffected. Almost consistently the reason given for this was that the adopters had protected them from knowing what was going on:

> *We kept the bad things away from our extended families. My husband's family was too old and unable to do anything but worry. My family have no knowledge of adoption and were really unaware of our problems. I think my husband and I tested our marriage to the limits during this time but luckily it survived.*

> *We tried not to say too much because we didn't want to keep going over the same stress.*

> *Although they were very supportive of us, we spared them from many of the worries by not informing them of all the facts.*

Obviously, the protection of others could magnify the stress for the adopters themselves and there is an indication of this in the three quotations above.

Thirty-one described the adoption as a stressful or very stressful experience for their family, in which in some instances the negative consequences had endured. These responses were broken down into clusters, since there were five principal themes which could be identified.

Eight described their relatives as supportive, but recounted that the adoption had created anxiety and worry for them:

> *Both our extended families were worried about what was happening but were very supportive of us.*

> *It was very anxious for them I guess, but they supported us and the child throughout.*

Another four described their relatives as sympathetic but placed under such stress themselves that they were effectively incapable of giving support:

> *My mother worried to the extent of a nervous breakdown. Our daughter is the only granddaughter in the family. . . . My mother-in-law became a bundle of nerves over it all. She died just before the case went to court. It was very sad. She went to her grave not knowing if our daughter was ever legally ours. That is one of the saddest aspects of our daughter's adoption.*

Six recorded that the contested adoption had had a long-term negative effect on them and their child, since it had hindered their child's acceptance into the family mainly because of the fear that he or she would subsequently be lost:

It has put a lot of stress on relationships within the families, and we feel they have been slower to accept and form their own relationships with our child.

I think they expected him to disappear at any time. It may have affected how they took to him initially.

It was a long time after the children joined our family before the girls were seen as ours and not just 'that girl you look after'. I think it has been a hindrance to their acceptance by the extended family.

Another five described how the contested adoption had strained their relationships within their family networks:

The adoption gave them an opportunity to criticise us even more!

Our relationship with my Mum (maternal Gran) deteriorated sharply. She didn't want us to adopt anyway and really wanted B's family to win. The situation has now improved and strangely enough B has more in common with my Mum than either of my two boys has.

In three instances respondents described how the contested adoption created a sense of anger amongst their wider families, born of powerlessness and frustration:

They couldn't understand what was going on and they just got very angry about the effect it was all having.

Lack of understanding by relatives and others and a consequent lack of support and understanding, was the principal effect recorded by another five respondents:

It strained relationships with parents as they didn't fully understand what was happening. This didn't help at the time – being told how easy it is for everyone else to adopt.

You can always have another child placed . . .

There were also comments about the effects of contested adoptions on children. These were linked by the common themes of uncertainty and confusion. They are effectively summed up in the following extract:

For our son I think it kept him in 'limbo land'. He was leading up to adoption for years, with every other sibling settled . . . It was not the birth mother's fault that it dragged on or ours. It was to do with the social worker not getting a move on . . . I do wonder if some

of our difficulties have been because we waited so long to get to court. We bonded to him but he doesn't seem very attached to us . . .

Conclusion

Extent to which initial conjectures were supported

There was a measure of support for the second and third conjectures that shaped this research, but the first, that the adversarial process would be likely to lead to minimal levels of post-adoption contact, was to a surprising degree not supported, as has been noted. Often it seemed to be due to the generous spirit of adopters, motivated both to do what they perceived to be best for the children, and to help the birth families. This was contact achieved or maintained in spite of, rather than because of, the court contest. Even where there was no contact there was a significant group who wished and hoped for it.

The second conjecture was that the adversarial process would be likely to lead to negative views on the part of adopters about birth parents. Clearly, this could not be properly assessed without a control group, matched in particular in relation to reasons for placement, to draw comparisons. There were two findings of possible significance, however. One was that the court process itself tended to be a time when feelings towards birth parents were at their most polarised, and where the most strongly held negative views were present, lending a measure of support to the view that the adversarial process itself actually generates antipathy, or a greater measure of antipathy. It is especially unfortunate, therefore, if irrevocable decisions are made at this time, as is all too often the case. This thought was expressed very clearly by one respondent:

> *The assumption is* [from the time of the hearing] *that negative attitudes are fixed. But they may not be. There should be recognition of this, like being able to contact birth parents through an independent third party some time after the heat of the legal proceedings, to request and offer information.*

Regrettably the White Paper (DoH, 1993, p.7, paras 4.14, 4.17) seems largely to be informed by views which regard the feelings of adopters about contact as likely to remain static, and does not seem to recognise the potential for these to change over time, and the need for arrangements that can take this into account.

The other finding was that, where contact was maintained, adopters expressed significantly more positive views of birth parents. The importance for children who are adopted of receiving, as they grow, positive

messages about their families of origin has been identified by a number of adoption researchers and theorists (see for example Frisk, 1964; McWhinnie, 1967; Raynor, 1980; Ryburn, 1992; Triseliotis, 1973, 1983), and where children receive predominantly negative views about their families of origin it is but a short step to begin to internalise them as messages also about themselves.

Birth parents without contact showed a fairly even balance of positive and negative views about adoptive parents, while those with contact contributed twice as many positive views as they did negative. We might speculate that, for adopters who are solely reliant on agencies to give them information, or where their last major impression of birth families dates from an adversarial court hearing, it is understandably more difficult to muster positive views than for those whose impressions from the court hearing have been ameliorated over time by an experience of contact which, on balance, they describe as positive. Those with contact were significantly more likely to take the view that courts and the legal system could have done more to reduce conflict. They might not have achieved this without the benefit of contact.

One of the ironies of contested adoptions for a significant number of respondents was that they believed they thereby received more full and detailed information about the birth families of their children. It may well be true that they did receive more information and, if it is, it is important to question why such a level of information is not available in all circumstances, given that it must be easier to assemble in instances where there is not a high level of conflict between the parties.

The other consideration is a point that I make in chapter 14. Where adopters are dependent on the court documentation of local authorities to meet their information needs and those of their children, it is important to recognise in this information the possibility of significant bias. It is information that has been carefully marshalled and presented with the intention of convincing a court of the need for adoption and, if it is necessary, of damaging the case of any contesting birth parents. There are likely in birth parents and their wider families to be many more positive attributes and qualities than those advanced as evidence in a court case, where the local authority is seeking to dispense with their agreement to adoption. Where adopters had contact with birth parents it did seem that they were able on balance to express more positive feelings towards them and this is likely to be because, through various forms of ongoing contact, they have been able to widen their field of view. It seems reasonable to surmise that for these adopters it will be correspondingly easier to portray their children's birth parents in more positive ways. This in turn may help children to achieve more easily a greater sense of self-worth.

A significant number of those who adopt following contested proceed-

ings say that they do not have the information that they need readily to answer all their children's requests for information. Similarly, a number believed the contesting of their adoptions had influenced the nature and availability of information. Adopters with contact were much more likely than those without to perceive, with hindsight, a more effective role for themselves, agencies and the legal and court system in the reduction of conflict, and the strategies they would now suggest would focus almost exclusively on early attempts to introduce contact.

Of the three conjectures shaping this research study, the clearest support was for the third. The stress produced for adopters and their wider network by contested adoptions is severe, and is reported in some instances to be long-lasting. We can only speculate as to the added measure of difficulty that this contributes to a task which already demands an enormous amount of parents. This study considered adoptions where placements were intact, but with such extreme descriptions of stress we must surely ask how many otherwise viable placements for children founder not because of lack of will, commitment or skill, but purely through the debilitating stress of protracted and often bitter court contests. It is a process, as one respondent remarked, that meant 'we began to doubt ourselves and our ability to care for a child', while, in the view of several, it creates an 'insecurity for the child that can affect them for the rest of their lives'. 'There has', as one adopter despairingly put it, 'got to be a better way.'

There are two routes to a better way. One is to recognise, as so many of the respondents to this survey point out, that with proper attention to issues of contact, a great deal of the conflict might be avoided. The other is to recognise, as the Adoption Law Review (DoH, 1992, p. 14, para 6.1) and now the White Paper (DoH, 1993, p. 13, para 5.23) do, that adoption is not the only or necessarily the preferred means to provide children with permanent stranger care. Other placement options, which avoid the bitterness of a battle based on the potentially irrevocable severance of a child's links with its original family, may well be preferable for all concerned.

Postscript

One prospective adopter, whose questionnaire could not be included in the survey since the adoption of the child placed with her and her partner still awaited a final court hearing, offered some concluding comments about the whole process of being assessed as an adopter and what it can feel like to be in 'competition' through a court contest:

The whole enterprise of trying to adopt involves effort and struggle, whether real or

imagined: overcoming feelings of grief and inadequacy at miscarriage and infertility, going through the most exacting examination of one's life, marriage and moral being during assessment; attempting (and failing often) to be supermum and superdad to a lovely but damaged child placed at a very difficult age. . . . [contested adoption] *is a deeply uncomfortable experience, not so much because of the element of uncertainty added . . . but rather because of a further element of struggle and 'competition' introduced.*

Infertility carries with it the almost inevitable burden of low self-esteem, guilt, a sense of worthlessness, irrational as this is. I feel I've had to prove my fitness to be an adoptive parent at a time when inwardly I didn't think I had much basis for proving anything. The adoption assessment process (rightly) has an agenda directed at a potential child's benefit, but the spin-off for the person being assessed is that s/he is 'competing' both against the rest of the human race and against an unknown set of rules and desiderata to prove 'fitness'. Even when the contest is 'won', and the adoption panel has pronounced in favour, the self-doubt is not assuaged, even if it can be coped with . . . and must be of course.

A contested adoption in my case involves competing with the birth mother for the care of her child.

(1)   As a 'competitor', I need to feel sure of my ground. Infertility has cut the ground from under my feet, so I can never feel quite emotionally sure, no matter how rational I am.

(2)   As 'competitors', we are inevitably struck by questions of equity and fairness. Rationally I know we are likely to 'win' our daughter, because we are a nice, secure, middle-class intellectual couple with all the advantages. As a human being, I am only too aware of how the dice are loaded against our daughter's birth mother who had a deprived childhood herself, lost a baby to cot death previously, had no income or education to speak of . . . I don't like competing against someone who is so disadvantaged, even if she did commit an act of violence which I abhor. There but for the grace of God go I, and who am I to say that I would have coped any better?

References

DoH/Welsh Office (1992), *Review of Adoption Law: Report to Ministers of an Inter-departmental Working Group: A Consultation Document*, London: DoH/Welsh Office.

DoH/Welsh Office/Home Office/Lord Chancellor's Department (1993), *Adoption: The Future*, Cmnd. 2288, London: HMSO.

Festinger, L. (1957), *A Theory of Cognitive Dissonance*, Stanford, CA: Stanford University Press.

Frisk, M. (1964), 'Identity Problems and Confused Conceptions of the Genetic Ego in Adopted Children During Adolescence', *Acta Paedo Psychiatrica*, **31**, 6–12.

Iwanek, M. (1987), 'A Study of Open Adoption', 14 Emerson Street, Petone, Wellington, New Zealand: Unpublished.

Kaye, K. and Warren, S. (1988), 'Discourse About Adoption in Adoptive Families', *Journal of Family Psychology*, **4**, 406–33.

Kirk, D. (1964), *Shared Fate: A Theory of Adoption and Mental Health*, New York: Free Press.

Kirk, D. (1981), *Adoptive Kinship: A Modern Institution in Need of Reform*, Toronto: Butterworths.

Lambert, L., Buist, M., Triseliotis, J. and Hill, M. (1990), *Freeing Children for Adoption*, London: BAAF.
McRoy, R. (1991), 'American Experience and Research on Openness', *Adoption and Fostering*, **15**(4), 99–110.
McWhinnie, A. (1967), *Adopted Children: How They Grow Up*, London: Routledge and Kegan Paul.
Raynor, L. (1980), *The Adopted Child Comes of Age*, London: Allen and Unwin.
Ryburn, M. (1992), 'Advertising for Permanent Placements', *Adoption and Fostering*, **16**(2), 8–15.
Ryburn, M. (1994), 'An Analysis of Post Adoption Contact Following Contested Adoption Proceedings', in preparation.
Sachdev, P. (1991), 'The Triangle of Fears: Fallacies and Facts', in Hibbs, E. [ed.], *Adoption: International Perspectives*, Maddison, CT: International Universities Press.
Triseliotis, J. (1973), *In Search of Origins*, London: Routledge and Kegan Paul.
Triseliotis, J. (1983), 'Identity and Security in Long Term Fostering and Adoption', *Adoption and Fostering*, **7**(1), 22–31.

12 Contested adoption – the perspective of birth parents

Murray Ryburn

Introduction

A family can suffer few more public judgments of social failure than to have a child compulsorily removed from its care. This chapter records the views and experiences of 12 such families, and considers whether the recommendations of the Adoption Law Review Working Party, and the subsequent White Paper, would ensure that their voices are heard in future.

Among consumers of social services there is probably no more disenfranchised group than the families whose children have been compulsorily taken from their care. Little credence is given to their views which are readily dismissed as anger and hostility towards a system that found it necessary to remove their children. It is however a test of the commitment of professionals to respecting those who use their services that they listen to their views, even where they are service users who have minimal power to effect change.

This chapter is based on interviews with members of 12 such families: eight mothers, five fathers, two grandparents and a sister of children now adopted or about to be adopted. Despite the small sample some clear themes emerge suggesting a need for change in professional approach and practice in contested adoption proceedings. Recommendations of the Adoption Law Review Consultation Document (DoH, 1992) and of the White Paper (DoH, 1993) will be considered in terms of how likely they are to address the concerns which families raised.

The context for decision-making

Decision-making in care and protection has been described as tending towards compulsion, whimsical, ill-defined and lacking in any consistent standards of judgment (see for example Parton, 1991, who highlights the growing use of compulsory powers; Packman et al., 1986, whose research highlighted the speed of decision-making; Millham et al., 1986, who revealed a lack of careful planning; Higginson, 1990, who pointed up the lack of consistent standards for decision-making; and the inquiry in Cleveland (DoH, 1988) which highlighted failures to follow guidance and procedures). There is, by contrast, an uncanny and alarming similarity in the accounts of birth families of the ways in which key decisions have been taken in their lives and in those of their children and young people. Their narratives may be those of a disaffected and disenfranchised group, yet there is a compelling consistency in the themes they identify and in their demands for a service which respects its users. The examples used in this chapter are from interviews with these families. All identifying details have been changed.

First contact

None of the families denied that there were areas of difficulty in their lives at the point of first contact with social services. What is often in dispute is the nature and extent of those difficulties when compared with the accounts of social workers and guardians *ad litem* in available documentation. Families seemed, in the main, to have embarked on their encounters with social services with both a belief in their own reasonableness and the expectation that any ordinary person in similar circumstances could expect to have similar difficulties. The word 'reasonable' was in fact used by three families, although others said the same thing in different ways.

'Reasonable' is a word that is often used in the law, and it is employed frequently in the judgments that social workers and the judiciary make about families. However, the legal definition of 'reasonableness' rests largely upon legal precedent, and bears little relation to the reasonableness of the circumstances to which it is applied. The reasonableness of those who seek or require services can, of course, only be made sense of in the wider context of the reasonableness of the services that are offered and provided and the reasonableness of those who are providing them.

If one assumes that reasonable parents might have an idea about the services that would best help them successfully to parent their children, there were in ten families accounts of parental requests that fell on deaf ears, and of services requested that were not deemed relevant. There were reports too of a lack of adequate provision that could be seen subsequently to have played a key role in children's later admissions to permanent compulsory care:

> When I said I was desperate and I had to have him in the nursery, she said there was a panel that decided all the places and that I would have to wait until the end of the month. It was two months before she came to talk to me about it again and then she told me there were so many cases for the panel that she couldn't put my papers forward. I said, so what was I meant to do, and she said well there was still child-minding and there might be a chance of getting that paid for still but that had to go to the same panel as the nursery care. If I could have got some help with Michael when I needed it, I know he wouldn't be where he is now.

These families' beliefs that realistic requests for help were ignored are consistent with findings in other research, indicating a failure on the part of professionals to attend to the family situation (see for example Fisher et al., 1986; Rowe et al., 1984). Responding first to what is asked for by those who use services is a fundamental requirement for a (respectful) service. Where this does not occur it will have a profound impact on all subsequent decisions.

The Adoption Law Review report (DoH, 1992, p. 64, para 32.4 (a)) recommends a duty to publicise adoption services and access to the complaints procedures required by the Children Act. The White Paper promises to strengthen adoption panels by including more independent members, and to introduce a complaints procedure, 'although no such procedure could reverse or re-open court adoption orders once they are made' (para 5.15). Complaints procedures are by definition bureaucratic and those using them effectively are likely to be relatively articulate and persistent. It would therefore be helpful if guidance were forthcoming which encouraged social services departments to direct users who feel unable to take advantage of such procedures independently, to sources of advocacy and support.

Initial decisions

Most families recounted initial decisions on the part of social workers that foreclosed on other options, with the effect of narrowing the range of future courses of action. Typical were the sorts of decisions that had been

identified in other studies (see for example Fisher et al., 1986) relating to a lack of planning around early admissions to care:

> *When I first came to London after being home it was so hard with my Mum and everyone still in Jamaica. I will admit I was not coping well and that I did hit Michael, but who did social services think they were? They didn't even tell me where Michael was at first. I just knew he was with white people.*

The sense of abandonment Michelle's young son doubtless experienced and Michelle's guilt at having been forced to leave him are bound to have marred any future attempts at reunification. The initial delay experienced as a result of lack of careful planning, and the failure to involve Michelle immediately in maintaining contact with her son, have been shown by the Dartington researchers (Millham et al., 1986) and others to be potentially critical factors in determining whether children are likely to remain long-term in care. Emphasis on the avoidance of delay in both the Children Act and the Adoption Law Review report and the White Paper (DoH, 1993), and the practice in most cases since the introduction of the Children Act in October 1991 to tell parents where children are, should therefore be welcomed.

Yet the Children Act can do little to remedy the informal barriers to contact that research has indicated are the key means by which relationships deteriorate (see for example Millham et al., 1986; Vernon and Fruin, 1986). The failure to provide Michelle with the financial means and the emotional support necessary to visit her child in the care of someone else were, by her account, critical factors in the breakdown of her relationship with him. The Children Act regrettably, creates only a power, not a duty, for local authorities to make supportive financial provision to facilitate contact, and it has nothing to say about the high levels of emotional support without which contact may never happen.

More significant still from Michelle's perspective than lack of support and early planning for contact was the fact that her child was placed with 'white people'. The sense of alienation that this provoked, doubtless did incalculable harm to any attempts at restoration:

> *Just knowing he was there and that he would be eating white people's food and no one knowing to use his skin grease and no black face to look at – I couldn't stand it.*

Recognition of the importance of race, culture, language and religion in the Children Act is echoed in the Adoption Law Review Consultation Document (DoH, 1992, p. 56, para 28.2) but not set out in recommendations. While the White Paper promises to introduce 'a broad requirement' in line with the Children Act, it expresses concern at factors of race and ethnicity having been given too much weight in the assessment process

and concludes: 'There is no conclusive research which justifies isolating such questions from other matters needing assessment; or which supports the proposition that children adopted by people of a different ethnic group will necessarily encounter problems of identity or prejudice later in life' (para 4.33). (See chapters 8 and 9.)

Sometimes the likely future consequences of initial decisions were even more starkly obviously than in the example above:

> *And I said 'no we had to convince these people because all their decisions have been based on paperwork not on actually seeing us'. They actually took Carl away at birth without ever actually having spoken to us.*

This was one of two families interviewed who had children removed at birth on the basis of past family history. The likelihood of reunification in such circumstances is remote. Such decisions seem extraordinary given that social work is founded on a belief in the capacity of individuals and groups to achieve change.

Lack of clarity about the social work role and planning

The Guidance accompanying the Children Act 1989 (DoH, 1991, Volume 3) recommends a partnership style of working even in situations of compulsory care. Yet partnership can clearly only operate when the necessary pre-conditions, including the full and thorough sharing of information, have been established. The quotation below, from a parent of a child who has now been adopted, illustrates the confusion about the role of social workers in voluntary situations, that can subsequently make it impossible for families to work with any degree of partnership once compulsory involvement has occurred:

> *In the end we made the mistake of actually treating the social worker as part of the extended family, without realising that she was not just a help, not just a friend, she was a social worker.*

The emphasis in the Adoption Law Review report (DoH, 1992, p. 55, para 28.1) on proper information-sharing and planning with parents of children who may be adopted is to be welcomed, though regrettably there is no recommendation specifying the services that should reasonably be offered. Families recounted many instances where key decisions were taken without any consultation with them:

> *The day we were to see her for our access visit they asked us whether we could come in half*

an hour early. We arrived and were taken into an interviewing room where our social worker was sitting with someone else. They told us they had had a meeting a few days before where they decided that adoption was the best plan for Julie. They said we would be allowed to see her two more times but then access would be stopped.

These parents were then expected to proceed with their visit to their child as if nothing had happened. Their account was confirmed in local authority documentation.

The recommendation of the Adoption Law Review report that there be a duty on agencies 'to offer birth parents the services of a social worker who is not involved in the adoption plan' (p. 55, para 28.5) coupled with the recommendation (p. 58, para 29.2) that local authorities be required to maintain a service in adoption that meets also the needs of relatives of children who 'have been or may be adopted', underlines the recognition that effective services for children are best delivered in partnership with their wider families. Given that very few agencies currently offer much in the form of post-adoption services, however, it is difficult to see how new requirements such as those outlined above will be likely to lead to any radical improvement in practice.

The White Paper would also appear to be more equivocal on contact, giving the views of adopters who oppose contact the greater weight (DoH, 1993, para 4.15), and observing in relation to the Children Act that, 'There is also some feeling that planning for a child who needs a permanent new family can be more difficult because of the emphasis in the Act on maintaining contact with birth families' (para 3.16).

Knowing best   *Consultation/ partnership*

All of the families interviewed referred to social workers and their managers as 'knowing best'. I have written about the effect this can have on the planning process (Ryburn, 1991b). For these families, their perception of practitioners 'believing that they know best' served more than anything else to exclude them further from any feeling of participating in making decisions about their own children:

When dealing with them, it's a feeling of you can't disapprove of us because we know what's best.

No one parent's got all the answers, I mean you just go on and do the best you can, but what I can't understand is why social services has to behave as if they do have all the answers, as if they do always get it right. As if they always know what's going to be best.

A belief by social workers and other professionals that they necessarily

know best and have a sound ability to make judgments that will have predictive value for the future cannot be sustained by research findings and it is of course a potent encouragement not to seek the views of families. It is a belief likely to pose one of the greatest future barriers to a model of practice under the Children Act or new adoption legislation which is founded on partnership.

Overriding cultural norms and values

The inclusion for the first time in the Children Act 1989 of provisions relating to race, culture, language and religion is a milestone in primary legislation relating to children. Five of the families who were interviewed were from minority ethnic groups and felt that the social work decisions affecting them had a strong white cultural bias.

One of the factors which has most militated against the recruitment of permanent new families for children of minority ethnic groups is the belief that adoption is necessarily the most desirable form of substitute permanent care. This is coupled with the assumption that because formal legal adoption finds acceptance in the non-black community it is right for all communities. Permanent and long-term substitute care for children, where links with original family are usually maintained, are common in many societies. The concept of a legal severance and the complete transfer of a child from one family to another may be an alien concept for many ethnic groups in Britain, and in Muslim countries, for example (with the exception of Tunisia), it does not exist. It should not be surprising that recruiting formal adopters in some communities has often been difficult, especially where children could only be adopted following contested proceedings.

These five families also believed that a white social work decision-making bias showed itself in the restrictive view taken of the nature of family and social kinship. This young mother, whose family in Jamaica was very willing to take on the parenting of her child, has been left with a deep sense of outrage that this was not even considered:

> *They wouldn't listen when I kept telling them how my mum would take him, they just wouldn't listen . . . They had to see he was safe, they said. How could they do that in Jamaica.*

One of the critically important aspects of the Adoption Law Review Consultation Document and the White Paper is the recognition that there are different routes to permanence and that adoption does not offer an

inherently better placement in permanent substitute care (see for example DoH, 1992, p. 15, para 6.1; p. 18, para 7.6; and DoH, 1993, paras 5.18–5.27). This is consistent with research findings such as those of Rowe and Thoburn (in Fratter et al., 1991), which show that permanent foster placements are no less secure than adoption. The emphasis on the importance to children of other relatives (see for example DoH, 1992, p. 18, para 7.6; p. 58, paras 29.1–29.2) echoes the Short Report in recognising that the invaluable resource of original family has far too often been ignored at a cost to its children. Implementation of the recommendations concerning alternative orders and the importance to children of their wider families, coupled with greater power for children to exercise their own choice in decision-making (DoH, 1992, p. 20, para 9.5; DoH, 1993, paras 2.6, 3.14, 4.3), may do much to address some of the concerns expressed by original families, including white families, about the tyranny of the thinking that equates permanence only with adoption and which excludes wider family from active consideration as a placement resource.

No room to renegotiate

All families expressed in different ways the belief that once decisions had been made by the local authority these were finite. They allowed, they believed, no scope for renegotiation in view of changing circumstances as this parent describes:

> *Before I knew anything about it, I was told Michael had been placed in a family who would adopt him.*

This was clearly expressed by another parent too:

> *Nobody ever asked down the road what sort of family we are. Nobody has ever considered the possibility of adoption in our extended families on both sides, and nobody has ever considered guardianship or something like that, because they just had their minds made up that it had to be adoption and that it had to be adoption arranged by them.*

Just as decisions at the outset of social work involvement with these families seemed very often to foreclose on future options, so too did decision-making at the point where long-term plans were being made for substitute care for children. This father expresses it very clearly:

> *The moment you terminate access you begin to load the dice because now you can say the link is broken and perhaps it shouldn't be re-forged because if you re-forge it you might be disturbing the child, and it is a deliberate policy. Why is it that before anybody considered*

my consent to adoption, adoptive parents were found for Suzanne, accepted, accepted possibly even by Suzanne, before the court gives permission for it? If that's not loading the dice, then what is?

Security is not best provided for children and young people by rigid decision-making that eliminates from future consideration options which are not seen to be consistent with it. That local authority long-term planning for children can be fundamentally flawed is well borne out by Jackie Trent's study described in *Homeward Bound* (1989).

The Adoption Law Review report takes seriously the injustice to original families of decision-making processes which exclude them from renegotiating the decisions of local authorities once planning for adoption has begun. If the recommendation that freeing be abolished (DoH, 1992, p. 31, para 14.8) is followed this will be a major step towards fairer proceedings. Freeing, where it has been contested, has led to decisions about parental unreasonableness in withholding consent where no particular placement is being considered. This is now seen to be manifestly unjust. The recommendation that consent be given in respect of each proposed adoption placement (pp. 21–2, para 10.4) is also welcome.

Placement orders in non-consenting adoptions (p. 30, para 14.6) were recommended in the Adoption Law Review as a way of ending the injustice of *de facto* adoptions such as that described above. However, much concern that such a new form of order will become little more than a freeing order in a different guise was expressed during the consultation period, and is set out in detail in chapter 3. The White Paper acknowledges that the proposal might prove 'cumbersome' and promises further discussion before new legislation is framed (DoH, 1993, paras 4.8–4.13). The decision about whether adoption is best for a child or young person should be clearly separated in time from discussion of specific adoption placements, and consideration should be given to requiring all planned permanent placements to be considered by panels. The White Paper also proposes further consultation on the functions and membership of adoption panels (paras 4.43–4.45). Hopefully, this will result in a recommendation that parents may be accompanied by an advocate of their choice, and that relatives will also, where appropriate, be allowed to attend.

The selection of evidence

All the families interviewed believed that evidence had been presented about them in court which was very selective, biased, and in some instances untruthful:

Social services is putting things down to try to paint as bad a picture as possible because they think ends justify the means. They will win their case no matter what and truth is the first thing to suffer.

The effect that the adversarial nature of court proceedings has is discussed in chapter 14. It is suggested that above all they create a context in which winning is more important than an exploration of all possibilities and options. Social workers do seek to have their plans ratified in court hearings on the basis of selected and selective evidence. Families, as they are presented in court, can easily be reduced to the equation of their parenting failures:

In that adoption report to the court there is no mention of all the hundreds of phone calls that my parents made saying can we see our granddaughter. There is no mention of the special arrangement that was made at Christmas time for them to be able to see her that was then later cancelled by the social services without any explanation at all, other than it wasn't convenient.

There is another element to the selection of evidence which is clearly expressed in the following quotation:

Such a black picture has been painted of us that the foster parents' [and prospective adopters in this case] *attitude has changed from one of, we want help with him from his own parents to, now we don't even want to meet his real parents because of what we have been told about them.*

I have written elsewhere (Ryburn, 1991a) about the potentially damaging effects that the selective information adduced by local authorities in adversarial court proceedings may have on children and young people, in their attempts to acquire a positive sense of self-worth and identity. Many of the families interviewed expressed fears that their children would go through the rest of their lives with only negative messages and images of them. Sadly, these fears may sometimes be justified and it is certainly arguable that adversarial proceedings add a dimension of difficulty for adopters in giving positive messages to children about their original families. Although the Adoption Law Review report recognises both the need for better information to be given to adopting parents (DoH, 1992, p. 53, para 27.5) and the need for a social worker for original families who is independent of the adoption process, it fails effectively to address the question of who will select the information given and by whom it will be conveyed. If this continues to be the responsibility of workers who have been opposed to parents in adversarial proceedings, it will almost inevitably be information which reflects their views.

Birth families spoke not only of the selective use of information in court

hearings, almost all complained of the lack of information that was given to them about their children:

> I've pleaded with them over the past nine months for some information about her. But only once in all those nine months have I heard anything at all that is real news about her life and what she is doing, and that was that she had been scratched by a cat when she was playing with it. Whenever I phone up and whenever I go to see the social services I am told she is 'flourishing', she is 'thriving', she is 'OK'. The only information I get is third party and it seems like the social workers have decided that if we tell him anything that is real news, he will go on and on and keep wanting to see her. Not telling me has the opposite effect, the less you know the more desperate you get to know something.

The lessons from studies of birth mothers in adoptions by relinquishment (see, for example, Winkler and van Keppel, 1984) give clear messages about the tragic effects for many of the lack of information about their children. There is no reason to think that this will be any less so for birth families in contested adoptions, and we could surmise that their lack of agreement to the plans for their children may compound their future anguish.

The Adoption Law Review recommendation (DoH, 1992, pp. 57–8, para 28.9) of a duty on local authorities to pass on information, where they receive it and birth parents request it, is to be welcomed. The White Paper echoes this recommendation, but is concerned throughout not to undermine the potential stability of a new placement (DoH, 1993, paras 4.14–4.20). Unless programmes for the preparation of adopters help them to understand how crucial this can be to the emotional and psychological welfare of birth families, they may often not forward information in the first place. The recommendation should also acknowledge the loss adoption brings to other relatives. They should be included specifically in the provisions for information-forwarding, rather than leaving this to the interpretation of different authorities under the terms of the general recommendation for the provision of a pre- and post-adoption service to meet their needs (DoH, 1992, p. 58, para 29.2).

Observation and opinions as facts

There were many instances in which families felt that *observations* made of them by social workers were presented as evidence and given the status of fact. Typical examples were observations about attachment made during contact visits, even though some years ago the Dartington researchers (Millham et al., 1986) highlighted the potentially tendentious nature of such judgments. Families rightly claimed that difficulties they encountered, for example in visiting their children in distant placements, or in

settings which they experienced as hostile, should also have been part of the court evidence:

> *No one said that it was two bus rides away and that I had to take Jamie and the baby with me.*

They also knew that local authorities would seldom, if ever, present a picture that ameliorated their parental 'failures' in a court setting.

False evidence

Many families had strongly held beliefs that evidence upon which decisions had been based had been deliberately falsified. Obviously in most instances the opinions of families about such matters are essentially contestable. There was one instance, however, in which other documentation supported the truth of the family's allegation:

> *They said in the affidavit that our attendance at the family centre had been very patchy so I went to the office and I said 'this isn't true is it?' and she said 'no and I will testify to that fact.' Come the date of the court hearing the man had to get up and apologise for the affidavit being wrong, but what was never made clear in court was why was it wrong, what made them make that mistake. It was after hearing all the reports from others about us that actually convinced this man to put this in the affidavit.*

One can only assume in this case and other instances that families reported, if they are to be believed, that social workers took the view that the end justifies the means. Recommendations for more open access to records (DoH, 1992, p. 69, para 35.3) may offer some redress to families where they are victims of wrong information, but the uptake of access to records depends crucially on advising those concerned of their rights. A duty on authorities, especially in all contested proceedings, to advise family members of the right of access to records would be helpful.

The treatment of families

Despite the requirement of the Adoption Act 1976 to offer a service to parents of children who have been or may be adopted, the families interviewed reported many instances when there was a complete failure to offer them any service and where sometimes even basic courtesies were ignored:

> *Sure I was invited to meetings, but whenever they asked me to come they were already meeting and I was kept waiting outside for so long that once I just went home.*

Now when I go there I'm interviewed by two social workers. I'm not allowed to bring anybody along apart from once when I went with my probation officer who was absolutely astounded to know what was going on. The social worker was talking to me but it was all directed via her.

No appeal

All families expressed feelings of anger and hostility towards some social workers or other professionals. This, of course, is scarcely surprising. What is interesting about their comments, however, is that they were selective. By no means all social workers or professionals were regarded with outright hostility, and it was the individual characteristics and behaviours of workers which earned them the respect or anger of families:

At least when she got involved she always put you in the picture and told you what was happening.

Families seemed consistently to reserve their anger for social workers who failed to give them information and to listen to their opinions as if they were worth noting. Several families who had had experience of a considerable number of social workers in their lives over a relatively short period assumed that these changes related to administrative decisions or to social workers leaving. There is no mechanism for families to change their social workers.

Some of those interviewed spoke specifically of their fear of fighting for what they saw as 'their rights', because they were afraid of the effect that this might have on the ways that decisions were taken and the sort of decisions that were made. Two families recounted being given legal advice that it was not worth pursuing matters in court and that this would only make things worse for them. Most failed to get effective advice and help until the court proceedings had actually begun. Some bitterly regretted that they had not sought legal advice much earlier. As this parent expressed it:

She kept saying 'don't worry it won't come to that, we'll work it out', and then by the time it was decided it was too late for me to do anything about it.

There is a definite argument for the involvement of a social worker independent of child care planning at a much earlier stage than the Adoption Law Review report recommends (DoH, 1992, pp. 56–7, para 28.5). The resource implications would be great, but so is the potential cost to children and families of the breakdown in partnership that all too often can occur if there is a blinkered and unhelpful concentration on the child, to the exclusion of their family and the wider context of their lives.

The fact that the plans of social workers, and their professional judgments, are so often endorsed by the courts cannot be taken as a measure of their validity. Social work decisions and the professional opinions of social workers can be shown by research to be hastily made, ill-conceived, and flawed. The congruence between social work views and court decisions can perhaps only adequately be explained in terms of the institutional power that professionals hold and which they can readily wield if they choose to override the wishes of those who are less powerful. The advice to families or the decision of families not to challenge the views of professionals is made in this knowledge and in the fear that challenge could lead to greater punitiveness. Some of the Adoption Law Review report recommendations encouraging a fairer representation of family views could begin to redress this situation.

The breakdown of trust

Families interviewed ultimately described their relationship with social services as a process leading to a complete breakdown in trust:

> *How do I know that I can trust the things that I am told about her and about what she says and how she is, when there is no trust there anyway.*

More sadly, perhaps, it was not that families so much described a lack of trust in those whose duty it was to offer them and their children a service, but rather that they recounted a lack of trust and conviction in themselves anymore. Beneath the anger that was usually present there seemed often to be a profound sense of failure:

> *The stigmatising that I feel as a result of all this, I have felt almost not a man anymore. I haven't had a relationship since that time because I thought to myself, 'what have I got to offer anymore?'*

What would have made a difference

Families had some very clear and simple messages about what could have made a difference to them in terms of the process, even were the outcome to be the same:

> *We felt like we was nothing, the amount of waiting and time-wasting that went on. We wanted to be treated the way they were treating all the others that was involved.*

> *Not once in that whole time did any social worker think about what it was doing to me and*

to my family. Just one word, one word of 'how are you getting on?' would have made all the difference to me.

We could have done it. It really could have worked. We just needed someone to believe in us.

I don't hate social workers, at least I don't hate all of them. Most of all I hate myself for letting this happen. But if they had been different, if they'd told me straight, at the very first when they were worried, then I might of been able to do something to stop it all going wrong.

Conclusion

A decision that children and young people should be permanently parented in substitute care against the wishes of their original families is for those families a very public declaration that brings with it anger, shame, guilt and bitter recrimination. Perhaps on the balance of the best available evidence those decisions were sometimes the right ones. It is hard, however, not to believe that there are very many children lost to their families through compulsory care who could have been effectively parented within the networks of their families of origin.

The accounts of families who have lost children permanently to compulsory care often detail the failure of social workers to pay even lip-service to their profession's cardinal principles of respect and empowerment. It is a sad irony that even where families may have wished to admit that they were not able effectively to parent their children, the ways that they had been treated and the lack of respect that they felt had been accorded them, prevented any co-operative partnership with social workers to achieve new permanent families for their children:

The whole concept of adoption, the way it's been done in our case, is completely wrong. Not even so much what they've done, it's the way that they've done it that is so hard for me to understand.

There are many recommendations in the Adoption Law Review Consultation Document, some of which are echoed in the White Paper, which could help shape fairer proceedings in adoption – recognition that there are perfectly viable ways of making permanent placements other than by adoption; access to a complaints system; the appointment of guardians in all agency adoptions; reform of panels and attendance at panels; access to records; separate workers; a clearer role for the extended family; the need for a 'whole of life' perspective in adoption; abolition of freeing; and the reform of dispensation of parental consent provisions.

Even if most of the recommendations are implemented, however, the weight of institutional power in adoption will still bear heavily against original families as long as disagreements are settled in adversarial court proceedings. Adoptions made without family consent represent the loss of a lifetime for children and their original families. Many such placements have been made with far too little consideration for the gravity of the consequences for all parties involved, and far too little regard for a process that is fair and just.[1]

References

DoH (1988), *Report of the Inquiry into Child Abuse in Cleveland 1987*, London: HMSO.
DoH (1991), *The Children Act 1989 Guidance and Regulations: Family Placements*, Vol. 3, London: HMSO.
DoH/Welsh Office (1992), *Review of Adoption Law: Report to Ministers of an Interdepartmental Working Group: A Consultation Document*, London: DoH.
DoH/Welsh Office/Home Office/Lord Chancellor's Department (1993), *Adoption: The Future*, Cmnd. 2288, London: HMSO.
DHSS (1985), *Social Work Decisions in Child Care: Recent Research Findings and their Implications*, London: HMSO.
Fisher, M., Marsh, P., Phillips, D. with Sainsbury, E. (1986), *In and Out of Care: The Experience of Children, Parents and Social Workers*, London: Batsford/BAAF.
Fratter, J., Rowe, J., Sapsford, D. and Thoburn, J. (1991), *Permanent Family Placement: A Decade of Experience*, London: BAAF.
Higginson, S. (1990), 'Distorted Evidence', *Community Care*, 17 May.
London Borough of Lambeth (1987), *The Tyra Henry Report*, London: London Borough of Lambeth.
Millham, S., Bullock, R., Hosie, K. and Haak, M. (1986), *Lost in Care: The Problems of Maintaining Links between Children in Care and their Families*, Aldershot: Gower.
Packman, J., Randall, J. and Jacques, N. (1986), *Who Needs Care? Social Work Decisions About Children*, Oxford: Blackwell.
Parton, N. (1991), *Governing the Family: Child Care, Child Protection and the State*, London: Macmillan.
Rowe, J., Cain, H., Hundleby, M. and Keane, A. (1984), *Long Term Foster Care*, London: Batsford/BAAF.
Ryburn, M. (1991a), 'Openness and Adoptive Parents', in Mullender, A. [ed.], *Open Adoption: The Philosophy and the Practice*, London: BAAF.
Ryburn, M. (1991b), 'The Myth of Assessment', *Adoption and Fostering*, **15**(1), 20–7.
Trent, J. (1989), *Homeward Bound: The Rehabilitation of Children to Their Birth Parents*, Ilford: Barnardos.
Vernon, J. and Fruin, D. (1986), *In Care: A Study of Social Work Decision Making*, London: National Children's Bureau.
Winkler, R. and van Keppel, M. (1984), *Relinquishing Mothers in Adoption: Their Long Term Adjustment*, Melbourne: Institute of Family Studies Monograph, No. 3.

1   An earlier version of this chapter appeared in *Adoption and Fostering*, **16**(4), 29–38.

13 A view of wider family perspectives in contested adoptions

Noreen Tingle

Introduction

It would normally be considered foolhardy to enter a contest where the opposing side was in a much stronger position to win. So what is it that drives grandparents to literally risk all in the sort of mismatched contest that the contested adoption of a young relative is almost bound to be? The answer is, like so many lives, not straightforward.

This is a chapter that has been informed by my personal experience as well as my experience as the founder of the UK Grandparents' Federation more than five years ago. The Grandparents' Federation was born in 1987 out of the need to change an unjust law that gave scant recognition to the important part that many grandparents play in the lives of their young relatives. A law regarding contact with their grandchildren, if for any reason this was not being allowed, was non-existent. Children – as well as their grandparents and members of their wider families – were suffering because of this, so our members joined forces with other like-minded people and organisations to work for change.

It was with great excitement that we recognised that contact with children would be enshrined in law, in the Children Act 1989. But for many of our members the 'victory' had a hollow ring, because their well-loved grandchildren had been adopted. Obviously, this was a great obstacle to contact, but by the same token, it was a great challenge: a situation we were determined to explore not only for our peace of mind, but for our adopted young relatives.

This chapter offers a glimpse into the lives of grandparents who have compulsorily lost grandchildren through decisions of the court. Ours is a perspective which is rarely heard and we represent a group which is

largely ignored by professionals as a placement resource or source of help for its children and young people when things go wrong in their immediate families. It is a great sadness to us that nothing seems really to have changed much since nearly ten years ago, when, in an important study of long-term care, Jane Rowe (1984) highlighted the almost 'wholly beneficial' role that we could play when children come into care. One of the most salutary findings in her study was that in only one of six local authorities in the survey were significant links with grandparents actively maintained by social workers. In very many ways the attitudes, beliefs and practice of professionals will determine just how much help we can give when things go wrong.

Being disregarded

The reasons why some children are adopted against the wishes of their families are many. A large proportion of our members are those who have had a grandchild taken into local authority care – a desperately painful situation in itself, but catastrophic if that child is subsequently adopted. The older generation recognise that they cannot be their own adult children's keepers, but, nevertheless, when this happens they are likely to feel terribly shocked and deeply saddened. They grieve for the loss of the child from the family circle.

Wanting to care for the child and being dismissed by professionals as 'too old, or too sick or too involved' – or just about 'too' anything – is both hurtful and frustrating. These are very often simply the opinions of professionals who do not really know the people at all well and yet are prepared to make what the grandparent views as damning statements about them. Witnessing the subsequent downhill process as social services reduce, then terminate contact with the child, as the apparently professional prerequisite to adoption, makes many grandparents very angry. More than this, they are filled with an overwhelming desire to protect their grandchild from the possibility of believing that they had been given away because nobody loved them. That, they say fervently, is too big a burden for any human being to believe; most of all for their grandchild to believe.

Another scenario is if a child is placed for adoption at, or soon after, birth. The grandparents, once again, are very frequently denied contact with the child. The old adage of 'what you haven't known you can't care about' has a hollow ring, as grandparents of adopted babies peer into prams, thinking of their lost grandchild and what might have been.

They are fearful, too, of their adopted grandchild growing up not knowing its family of birth and of being rootless because of it. We all have

our perspectives of reality which are made up not only of the here and now, but of our family history. To deny a child contact with that root is to risk producing a person who is forever fantasising about the unknown family of birth, to the detriment of his or her own mental stability and to the discomfort of the adoptive family. This is surely not in anybody's best interests. Grandparents are at a loss to understand why adoption law does not reflect this common-sense view. Quite a lot of grandparents are old enough to remember the times of large families, when some of the children of such broods were very often brought up by their grandparents. Social forces have, to some extent, put a halt on that, but this is no reason for a Draconian law which declares that there shall be no contact after adoption. Especially when research – and common sense – shows that this is not in the adopted child's interests, nor anybody else's.

Family life is complicated and the older generation usually tries to steer a middle course in its choppy stretches with its sometimes treacherous undercurrents. They usually 'go along' with decisions made by family members, recognising that they must not interfere, whilst at the same time being ready to listen to the family's problems and offering suggestions as to how to overcome them. Theirs is a supportive role and never more so than with the grandchildren. In them they see their hopes for the future; in the children's looks and characters they capture a glimpse of immortality. As such, the children are very precious.

What makes this relationship between the generations so special is that the children themselves seem to sense at a very early age that they have with their grandparents a wonderful affinity. Nature seems to have made it thus: it is a reciprocal balance of youth and maturity, each feeding off the other to obtain that sense of wholeness and identity which is so necessary for the 'well-rounded' personality. Children who have been removed from their families must inevitably grieve for aspects of their family life which may be lost for ever, for even the child who has been abused is likely to have known love and affection, too. How does the child come to terms with a world where nothing seems permanent, where people who showed him love no longer come near, nor have contact, even at birthdays and Christmas? These impressions, learned at such a formative age, could have a lasting effect on the way he in turn behaves when adult, to those he loves.

A living loss

As for the families caught up in the trauma of having a child adopted – well, it has become commonplace for social workers to tell grandparents to

look on the adoption of their grandchild 'as a bereavement'. But adoption is not death: death is part of life and something that we have to accept. When it happens, even as we grieve we give thanks for that life that is no longer. We bury our dead and tend the grave. But with adoption, as it is now, the child is removed and the family will be lucky to be granted a final hour to say good-bye. What's more, under the watchful eyes of social workers, the family must keep cheerful and give no sign of regret or sadness to the unsuspecting child. There is no priest on hand to offer a blessing; no words of comfort. No, it is certainly not a bereavement, for death can be merciful and a funeral a place to say a sad and tearful farewell. But a last hour to play with a healthy child, and then good-bye . . .?

Death as a reason for adoption

My experience in the Grandparents' Federation has shown me that death is by no means an uncommon reason why children are adopted. One member's wife, then daughter, and finally son-in-law all died in the space of 16 months, leaving behind a two-year-old child. The grandfather was not allowed any contact with his grandchild, who was placed for adoption. The humanity of the judge hearing the adoption application, who suggested that the prospective adopters might make our member an 'honorary grandpa' has transformed the life of this elderly gentleman, and of the child, who has been given the privilege of knowing this wonderful man is a member of his birth family.

But it should not be 'a privilege': it should be a right. However, a cruel law denies this right to so many adopted children. Another couple wrote and said that their daughter had died, leaving two children living with them, with whom they had always had a close relationship. There was no father, and the grandparents were no longer young. Because of their age, they were fearful for the future, wondering if they would live long enough to care for their grandchildren until they were grown up. They recognised that for the children to be brought up by a young and active couple would, in some ways, be better for them. But they felt strongly that to let them be adopted, with no contact with themselves, would be very cruel to the children – an added sadness that their young lives could not bear. As there was no guarantee that they would remain in contact if the children were adopted, they kept their fears for the future to themselves, not breathing a word to the social workers.

Then there was the child said to have been neglected by her young parents, and so removed from their home and placed in long-term foster care with a view to adoption. The grandparents wanted to adopt the child,

but the parents disagreed with this – the sort of attitude that says 'if we cannot have the child, they cannot either'. So the child was freed for adoption and contact was terminated. But within two months the young man had succumbed to leukaemia. The grief-stricken young wife faced a double loss and quickly realised the terrible mistake of saying that the grandparents could not have her child. But it was too late: although not yet adopted, the family was refused legal aid to take their case back to court and the local authority refused any let-up in the no-contact regime – even to the extent of informing them that they must only give a brief acknowledgement on seeing the child, should there be a chance encounter. How could this be explained to the youngster, if she asked why her grandparents had not stopped to talk to her? The truth could well lead to this person growing up with a grudge against society. The experience has done nothing, either, for the equilibrium of either the grandparents or the child's mother.

Adoption following mental illness

Let me tell you next some of the case histories of another large group of our membership: that of grandparents who have a son or daughter with mental illness – often schizophrenia. The birth of a child to a person with this sometimes terrifying illness presents social workers with a particularly difficult problem. This appears to be made worse by the variety of theories surrounding the aetiology of the condition, and this in turn seems to influence the outcome for the child. Is the illness precipitated by the patient's family? Is it an inherited tendency? Has it been caused by drug abuse? Is it a chemical imbalance like some other illnesses? Some parents have been labelled the cause of their adult child's illness, so if their grand-child is removed from its parents' care, contact with the grandparents is quickly terminated, much to their distress and no doubt adding to the child's. For children who have two parents with schizophrenia, there appears to be a high risk that they themselves will develop the illness. This was not accepted by the prospective adoptive family of one such child and, the social workers believing this 'genetic' theory of schizophrenia, the adoption was stopped at the last minute. Contact with the child's family having been terminated, the local authority at this stage did an 'about turn' and subsequently allowed the child to be adopted within the family.

Had the prospective adopters accepted the genetic theory of the child's parents' illness and gone ahead with the adoption, and were the child to have succumbed to the illness, it would have been greater reason for contact to have been maintained with the family of birth who, with their

experience of the illness, could have offered considerable support. Presumably, in such cases, social workers are faced with the fixed idea of the 'clean slate' approach to adoption, so maintaining links with the birth family is not pursued even though such contact could prove invaluable to the adoptive family as well as to the child, should he become ill with the same condition.

One grandmother not infrequently looked after her school-aged grandchild when her son-in-law was going through a psychotic state, because at these times the man became violent and sometimes beat the child. On one such occasion, she was not quick enough to take the child home before he received a bad beating. Teachers saw the bruises the following day, social services were alerted and the child was taken into care. Contact between this child and grandmother was thereafter cut drastically. The grandmother's pleas to be given news of the child were met with blank refusal and, in fact, that morning when they walked to school together was almost the last time in seven years that she had contact with her grandchild. This was despite the fact that the sick father committed suicide two years later, so was no longer a threat to the child.

Her grandchild was subsequently adopted, but nevertheless our member continued to send birthday and Christmas cards to the child via the social services, and ask for news of him. But the only answer she received from them was a curt letter to say that the child was no longer part of her family, so they could give no news of the child. As a result she was not informed when the adoption failed. Then, apparently, the child became very disturbed and had to be placed in a therapeutic community. At this stage, the local authority, enlisting the help of a nun to accompany a social worker, asked the grandmother's help with the teenager. She gladly agreed to this, but she was naturally angry at all the lost years when she could have been of assistance, both to her grandchild and to the adoptive parents. She was shocked at her grandchild's appearance and it was painfully obvious that the youngster felt no trust in her, nor in anybody. However, the grandmother persevered with the contact arrangements and now, after two years, her grandchild's behaviour is so much improved that a normal schooling can be resumed.

Sometimes, behaviour that appears to the layperson to denote schizophrenia is labelled by professionals as 'personality disorder'. One couple had a daughter who was diagnosed thus. When her marriage failed, after she had given birth to her third child, she seemed to lose interest in life altogether, taking to her bed and neglecting the children, who were taken into care. At this point, the husband left them. The grandparents were not allowed to look after the children and contact with them was at first severely curtailed and then terminated. They were never told why. The judge, when freeing the children for adoption, said that the family should

receive news of them every six months. But this has never happened and social workers have never intervened. The family still grieves for them, and put an advertisement in newspapers last Grandparents' Day, hoping against hope that someone who knew the boys might tell them of the entry in the newspaper. The grandparents have been denied giving any information to these children about their mother or their other relatives. What must these children make of such inexplicable behaviour?

Of course, any person can become ill, but for the prospective adoptive mother of a child to become more ill than the child's natural mother – whose child was removed because of a similar illness – presents social workers with a complex problem. Such is the case that a member related to me. Her daughter suffers from epilepsy and both her children were looked after in foster homes, with the younger child having been freed for adoption. Relieved of the stress of caring for the two young children, the mother's health improved and there is no plan for the older child to be adopted. In the meantime, the younger child has now become epileptic and the prospective adoptive mother has had a stroke and now suffers fits. Living in an upstairs flat, the child cannot go out often because the prospective adoptive mother is now no longer mobile. This poor sick woman is so fearful that the child will be removed that she has stopped all contact with our member, the child's grandmother. Are the best interests of the child really paramount in such cases?

Relationships with social workers

It is very common for me to hear from members of the Grandparents' Federation that the relationship with the professional workers on their grandchild's case is very strained, to say the least. Indeed, I sometimes feel that the apparent antagonism between the parties detracts from what should be the main focus of attention and concern – the child. Grandparents who have a young relative in local authority care are often confused, desperately unhappy, bewildered by official terminology and frustrated beyond measure by the legendary slowness of official responses. Recently, a grandmother who turned up, after a long journey, a few minutes early for a contact visit with her grandchild who was likely to be adopted, confided to the social worker who was waiting that she was desperate to visit the lavatory. She asked if she could let the foster carer know that she had arrived a little early and ask to visit the toilet before seeing her grandchild. The social worker would not allow this, so the grandmother, unable to wait any longer, knocked on the next door neighbour's door and, explaining her need, asked if she could use the

neighbour's toilet facilities. The neighbour unhesitatingly agreed to this. The social worker, however, was very annoyed and this incident prompted a letter being sent, later, to the grandmother from the local authority, complaining about the incident.

Incredible! It is hard to believe that anything akin to the ideal of working in partnership will be able to exist between these two people. Both believe they have the child's best interests at heart, but the balance of power obviously lies with the social worker. As things stand, without either a change of worker – or a change of heart by the present one – contact with this child and the grandmother could wither. If this happens, a judge hearing a freeing order for adoption could make the assumption that the grandmother didn't care about continuing contact with her grandchild, so no contact order would be made. The kind of animosity witnessed in the last case paves the way to very bad reports being written about relatives by social workers, and this could influence the court's decision regarding granting a contact order if the child is freed for adoption.

Court hearings

Occasionally, though, social workers are overruled. A guardian *ad litem*'s report made all the difference to the outcome of a member's case recently. If social workers had had their way, the grandmother would have had no contact with her grandchildren who were to be adopted. But the guardian *ad litem* gave a glowing report of the obvious love the grandmother had for her grandchildren and of how pleasurable were the children's visits to her home. So a meeting was set up between the local authority's legal department and our member, accompanied by her solicitor. The contact arrangements, after the children's adoption, were agreed. This happy conclusion, having been all arranged before the court hearing, saved a good deal of Legal Aid money, local authority money and court time. Unhappily, all too often social workers ignore court recommendations, and grandparents very often cannot afford to pursue these matters, so justice is not done, despite the court's directions.

Justice can hardly be seen to have been dispensed if a family sees the judge apparently asleep whilst their case is being heard, and who then rouses sufficiently to decide the case. Imagine, too, the feelings of the grandmother, not yet fifty, when she heard the much older judge say to her that 'at your time of life you should be sitting at home putting your feet up, not worrying about contact with your grandchildren'.

Family members feel very aggrieved when they hear psychiatrists – paid for by the local authority – comment extremely unfavourably about a

child's family of birth, after a ten-minute interview with them. They feel it nonsensical, too, to hear that it has been decided that siblings should be parted when adopted, because they have different needs and personalities. It all adds up to a feeling of fighting a losing battle, where the odds are extraordinarily high, but where the chance of winning will give such joy to the family, and long-term benefit to the child who is to be adopted.

The cost of proceedings

Not obtaining Legal Aid is, not surprisingly, the reason why many grandparents cannot proceed with a court case for contact with a grandchild who is to be adopted. Too beset with anxiety and sadness, they feel in no position to represent themselves in court. What very small financial resources they do have, they feel they must hold on to for their old age. So, like their young grandchildren who have no say in the matter, they lose the fight for continued contact.

Two of our members believed that they had got Legal Aid for their contact order cases. They now find, to their intense concern, that they have not. One couple have been sent a bill for £1 500. They lost their case for contact with their grandchildren and the wife is now being treated for severe depression, heavily in debt and fearful of the bailiffs arriving. The other member also lost the case, after 11 days in court, and then was horrified to receive a bill for £25 000 – a sum that he cannot pay, and has no intention of paying, because his solicitor had informed him that he was to get Legal Aid. Not surprisingly, with so much stress, very many of these grandparents suffer serious illness. Such is the frequent aftermath of a child's adoption from a family.

Anything for a glimpse of their grandchild

With adoption in this country meaning a complete severing of the birth family's relationship with the adopted child, some of our members go to extreme lengths to literally 'steal' a glimpse of their grandchild who has been adopted. One lady, crippled with arthritis, waited for five hours at a ferry terminal in the hope of having a fleeting look at her grandchild, whom she had been told would be going on a school trip that day from the port. Unhappily, she didn't see the child. Others hang around school gates at playtime and lunch-times, not intending to speak to their loved

grandchild for fear of being moved on, just wanting to see them. It is a glimpse that keeps them going until the next sighting.

On one occasion, a couple got a good look at their adopted grandchild, even though it was not in the flesh. They were on holiday and idly window-shopping. Stopping at a photographer's shop, they looked at the pictures in the window and there was a picture of their grandchild! Excitedly, our members went inside and asked if they could have a copy of the picture, but the photographer said that he could not do this. At this, the grandmother explained why they wanted a picture of the child. After a pause, the photographer declared that he would put the awning down so as to stop the window reflecting light – and look the other way whilst they took snaps of the picture with the camera they had with them!

Another member moved away from the district after her grandchild was adopted from 'care' as she had too many unhappy memories of the town. She settled into the new area and took a job helping in a playgroup and – much to her astonishment and delight – her grandchild was one of the toddlers who attended every morning. As this member said to me 'it's just as though it had to be'. Not surprisingly, she didn't tell anybody of her relationship to the little child. Very occasionally, divine intervention seems to happen.

Would that the law made it more than just 'sightings'. Now that the Children Act has provided families with the opportunity of asking for contact with their young relatives, we are beginning to hear poignant accounts of how the children themselves react to the kind of order which prevents any physical contact with their family of birth. Imagine then a four-year-old child who had been adopted from local authority care and whose grandmother had won for her the present of a video cassette film of her family, for her fourth birthday. The little girl kept viewing it over and over again, saying to herself 'and this is my first mummy and daddy, and this is my nanna and this is my baby sister', and then kissing the glass. Why, oh why, must this child be like the Lady of Shalott, having to view her loved ones through a kind of mirror? Where is the justice in such a cruel law? Are the interests of the child really being served? We emphatically believe that they are not.

Conclusion

It is only very occasionally that we hear of the happiest of endings to the adoption of a child. One concerns the grandparents of an adopted child who took flowers to the court on the day of the adoption and thanked the new parents for loving their grandson so much. The local authority was in

strong disagreement with the grandparents over any kind of contact with the child, so they felt this would be their only chance of thanking the adoptive parents of their only grandson. Imagine their joy and astonishment to get a phone call from them just a short time later, inviting them to tea. Both sides kept the meeting a secret, for fear of reprisal by social services.

I will finish by relating a conversation overheard by the grandfather whose tragic experience of three deaths I recounted at the beginning. He was staying overnight at the home of his grandchild's adoptive parents and had put the little boy and the natural child of the family to bed. Hearing them chattering away, he crept upstairs. Listening at the door, he heard one child say 'Do you think your mummy who died would have liked me?' 'Oh yes, I'm sure she would, 'cos we're brothers, aren't we?' And Jim is happily grandpa to them both. That's what open adoption can bring to a family – wholeness. Surely, if we really care about children and their families, open adoption is what we must all strive to achieve in adoption law.

References

Rowe, J., Cain, H., Hundleby, M. and Keane, A. (1984), *Long-Term Foster Care*, London: Batsford/BAAF.

14 The use of an adversarial process in contested adoptions

Murray Ryburn

Introduction

The process by which decisions are made for the compulsory adoption of children is one which has been largely ignored in adoption literature (Ryburn, 1992b), yet it is the context against which all other matters must be considered. This final chapter examines the use of the adversarial court process to make decisions in adoption and considers the effect of this process on social work assessments in contested situations.

Forced adoptions find moral justification in the view that the state has a duty to intervene in certain circumstances on behalf of its citizens, or its future citizens, where they would otherwise be at significant risk. State intervention on behalf of children aims to restore to them full rights so that they may participate in society as accountable and responsible citizens.

Beyond perhaps some consensus about compulsory intervention at this general level, all else is a matter of discretion. The debate about compulsory adoption is a moral debate which originates in evaluative rather than descriptive premises. It centres on questions such as 'what constitutes adequate parenting for children?', 'what forms of family life should we endorse and support and which should we reject?', and 'in the event of a perceived conflict between the wishes of adults and children, whose views should we support?' It is a debate in which the arguments will always be politically- and ideologically-driven.

This concluding chapter suggests that the moral persuasiveness of arguments to repeal provisions in our legislation for forced adoption is undeniable and calls for a model in contested situations which is based upon negotiated agreement.

Status, contract and the law

Comparable jurisdictions, where often there was legislation for adoption long before our own, have either not had or do not make use of provisions of the law to force adoption against parental wishes. They rely instead on permanent orders such as guardianship which secure for children all the advantages of a permanent family without breaking irretrievably their links with their birth families. European jurisdictions, though not always comparable, since their origins are in Roman law, almost universally eschew the idea of forced adoption. The starting point for any consideration of the legal process in relation to contested adoption is a recognition therefore that our legislation is fundamentally out of step with that of many other Western countries. Until the Children Act 1989 we emphasised the rights of parents over children much more than we did their duties to them. Adoption law provisions, as Bill Jordan has highlighted in chapter 2, are out of step with much of the thinking and the philosophy of the Children Act. Children who are subject to forced adoption are still in many respects treated as transportable pieces of personal property who can, by a legal fiction, have past links extinguished and join a new family as if they were born to it.

Sir Henry Main (Allen, 1993) characterised the modern development of Western law as a move from status to contract. In other words, with the expansion of the law as a means to societal regulation, there was a corresponding diminution in the regulatory role of traditional structures such as kinship systems. While there may be advantage, in terms of clearer accountability, in the move from status to contract, there is also grave disadvantage.

The move to contract is the move to legally assignable relationships. It is an essentially reductionist process, in which all meaning must be subsumed within what can be presented in terms of evidence. In the court-room, in contested adoptions, the subtleties and complexities of family living and relationships and the needs of children within them are systematically re-interpreted to create the necessary polarities for court decision-making. The parties to proceedings tend to be represented as one-dimensional figures by their legal advisers in what, to an observer, may well appear to be an orchestrated battle between good and evil.

The judgments that are finally given are also indicative of the same reductionist process. Often they are founded on simple propositions which are assumed to have a universal applicability across class, culture and diverse forms of family life. These are propositions such as: 'it will be disruptive of new placements for past links to continue', or 'adoption offers the only secure permanent future for children outside their families of

origin'. As a vision of family life they represent the hegemony of the white, two-parent, heterosexual, nuclear family unit. These judgments also serve a wider social purpose. They can be taken to give clear and resounding messages about protection of the vulnerable, rewarding the supplicant and the punishment of the wrongdoer.

Evidence and the adversarial process

The adversarial courtroom process can often distract professionals from any genuine search for what is likely to be best for those they serve, and for negotiated settlements wherever possible, into a drive for victory at any cost. Any commitment to the interests of children and the interests of truth may sometimes be hard to discern, and as the quotation below from a recent interview indicates, it is a process which does little to engender compassion and sensitivity:

> *What I can't believe is that here we've got this barrister and at lunch time he's all best friends with the barrister for the council. It might be fun and work for them. It's our lives.*

The evidence that is advanced in contested proceedings is selective. Care is taken to ensure that nothing is included that will reduce the persuasiveness of the case (Ryburn, 1992b). This is well-illustrated in a recent case.

The long-term plan of the local authority was for the adoption of a two-year-old child against the wishes of her mother. The mother's parental failures were largely attributable to her mental ill health. In the course of an interview with the mother she said that she was taken on a fortnightly basis to the foster carers to see her child. This was also the evidence of the local authority which portrayed this as indicative of the mother's lack of ability or motivation to maintain contact unassisted.

When the mother finally gave her evidence, it emerged that she first took two bus rides to get to the social worker's office. The mother did not recognise the significance of this information so she did not reveal it in interview and it therefore emerged purely by chance in the court. The local authority however was well aware of its significance. They had elected in this instance to suppress a vital piece of evidence which cast an entirely different complexion on their account of the mother's motivation and her links with her daughter. The process of the careful selection of evidence is one that accompanies the presentation of any case in contested proceedings.

Sometimes the drive to win in the adversarial process leads to deliberate

falsification of evidence. We can only assume here that professionals believe the end justifies the means. Family members interviewed recently (Ryburn, 1992b) gave many accounts of what they saw as the deliberate misrepresentation of the facts. In most instances this was impossible to verify, but there were examples where this could be confirmed by court documentation. In general this evidence sought to lend support to portrayals of parents as irresponsible and unco-operative.

Another consequence of a judicial process which aims to reduce complexity to provable propositions of truth or falsehood is that witnesses are constantly pushed to exceed their limit of confidence in the opinions that they offer. In a choice between right and wrong the middle ground does not exist. Social workers, guardians and experts are not permitted not to know – unless they are prepared as a consequence for the likely denigration of everything else that they may have offered in evidence. The court, as every witness is likely to learn, is a hostile environment. In a system where, despite mounting criticism, preferment for barristers depends upon secret recommendations by judges, barristers will vie to be noticed, often at the expense of eliciting from witnesses what it would be helpful and useful to know.

In the criminal law, where the adversarial process is substantially the same, but where standards of proof are more rigorous, recent cases of grave miscarriages of justice have attracted public outrage. Such cases have resulted from selective use of evidence, expert testimony that zealously exceeded justifiable conclusions, and deliberate corruption and falsification of evidence. We ought reasonably to have less confidence in the operation of a largely similar judicial process in contested adoption, where often fact can less easily be distinguished from opinion, where there may be less exacting examination of evidence, and where there is no jury system which can widen the field of vision.

Poverty and power in contested proceedings

Major studies such as that of Bebbington and Miles (1989), which considered the dynamic of poverty and deprivation in the lives of families whose children are admitted to care, demonstrated that 'deprivation is a common factor amongst all types of children who enter care'. They also demonstrate in their study, as Gerison Lansdown has highlighted in chapter 6, that whilst for families living in the greatest deprivation the chances of a child entering care are 1 in 10, for white two-parent families on good incomes the chances are 1 in 7 000. Children who will be adopted against the wishes of their families are highly likely to be children of the

poor. Our adoption and statutory substitute family placement practice has always been of the transfer of children across wealth and class barriers (Benet, 1976; Bebbington and Miles, 1989). As Kirk and McDaniel (1984) have also pointed out, the wish for the transfer of children from state-supported care to privately-funded care cannot be divorced from the motives of those who first introduced adoption legislation.

Poverty brings with it multiple disadvantage as the work of Townsend (1979) and others has indicated. The relationship between poverty and such factors as ill health and lower levels of educational attainment results in reduced ability to participate in citizenship and increased dependence on others to mediate transactions between the individual and state. The poor, who overwhelmingly are the users of compulsory child care services, are likely, because of the disadvantages that accompany poverty, to experience difficulty both in negotiating about whether there is a need for compulsory services, and in negotiating the nature of those services when they are imposed. This means that their wishes being voiced is more likely to depend on the ability of others, usually professionals, to advocate and mediate for them. Even where advocates are found, the delay for families in finding someone prepared to take their interests and wishes seriously often means that matters have by then achieved a momentum where choices are greatly reduced.

One of the factors that probably militates most against original families in pressing for the return of their children, when adoption plans are being formulated, is the fact that the children are now settled in a life in which the original family no longer has any (obviously) significant role. We know from a variety of research studies (see for example Millham et al., 1986) that where children spend six weeks or more in foster care, the chances of their returning home successfully are greatly diminished. Many families express great bitterness at the level of resourcing by way both of foster care allowances (and later adoption allowances), that goes into helping substitute families care for their children, so that a secure alternative family base can be established. They argue that with this level of income they would have been able to manage the care of their children so that substitute families were not needed.

If we compare the level of resourcing available to poor families dependent on Income Support, we find that they receive an allowance of £15.05 for looking after a child of ten years. The National Foster Care Association recommends a minimum foster care allowance of £63 for a ten-year-old. The National Foster Care Association figures include no element of reward or salary and are determined by the actual cost of bringing up a child in the UK today. In fact since local authorities often pay enhanced rates to foster carers, the actual per capita spending on foster care across all ages in England in 1990–1991 was £102 per child per week (Verity, 1993).

The average child care allowance across all ages received by those living on state benefit, which will include most of those whose children are adopted without their consent, is £18.

On the other hand the ultimate reliance on a court-led adversarial system for decision-making in compulsory child care cases is largely antithetical to any model of negotiated conflict resolution and works to reduce any emphasis on mediated and facilitated settlements. As the Adoption Law Review (DoH, 1992) with its greater attention to services for original families has to some extent recognised, from the point of compulsory care and thereafter up to the moment of forced adoption, original families cease to be the unit of concern. There is often a focus on children and young people which presumes the ready separability of their interests from those of their family networks. Where poverty is a factor in original families, invidious comparisons between new and original families can also influence the views of professionals concerning the best interests of children and young people.

The adversarial court-led system for dealing with conflict in child care cases is a major consumer of public resources. It is not uncommon for costs in individual cases to run well into six figures. With this in mind it is appropriate to consider the words of the 1984 All Party House of Commons Social Services Committee (the Short Report):

> If half the funds and intellectual effort that has gone into finding alternative families for children had been spent on what we can only lamely call preventive work, there would be unquestionable advantage to all (p.xix, para 30).

When we acknowledge poverty as the clearest predictor of whether children will be adopted against the wishes of their families, and set the vast sums spent in adversarial court proceedings, foster and residential care against the small amounts still spent on supporting original families, then the words of the Short Report should continue to resound. Since 1926 children have been adopted because of poverty. It remains a key element in the adoption equation in 1994.

The apparent ability of those with institutional power to override the wishes of others who are less dominant is evident in the outcomes of contested adoption proceedings. In the Bristol Pathways research (Murch et al., 1993, p. 28) 97 per cent of contested freeing applications, where a final decision had been made by the courts, were granted. The study found that 95 per cent of contested adoption orders were granted (p.28). This represents a dramatic endorsement by the courts of local authority plans. So much so that it is not surprising that some families reported in a recent study (Ryburn, 1992b) being advised by lawyers that it was not worth pursuing their wishes in court, because the scales, regardless of the merits of their case, were so weighted against them.

In contrast, Jackie Trent's 1989 Barnardos' research project took, on referral, children for whom local authorities had determined that adoption was necessary. Instead they restored 36 of these children to their original family networks and achieved a success rate of 74 per cent. This compares favourably with adoption and permanent placement outcome studies (see, for example, Fratter et al., 1991; Lahti, 1982; Thoburn, 1989) here and elsewhere. The critical factor is that the project's restoration plans were properly resourced and thoroughly followed through.

Risk assessment

The necessary precursor to forced adoption is an assessment by social workers and their managers which concludes that inevitable and irremediable harm will occur if a child remains in her or his family of origin. Yet it is a reflexive process. It is the very nature of the court process itself that shapes the assessment. The possibility of a court hearing, and the dictates of the adversarial process in terms of how evidence must be gathered, assessed and presented, is always at the shoulder of any social worker involved in issues of child care and protection.

The search by practitioners for 'objective' measures to determine irremediable harm, measures that will, if necessary, offer the justification to a court for a forced adoption, has given birth to a new creature from the late 1980s. It is commonly called a *risk assessment*. Practitioners do not often articulate clearly the constituents of risk assessment, but where answers are given there is usually mention of the Department of Health's child protection publication, *Protecting Children: A Guide for Social Workers Undertaking a Comprehensive Assessment* (DoH, 1988b), which is popularly known because of its cover as 'the orange book'.

Practitioners most often talk about *doing* a risk assessment or *doing* an orange book assessment. Doing it to someone is very much the model promoted in the orange book. Its approach is largely to avoid any sort of interactive process. It centres on the collection and collation of information and data, and on reaching conclusions and judgments. It is a model that is peopled, according to the book itself, by those who are 'dangerous' (p.12) and those who are not. Those who are dangerous are some families (not as we might reasonably surmise some individuals within some families), and those professionals who lack a sufficiently interventionist stance so that, to use the words of the Beckford Inquiry (London Borough of Brent, 1985, p.295), they have failed to grasp that ' "authority" is not a dirty word'.

In a doubt-ridden world, and in the face of an increasingly hostile media, the orange book and its underlying philosophy seem to promise certainty

in the assessment of risk. Collaboration, partnership and reciprocity are largely alien to its system of meaning, so that we can look forward to a time when those coming to agencies for help will be offered not a service, but a risk assessment. If the professional is to be seen as dispassionate observer and as assessor, rather than proactive practitioner, there is a major risk that those who have a professional, legal and ethical duty to help will sit back to observe and monitor failure – and to employ their findings as evidence in contested proceedings.

The 'professional as dispassionate expert' model of assessment is a requirement for an adversarial court-led system. It calls for, in professionals, a binary vision so that complexity and the middle ground can be ignored. Some of its more obvious deficiencies are well-illustrated in a recent case.

A was the mother of two children. She was African-Caribbean and had been diagnosed as having a schizophrenic illness. She was offered a programme of help to restore her children to her. Just before this programme of planned involvement began she was told that it would instead be an assessment of her parenting capacity – in other words a risk assessment. What was proposed was a series of sessions in which she would be with the children and her interaction with them would be observed by workers in the room as well as being recorded on video. In fact there were only two sessions because it was decided that A could not fulfil any useful role in relation to her children and that they should be adopted.

In evidence it was said that A continued in the sessions, to the exclusion of all else, to plait extensions into her pre-school age daughter's hair. It was emphasised that A failed to recognise the dangers of hot drinks when these were brought into the room, and that she ignored the younger of the children. It was also stated that she demonstrated her inability to work with professionals when she entered into a heated argument with professionals at the end of the session because she did not wish to comply with a request to stop plaiting her daughter's hair, both because the session was at an end and because her daughter was crying.

The evidence included video recordings, a transcript of the dialogue and the reports of the professionals. It was presented as an objective assessment of A's incapacity to parent her children with safety and to demonstrate her attachment and affection to them.

Context

First, the assessment was outside the context of the normal setting in which A expected to be with her children. As Millham and his colleagues wrote in 1986, we should not rely on any assessments of attachment where

the fact of care has created unusual situations for parent–child interaction. The Dartington researchers highlight the injustice of creating the very sort of situation that A was placed in, where:

> ill-prepared and without a syllabus the family sit a 'love test' which is set and marked by social workers. (p.223)

During an interview A said she had been told to behave exactly as if she were at home with the children. If she were at home she said she would have wished to bath the children. When she asked to do this she was told it was not possible. No wonder A was confused. It is ironic, given A's psychiatric diagnosis, that the early work by Gregory Bateson and his colleagues (1956) in relation to schizophrenia suggested a causal connexion between it and just such confusing communication as that offered by the workers in this case.

The assessment of attachment and risk of harm by methods of direct observation usually fails also to acknowledge, as was the case here, that the dynamic of having others present in the room (let alone video cameras) will inevitably alter the interaction between parents and children. It is an acknowledgement seldom made because to do so would also be to accept that the process itself is essentially flawed.

Lack of ordinary parenting tasks

Second, parenting capacity and risk can only usefully be assessed in relation to the fulfilment of the ordinary tasks of parenting. It was A's search, in an unfamiliar setting, for an ordinary task of parenting, plaiting her daughter's hair, that led to the greatest censure by those assessing her.

Lack of role clarity

A third failure was the lack of any evidence that clarity had been established concerning roles and tasks during the sessions. Despite the statements of purpose in written reports, when A was interviewed she conveyed only the murkiest notion of what the purpose of the sessions had been. This could have affected the behaviour that was observed in at least two very important ways.

Her confusion would have communicated itself to the children, whom we could expect to have been similarly unsure and therefore anxious.

Additionally, if A was unsure of her own role then she would also be unclear about the roles of others in relation to her. It is quite possible, for example, that she expected the two workers who had made and brought in the hot drinks to ensure that they did not pose a safety risk to the children

– after all this was, from her perspective, their place. Since she had not been the primary carer of her two children for some time, it was also perhaps reasonable that she expected others to continue still to play a key role in their care. Thus she may have expected one of the workers to look after her young son while she attended to her daughter's hair – after all, what were the workers there for if they were not going to do something useful?

Failure to consider the wider family context

A fourth flaw was the failure of workers to take any account of the role that others in the family network might play, in tandem with A, in caring for the children. Thus there was no invitation for her to bring any of the family members with her who could have offered vital help were the children returned to her care. Their ability to work creatively alongside A should have been a vital ingredient in any assessment. As it was, neither the workers nor subsequently the guardian explored the help that could be available in the wider family, despite the comprehensive assessment that was said to have been made. In fact A had a wide family network, some of whom, when they were finally approached, not by the social workers but by A's solicitor, indicated that they were prepared to play a role. The workers involved in this case framed their assessment around a very restrictive definition of family and the results of their assessment were correspondingly skewed.

Parents as people

A fifth flaw was the failure to take individual account of A's circumstances – she was not, to paraphrase Butler-Sloss in the Cleveland Inquiry (DoH, 1988a, p. 245), an 'object of assessment', she was a person, and one of her personal characteristics was that she had a mental health problem. This meant that extra care should have been taken in explaining the process of assessment to her. It also meant that any observations ought reasonably to have taken account of the dynamic of her illness and its interaction with a process that was undoubtedly stressful.

Schizophrenia is an illness where disabling symptoms, such as auditory hallucinations, may be increased by stress. A reported that this had happened to her. One of the ways hospital staff had taught her to manage hallucinations was by concentrating on a task requiring digital and manual dexterity – something, for example, like plaiting her daughter's hair! In doing this A was certainly following the advice of at least one set of professionals. When seen in this light her behaviour probably tells us far

more about the assessment process than it does about A's relationships or capacity for relationships with her children.

Cultural perspectives

The assessment failed also to take account of cultural difference. A's children were at that time transracially placed. They were not receiving the hair care that she would have wished for them. Additionally the importance attached in A's culture to a mother's care of her children's hair should have been a crucial part of any conclusions that were drawn about her behaviour in persisting throughout the assessment process in plaiting it. Nor did the workers' accounts recognise the hair-plaiting as part of an interactive process. They described it solely as something that A did to her daughter, not something through which her daughter could have derived benefit through physical closeness with her mother.

Finally, we should note an additional point, which is obvious, but was clearly ignored. Once the process of plaiting hair has begun, it is not possible just to leave it, it needs to be finished, even if, as in this case, time was up. Furthermore, that A's daughter's was crying whilst having her hair plaited should not have been portrayed, as it was, as some form of cruelty. Plaiting can cause some discomfort, but it is something children cared for in their own black families become used to.

The 'reasonable' local authority

The seventh missing ingredient was any notion of the 'reasonable service provider'. Volume One of the Guidance to the Children Act indicates that it may be reasonable to take account of individual circumstances in the assessment of risk, and it has much to say about reasonable parents. However, where children need services that their parents cannot provide, the reasonableness of those parents can only be interpreted in the light of the reasonableness of those with a duty to offer services.

Reasonableness is not a word that is applied to professional behaviour in the process of assessing the risk of harm. We should do so. Was it reasonable in this case for two workers to continue their observations and ensure that everything was thoroughly recorded, or would it have been more reasonable for two paid professional helpers to have intervened effectively to help when they believed A was in difficulty? Any useful assessment might have focused on A's ability to respond to the helping initiatives of others, given the belief of workers that major changes would be necessary before she could be considered as a parent for her children.

Objectivity and the judicial process

It is not only the activities of social workers that can be distorted by the adversarial process. It is a system for making decisions in which the attention of the judiciary focuses on how the received version of events can fit the strait-jacket of legal precedent and opinion. While in contract law the courts still agonise over a snail which was inadvertently pickled in a bottle of ginger beer (*Donoghue* v. *Stephenson*, AC [1932]), in contested adoption the path of legal correctness takes us back a year earlier to a 1931 Court of Appeal decision in *Re J M Carroll (an infant)* KB 1. Court decisions in general, including decisions in contested adoptions, are essentially wrong only where they fail to follow the rules of conformity. Having one's judgment overturned is the thing most to be avoided, and with adoption law requiring that consideration only be given throughout childhood, issues of long-term welfare beyond childhood do not get any serious consideration. The judicial process with its emphasis on legal correctness is one which tends to ignore that we inhabit a world of conjecture, prejudice, uncertainty and change. In doing so it is even more surely captive to these very influences.

There is no point of detachment in contested proceedings from which judges, social workers, lawyers, guardians or anyone else can apply objective tests to the lives of others (Ryburn, 1991). It is difficult to distinguish the reasonable conclusions of a professional observer from their personal beliefs, values and prejudices and, as June Thoburn highlights in chapter 8, even where evidence is based on empirical research there is enormous scope in the accounts of witnesses for bias in the way it is presented. Furthermore, few would dispute that statute law is framed to conform to a vision of family life, social organisation and the collective good that many would never share.

Capacity to make judgments with predictive value for the future

Even if courts could make judgments of which we could be certain today, would they hold any validity for a changing and uncertain tomorrow? This issue is at the heart of a number of longitudinal studies concerning the development of children, and the consistent message these give is that it is quite unrealistic to make judgments in respect of children in the belief that they will have predictive reliability in the future. Thus, for example, in

Berkeley, California, in 1928 and 1931, exhaustive information was gathered concerning two cohorts of infants in an attempt, amongst other things, to predict how they would develop in adulthood. On a 30-year follow-up the researchers (Elder, 1978, 1981) were amazed at how inaccurate their predictions had been, despite all the detailed information that had been available. If we had a '7-Up' programme to monitor the wisdom of judicial decisions in forced adoptions, we might well be similarly shaken.

It is hard to see how adoption decisions, with all their irrevocable consequences, can be the right ones for courts to be making in matters as complex and uncertain as those where there are conflicting views concerning the care of children. Where children cannot be permanently parented in their original families, there are, as June Thoburn indicates in chapter 8 and as the Adoption Law Review (DoH, 1992) also acknowledges, other routes to permanence. They are routes where the outcomes are as good as adoption (Fratter et al., 1991) and the consequences are far less Draconian in their effect.

Best interests of all parties

Even if arguments that the adversarial process is the wrong one for making adoption decisions are not accepted, there are other reasons why, taking a longer-term perspective, forced adoptions compare unfavourably with the advantages afforded by the other permanent care options.

First, we know unequivocally that the balance of evidence points to the importance of the maintenance of links and contact for those who are adopted, with their original families (for a review of the research see Ryburn, 1994). Forced adoptions (see chapter 11) are likely to create heightened anger, anxiety and fear in new carers, and deep hostility in original families (see chapter 12). They do not constitute a system for decision-making which facilitates the possibilities for contact, and where contact is achieved following contested adoptions, it is contact achieved against the odds.

Second, we know from research by Triseliotis (1983) and others that it can be vitally important for adopted people to have access to the fullest possible information regarding their backgrounds and personal history. In adversarial proceedings both the local authority and the prospective adopters need to believe in the starkest possible presentation of the parental failures of birth families. For workers, this alone can offer moral sanction to the action they have taken, while for prospective adopters any alternative view is also too awful to contemplate. Who would ever wish to

parent a child wrested from a family that, with the right help and support, could have cared adequately for her.

In this way a contested adoption narrows the range of information about birth families that is seen, conveyed or listened to. The information that is available to children and young people may often therefore be nothing more than a sanitised version of the unpalatable facts that have formed the basis of the local authority case in court. In addition, even where approaches are made to original families for information to help children to understand their personal histories, the antagonism created by the court contest is such that they often may not wish to co-operate (Ryburn, 1992b).

Finally, where adopters have received negative messages about original families it is probably impossible for them not to convey these to the children in various ways over the years. If children and young people internalise negative messages about their families of origin, it is but a short step, for example, during adolescence, for these to be interpreted either by parents or by young people in terms of ideas about 'bad blood', rather than in terms of the normal problems of development (Kaye and Warren, 1988). We know from research, on the other hand, that a positive sense of identity depends upon positive self-esteem (Triseliotis, 1983). Other forms of permanent placement, as Gerison Lansdown has suggested in chapter 6, are less likely to encounter these major difficulties.

Conclusion

Contested adoptions lead to polarised and extreme positions. They are antithetical to the sort of partnership that the Children Act encourages and are enormously expensive in human and economic terms. It is hard to see how they can ever serve the best interests of children and their wider families. A better approach calls for the repeal of provisions for freeing and the dispensation of parental consent, the abandonment of adversarial decision-making in favour of negotiated settlements,[1] and the recognition that there are alternatives to adoption as a form of family placement, which can offer children the advantages of permanence without the potentially irretrievable loss of their entire original families.[2]

1   For a full discussion of the use of Family Group Conferences to achieve negotiated settlements in child care and protection, see Ryburn, M. (1993), 'A New Model for Family Decision-Making in Child Care and Protection', *Early Child Development and Care*, **86**, 1–10.
2   A shorter version of this chapter appeared in *Adoption and Fostering*, **17**(3), 39–45.

References

Allen, G. (1993), in Allen, G. and Marsh, P., 'The New Zealand Development of Family Group Conferences', in Marsh, P. and Triseliotis, J., *Prevention and Reunification in Child Care*, London: Batsford/BAAF.

Bateson, G., Jackson, D., Haley, J. and Weakland, J. (1956), *Behavioural Science*, 1(4), 251–64.

Bebbington, A. and Miles, J. (1989), 'The Background of Children Who Enter Local Authority Care', *The British Journal of Social Work*, 19(4), 349–68.

Benet, M. (1976), *The Character of Adoption*, London: Jonathan Cape.

Bullard, E., Mallos, E. and Parker, R. (1990), *Custodianship Research Project: A Report to the Department of Health*, Bristol: University of Bristol.

DoH (1988a), *Report of the Inquiry into Child Abuse in Cleveland 1987*, London: HMSO.

DoH (1988b), *Protecting Children: A Guide for Social Workers Undertaking a Comprehensive Assessment*, London: HMSO.

DoH/Welsh Office (1990), *Interdepartmental Review of Adoption Law, Discussion Paper 2, Agreement and Freeing*, London: DOH.

DoH/Welsh Office (1992), *Review of Adoption Law: Report to Ministers of an Interdepartmental Working Group: A Consultation Document*, London: DOH.

Elder, G. (1978), 'Family History and the Life Course', in Haerven, T. [ed.], *Transitions: The Family and the Life Course in Historical Perspective*, New York: Academic Press.

Elder, G. (1981), 'Social History and Life Experience', in Eichorn, D., Clausen, A., Haan, N., Honzik, M. and Mussen, P. [eds], *Present and Past in Middle Life*, New York: Academic Press.

Fratter, J., Rowe, J., Sapsford, D. and Thoburn, J. (1991), *Permanent Family Placement: A Decade of Experience*, London: BAAF.

Kaye, K. and Warren, S. (1988), 'Discourse About Adoption in Adoptive Families', *Journal of Family Psychology*, 1, 406–33.

Kirk, D. and McDaniel, S. (1984), 'Adoption Policy in Great Britain and North America', *Journal of Social Policy*, 13(1), 75–84.

Lahti, J. (1982), 'A Follow-up Study of Foster Children in Permanent Placements', *Social Service Review*, Chicago: University of Chicago.

London Borough of Brent (1985), *A Child in Trust: Report of the Panel of Inquiry Investigating the Circumstances of the Death of Jasmine Beckford*, London: London Borough of Brent.

Millham, S., Bullock, R., Hosie, K. and Haak, M. (1986), *Lost in Care: The Problems of Maintaining Links between Children in Care and their Families*, Aldershot: Gower.

Murch, M., Lowe, N., Borkowski, M., Copner, R. and Griew, K. (1993), *Pathways to Adoption Research Project*, Bristol: Socio-Legal Centre for Family Studies, University of Bristol/DoH.

Ryburn, M. (1991), 'The Myth of Assessment', *Adoption and Fostering*, 15(1), 20–27.

Ryburn, M. (1992a), *Adoption in the 1990s*, Birmingham: Leamington Press.

Ryburn, M. (1992b), 'Contested Adoption Proceedings', *Adoption and Fostering*, 16(4), 29–38.

Ryburn, M. (1994), *Open Adoption: Research, Theory and Practice*, Aldershot: Avebury.

Short Report (1984), *Second Report From the House of Commons Social Services Committee, 'Children in Care'* (HC 360), London: HMSO.

Thoburn, J. (1985), 'What Kind of Permanence', *Adoption and Fostering*, 9(4), 29–33.

Thoburn, J. (1989), *Success and Failure in Permanent Placement*, Aldershot: Avebury/ Gower.
Townsend, P. (1979), *Poverty in the United Kingdom*, London: Penguin.
Trent, J. (1989), *Homeward Bound: The Rehabilitation of Children to their Birth Parents*, Ilford: Barnados.
Triseliotis, J. (1983), 'Identity and Security in Long Term Fostering and Adoption', *Adoption and Fostering*, **7**(1), 22–31.
Verity, P. (1993), personal communication, July.

Bibliography

Aboud, F. (1987), 'The Development of Ethnic Self Identification and Attitudes', in Phinney, J. and Rotheram, M. [eds], *Children's Ethnic Socialisation: Pluralism and Development*, Newbury Park, CA: Sage.

Adoption Agencies Regulations (1983), SI 1983/1964, London: HMSO.

Adoption Rules 1984, SI 1984/265, London: HMSO.

Ainsworth, M. (1940), *An Evaluation of Adjustment Based on the Concept of Security*, Child Development Series, Toronto: University of Toronto Press.

Ainsworth, M. (1962), 'The Effects of Maternal Deprivation: A Review of the Findings and Controversy in the Context of Research Strategy', in *Deprivation of Maternal Care: A Reassessment of its Effects*, Geneva: World Health Organisation.

Aldgate, J. (1990), 'Foster Children at School: Success or Failure', *Adoption and Fostering*, **14**(4), 38–48.

Allen, G. (1993), in Allen, G. and Marsh, P., 'The New Zealand Development of Family Group Conferences', in Marsh, P. and Triseliotis, J., *Prevention and Reunification in Child Care*, London: Batsford/BAAF.

Andujo, E. (1988), 'Ethnic Identity of Transethnically Adopted Hispanic Adolescents', *Social Work*, **33**, 531–5.

BAAF (1993), *The BAAF Response to the Review of Adoption Law*, London: BAAF.

Baldwin, S. and Twigg, J. (1991), 'Women and Community Care: Reflections on a Debate', in MacLean, M. and Groves, D. [eds], *Women's Issues in Social Policy*, London: Routledge and Kegan Paul.

Bateson, G., Jackson, D., Haley, J. and Weakland, J. (1956), *Behavioural Science*, **1**(4), 251–64.

Bebbington, A. and Miles, J. (1989), 'The Background of Children Who

Enter Local Authority Care', *The British Journal of Social Work*, **19**(4), 349–68.

Benet, M. (1976), *The Character of Adoption*, London: Jonathan Cape.

Berger, M. and Passingham, R. (1972), 'Early Experience and Other Environmental Factors: An Overview', in Eysenck, H. [ed.], *Handbook of Abnormal Psychology*, 2nd edition, London: Pitman.

Berridge, D. and Cleaver, H. (1987), *Foster Home Breakdown*, Oxford: Blackwell.

Bouchier, P., Lambert, L. and Triseliotis, J. (1991), *Parting with a Child for Adoption*, London: BAAF.

Bowlby, J. (1952), *Maternal Care and Mental Health*, Geneva: World Health Organisation.

Bowlby, J. (1979), *The Making and Breaking of Affectional Bonds*, London: Tavistock Routledge.

Brodzinsky, D., Schechter, D., Braff, A. and Singer, L. (1984), 'Psychological and Academic Adjustment in Adopted Children', *Journal of Consulting and Clinical Psychology*, **52**(4), 582–90.

Brodzinsky, D., Singer, L. and Braff, A. (1984), 'Children's Understanding of Adoption', *Child Development*, **55**, 869–78.

Browne, K., Davies, C. and Stratton, P. [eds] (1988), *Early Prediction and Prevention of Child Abuse*, Chichester: Wiley.

Bullard, E., Mallos, E. and Parker, R. (1990), *Custodianship Research Project: A Report to the Department of Health*, Bristol: Socio-Legal Centre for Family Studies, University of Bristol.

Bullock, R., Little, M. and Millham, S. (1993), *Going Home*, Aldershot: Dartmouth.

Charles, M., Rashid, S. and Thoburn, J. (1992), 'Research on Permanent Family Placement of Black Children and those from Minority Ethnic Groups', *Adoption and Fostering*, **16**(2), 3–4.

Cheetham, J., Fuller, R., MacIvor, G. and Petch, A. (1992), *Evaluating Social Work Effectiveness*, Milton Keynes: Open University Press.

Children's Legal Centre (1993), *Review of Adoption Law: Report to Minister of an Interdepartmental Working Group – Response of the Children's Legal Centre*, London.

Cole, E. and Donley, K. (1990), 'History, Values and Placement Policy Issues', in Brodzinsky, D. and Schechter, M. [eds], *The Psychology of Adoption*, 273–94, Oxford: Oxford University Press.

Cook, D. (1991), *Second Best*, London: Faber and Faber.

Cooper, C. (1980), 'Paediatric Perspectives', in Adcock, M. and White, R. [eds], *Terminating Parental Contact*, London: BAAF.

Craft, M., Stephenson, J. and Grainger, C. (1984), 'The Relationship Between Severity of Personality Disorder and Certain Adverse Childhood Influences', *British Journal of Psychiatry*, **110**, 392–492.

Dale, P. with Davies, M., Morrison, T. and Waters, J. (1986), *Dangerous Families: Assessment and Treatment of Child Abuse*, London: Tavistock.

Davey, A. (1983), *Learning to be Prejudiced: Growing up in Multi-Ethnic Britain*, London: Edward Arnold.

David, M. (1991), 'Putting on an Act for the Children?', in Maclean, M. and Groves, D. [eds], *Women's Issues in Social Policy*, London: Routledge and Kegan Paul.

DHSS (1985), *Social Work Decisions in Child Care: Recent Research Findings and Their Implications*, London: HMSO.

DHSS White Paper (1987), *The Law on Child Care and Family Services*, Cmnd. 62, London: HMSO.

DHSS (1988), *Review of Child Care Law: Report of an Interdepartmental Working Party*, London: HMSO.

Department of Health (1988), *Protecting Children: A Guide for Social Workers Undertaking a Comprehensive Assessment*, London: HMSO.

Department of Health (1988), *Report of the Inquiry into Child Abuse in Cleveland 1987*, London: HMSO.

Department of Health (1988), *Children in Care 1988, England*, A/F 88/1, London: HMSO.

Department of Health/Welsh Office (1990), *Inter-Departmental Review of Adoption Law: Discussion Paper 2, Agreement and Freeing*, London: DoH.

Department of Health/Welsh Office (1991), *Inter-Departmental Review of Adoption Law: The Adoption Process, Discussion Paper 3*, London: DoH.

Department of Health (1991), *Patterns & Outcomes in Child Placement: Messages from Current Research and Their Implications*, London: HMSO.

Department of Health (1991), *The Children Act 1989: Guidance and Regulations: Family Placements*, Vol. 3, London: HMSO.

Department of Health (1991), *Children in Care 1991, England*, A/F 91/1, London: HMSO.

Department of Health (1992), *Manual of Practice Guidance for Guardians ad Litem and Reporting Officers*, London: HMSO.

Department of Health/Welsh Office (1992), *Review of Adoption Law: Report to Ministers of an Interdepartmental Working Group: A Consultation Document*, London: DoH.

Department of Health (1992), *Child Care Statistics*, London: HMSO.

Department of Health/Welsh Office/Home Office/Lord Chancellor's Department (1993), *Adoption: The Future*, Cmnd. 2288, London: HMSO.

Department of Health/Welsh Office/Lord Chancellor's Department (1994), *Placement for Adoption: A Consultation Document*, London: DoH.

Earle, A. and Earle, D. (1961), 'Early Maternal Deprivation and Later Psychiatric Illness', *American Journal of Ortho-Psychiatry*, **31**, 181–6.

Elder, G. (1978), 'Family History and the Life Course', in Haerven, T. [ed.],

Transitions: The Family and the Life Course in Historical Perspective, New York: Academic Press.

Elder, G. (1981), 'Social History and Life Experience', in Eichorn, D., Clausen, A., Haan, N., Honzik, M. and Mussen, P. [eds], *Present and Past in Middle Life*, New York: Academic Press.

Erikson, E. (1968), *Identity: Youth and Crisis*, New York: Norton.

Fahlberg, V. (1981), *Helping Children When They Must Move*, London: BAAF.

Fahlberg, V. (1981), *Attachment and Separation*, London: BAAF.

Fahlberg, V. (1993), unpublished paper on 'Contact and Permanent Placement'.

Fahlberg, V. (1994), *A Child's Journey Through Placement*, London: BAAF.

Family Proceedings Courts (Children Act 1989) Rules 1991, SI 1991/1395, London: HMSO.

Family Proceedings Rules 1991, SI 1991/1247, London: HMSO.

Fein, E., Maluccio, A. and Kluger, M. (1990), *No More Partings: An Examination of Long Term Foster Family Care*, New York: Child Welfare League of America.

Festinger, L. (1957), *A Theory of Cognitive Dissonance*, Stanford, CA: Stanford University Press.

Fisher, M., Marsh, P., Phillips, D. with Sainsbury, E. (1986), *In and Out of Care: The Experience of Children, Parents and Social Workers*, London: Batsford/BAAF.

Fratter, J. (1988), 'Black Children with Black Families', in Argent H. [ed.], *Keeping the Doors Open: A Review of Post Adoption Services*, London: BAAF.

Fratter, J. (1991), 'Adoptive Parents and Open Adoption in the UK', in Mullender, A. [ed.], *Open Adoption: The Philosophy and the Practice*, London: BAAF.

Fratter, J., Rowe, J., Sapsford, D. and Thoburn, J. (1991), *Permanent Family Placement: A Decade of Experience*, London: BAAF.

Frisk, M. (1964), 'Identity Problems and Confused Conceptions of the Genetic Ego in Adopted Children During Adolescence', *Acta Paedo Psychiatrica*, **31**, 6–12.

Gill, O. and Jackson, B. (1983), *Adoption and Race: Black, Asian and Mixed Race Children in White Families*, London: Batsford.

Goldstein, J., Freud, A. and Solnit, A. (1973), *Beyond the Best Interests of the Child*, New York: Free Press.

Greer, S., Gunn, J. and Coller, K. (1966), 'Aetiological Factors in Attempted Suicide', *British Medical Journal*, **2**, 1352–5.

Grey, E. and Blunden, R. (1971), *A Survey of Adoption in Great Britain*, London: HMSO.

Haines, E. and Timms, N. (1985), *Adoption, Identity and Social Policy*, Aldershot: Gower.

Harper, J. (1990), 'Children's Communication of Anxiety Through Metaphor in Fostering and Adoption', *Adoption and Fostering*, **14**(3), 33–7.

Hayek, F. (1960), *The Constitution of Liberty*, Routledge and Kegan Paul.

Hayek, F. (1967), *Studies in Philosophy, Politics and Economics*, London: Routledge Kegan Paul.

Hayek, F. (1973), *Rules and Order*, London: Routledge and Kegan Paul.

Hayek, F. (1976), *The Mirage of Social Justice*, London: Routledge and Kegan Paul.

Heinicke, C. and Westheimer, I. (1966), *Brief Separations*, New York: International Universities Press.

Higginson, S. (1990), 'Distorted Evidence', *Community Care*, 17 May.

Hill, M., Lambert, L. and Triseliotis, J. (1989), *Achieving Adoption with Love and Money*, London: National Children's Bureau.

Hill, M., Lambert, L., Triseliotis, J. and Buist, M. (1992), 'Making Judgements About Parenting: The Example of Freeing for Adoption', *British Journal of Social Work*, **22**, 373–89.

HMSO (1972), *Report of the Departmental Committee on the Adoption of Children* (Houghton Report), Cmnd. 5107, London: HMSO.

Hogget, B. (1984), 'Adoption Law: An Overview', in Bean, P. [ed.], *Adoption*, London: Tavistock.

Howe, D. and Hinings, D. (1989), *The Post-Adoption Centre: The First Three Years*, Norwich: University of East Anglia.

Humphrey, M. and Humphrey, H. [eds] (1992), *Inter-Country Adoption: Practical Experiences*, Routledge: London.

Hunt, J., Thomas, C. and Macleod, A. (1993), *Statutory Intervention in Child Protection: The Impact of the Children Act 1989*, Bristol: Socio-Legal Centre for Legal Studies, University of Bristol.

Israel, J. and Tajfel, H. [eds] (1972), *The Context of Social Psychology: A Critical Assessment*, London: Academic Press.

Iwanek, M. (1987), 'A Study of Open Adoption', 14 Emerson Street, Petone, Wellington, New Zealand: Unpublished.

Kaye, K. and Warren, S. (1988), 'Discourse About Adoption in Adoptive Families', *Journal of Family Psychology*, **1**, 406–33.

Kelly, G. and McCauley, C. (in preparation), *A Study of Long Term Foster Placements in Northern Ireland*, London: BAAF.

King, P. and Young, I. (1992), *The Child as Client*, Bristol: Jordan's Family Law.

Kirk, D. (1964), *Shared Fate: A Theory of Adoption and Mental Health*, New York: Free Press.

Kirk, D. (1981), *Adoptive Kinship: A Modern Institution in Need of Reform*, Toronto: Butterworths.

Kirk, D. and McDaniel, S. (1984), 'Adoption Policy in Great Britain and North America', *Journal of Social Policy*, **13**(1), 75–84.

Lahti, J. (1982), 'A Follow-up Study of Foster Children in Permanent Placements', *Social Service Review*, **56**(4), 556–71.

Lambert, L., Buist, M., Triseliotis, J. and Hill, M. (1989), *Freeing Children for Adoption*, Final Report to SWSG, Edinburgh.

Lambert, L., Buist, M., Triseliotis, J. and Hill, M. (1990), *Freeing Children for Adoption*, London: BAAF.

Lansdown, G. (1992), 'UN Convention: Setting New Targets', *Adoption and Fostering*, **16**(3), 34–7.

London Borough of Brent (1985), *A Child in Trust: Report of the Panel of Inquiry Investigating the Circumstances of the Death of Jasmine Beckford*, London: London Borough of Brent.

London Borough of Lambeth (1987), *The Tyra Henry Report*, London: London Borough of Lambeth.

Lowe, N. with Borkowski, M., Copner, R. and Murch, M. (1991), *Report of the Research into the Use and Practice of the Freeing for Adoption Provisions*, Bristol: Socio-Legal Centre for Family Studies, University of Bristol.

Magistrates Courts (Adoption) Rules 1984, SI 1984/611, London: HMSO.

Main, M. and Solomon, J. (1986), 'Discovery of an Insecure Disorganized/ Disoriented Attachment Pattern: Procedures, Findings and Implications for the Classification of Behaviour', in Yogman, M. and Brazelton, T. [eds], *Affective Development in Infancy*, Norwood, NJ: Ablex.

McCord, W. and McCord, J. (1959), *The Origins of Crime: A New Evaluation of the Cambridge-Sommerville Youth Study*, New York: Columbia University Press.

McKay, M. (1980), 'Planning for Permanent Placement', *Adoption and Fostering*, **4**(1), 19–21.

McRoy, R. (1991), 'American Experience and Research on Openness', *Adoption and Fostering*, **15**(4), 99–110.

McWhinnie, A. (1967), *Adopted Children: How They Grow Up*, London: Routledge and Kegan Paul.

Millham, S., Bullock, R., Hosie, K. and Haak, M. (1986), *Lost in Care: The Problems of Maintaining Links between Children in Care and their Families*, Aldershot: Gower.

Millham, S., Bullock, R., Hosie, K. and Little, M. (1989), *Access Disputes in Child-Care*, Aldershot: Gower.

Mount, F. (1983), *The Subversive Family*, Harmondsworth: Penguin.

Murch, M. (1980), *Justice and Welfare in Divorce*, London: Sweet and Maxwell.

Murch, M., Lowe, N., Borkowski, M., Copner, R. and Griew, K. (1991), *Pathways to Adoption*, Final Report, Bristol: Socio-Legal Centre for Family Studies, University of Bristol.

Murch, M., Lowe, N., Borkowski, M., Copner, R. and Griew, K. (1993), *Pathways to Adoption Research Project*, Bristol: Socio-Legal Centre for Family Studies, University of Bristol/DoH.

Packman, J., Randall, J. and Jacques, N. (1986), *Who Needs Care? Social Work Decisions About Children*, Oxford: Blackwell.

Page, R. and Clarke, G. (1977), *Who Cares?*, London: National Children's Bureau.

Pannor, R., Baran, A. and Sorosky, A. (1978), 'Birth Parents Who Relinquished Babies for Adoption Revisited', *Family Process*, **17**(3), 329–37.

Pardeck, J. and Pardeck, J. (1988), 'Helping Children to Adjust to Adoption Through the Biblio Therapeutic Approach', *Adoption and Fostering*, **12**(3), 11–16.

Parton, N. (1991), *Governing the Family: Child Care, Child Protection and the State*, London: Macmillan.

Parton, N. and Martin, N. (1989), 'Public Inquiries, Legalism and Child Care in Britain', *International Journal of Law and the Family*, **3**(1), 21–39.

Pochin, J. (1969), *Without a Wedding Ring*, London: Constable.

Raynor, L. (1971), *Giving Up a Baby for Adoption*, London: ABAA.

Raynor, L. (1980), *The Adopted Child Comes of Age*, London: Allen and Unwin.

Rickford, F. (1993), 'Havoc in the Home', *Community Care*, 30 September.

Robertson, J. and Bowlby, J. (1952), *Responses of Young Children to Separation From Their Mothers*, Paris: Courier of the International Children's Centre, **2**, 131–40.

Robertson, J. and Robertson, J. (1971), 'Young Children in Brief Separation' *Psychoanalytic Study of the Child*, **26**, 264–315.

Rockel, J. and Ryburn, M. (1988), *Adoption Today: Change and Choice in New Zealand*, Auckland: Heinemann/Reed.

Rowe, J., Cain, H., Hundleby, M. and Keane, A. (1984), *Long Term Foster Care*, London: Batsford/BAAF.

Rowe, J. and Lambert, L. (1973), *Children Who Wait*, London: ABAA.

Rowe, J. (1984), 'Freeing for Adoption: An Historical Perspective', *Adoption and Fostering*, **8**(2), 10–11.

Rowe, J., Hundleby, M. and Garnett, L. (1989), *Child Care Now: A Survey of Placement Patterns*, London: BAAF.

Rutter, M. (1971), 'Parent Child Separation: Psychological Effects on the Children', *Journal of Child Psychology and Psychiatry*, **11**, 259–83.

Rutter, M. (1972), *Maternal Deprivation Reassessed*, Harmondsworth: Penguin.

Rutter, M. (1975), *Helping Troubled Children*, Harmondsworth: Penguin.

Ryburn, M. (1991), 'The Myth of Assessment', *Adoption and Fostering*, **15**(1), 20–27.

Ryburn, M. (1991), 'Openness and Adoptive Parents', in Mullender, A. [ed.], *Open Adoption: The Philosophy and the Practice*, London: BAAF.

Ryburn, M. (1992), 'Advertising for Permanent Placements', *Adoption and Fostering*, **16**(2), 8–15.

Ryburn, M. (1992), 'The Myth of Assessment Revisited, *Adoption and Fostering*, **16**(3), 3.

Ryburn, M. (1992), 'Contested Adoption Proceedings', *Adoption and Fostering*, **16**(4), 29–38.

Ryburn, M. (1992), *Adoption in the 1990s: Identity and Openness*, Birmingham: Leamington Press.

Ryburn, M. (1994), *Open Adoption: Research, Theory and Practice*, Aldershot: Avebury.

Ryburn, M. (1994), 'An Analysis of Post Adoption Contact Following Contested Adoption Proceedings', in preparation.

Sachdev, P. (1991), 'The Triangle of Fears: Fallacies and Facts', in Hibbs, E. [ed.], *Adoption: International Perspectives*, Maddison, CT: International Universities Press.

Schaffer, H. and Emerson, P. (1964), 'Patterns of Response to Physical Contact in Early Human Development', *Journal of Child Psychology and Psychiatry*, **5**, 1–13.

Secretary of State for Social Services (1988), *Report of the Inquiry into Child Abuse in Cleveland*, Cmnd 412, London: HMSO.

Seglow, J., Pringle, M. and Wedge, P. (1972), *Growing up Adopted*, London: NFER.

Scottish Office (1993), *The Future of Adoption Law in Scotland: A Consultation Paper*, Edinburgh, Social Work Services Group.

Short Report (1984), *Second Report from the House of Commons Social Services Committee, 'Children in Care'* (HC 360), London: HMSO.

Social Services Select Committee (HC 360) (1984), *Children in Care*, London: HMSO.

Stacey, M., Dearden, R., Pill, R. and Robinson, D. (1970), *Hospitals, Children and Their Families: The Report of a Pilot Study*, London: Routledge and Kegan Paul.

Tajfel, H. (1972), 'Experiments in a Vacuum', in Israel, J. and Tajfel, H. [eds], *The Context of Social Psychology: A Critical Assessment*, London: Academic Press.

Teague, A. (1989), *Social Change, Social Work and the Adoption of Children*, Aldershot: Gower.

Thoburn, J. (1985), 'What Kind of Permanence', *Adoption and Fostering*, **9**(4), 29–33.

Thoburn, J. (1990), *Success and Failure in Permanent Family Placement*, Aldershot: Avebury.

Thoburn, J. (1990), *Review of Research Relating to Adoption*, London: Dept of Health/Welsh Office (also Appendix C in DoH (1992), *Review of Adoption Law: A Consultation Document*, London: HMSO).

Thoburn, J., Murdoch, A. and O'Brien, A. (1986), *Permanence in Child Care*, Oxford: Blackwell.

Thoburn, J. and Rowe, J. (1988), 'A Snapshot of Permanent Family Placement', *Adoption and Fostering*, **12**(3), 29–34.

Thoburn, J., Rashid, S. and Charles, M. (1992), 'The Placement of Black Children with Permanent New Families', *Adoption and Fostering*, **16**(3), 13–18.

Tizard, B. (1977), *Adoption: A Second Chance*, London: Open Books.

Townsend, P. (1979), *Poverty in the United Kingdom*, London: Penguin.

Trent, J. (1989), *Homeward Bound: The Rehabilitation of Children to Their Birth Parents*, Ilford: Barnados.

Triseliotis, J. (1973), *In Search of Origins*, London: Routledge and Kegan Paul.

Triseliotis, J. (1983), 'Identity and Security in Long Term Fostering and Adoption', *Adoption and Fostering*, **7**(1), 22–31.

Triseliotis, J. and Hall, E. (1971), 'Giving Consent to Adoption', *Social Work Today*, **2**, 17.

Triseliotis, J. and Russell, J. (1984), *Hard to Place: The Outcome of Adoption and Residential Care*, Aldershot: Gower.

Verity, P. (1993), personal communication, July.

Vernon, D., Foley, J., Sipowicz, R. and Schulman, J. (1965), *The Psychological Responses of Children to Illness*, New York: C.C. Thomas.

Vernon, J. and Fruin, D. (1986), *In Care: A Study of Social Work Decision Making*, London: National Children's Bureau.

Wallerstein, J. and Kelly, J. (1980), *Surviving the Breakup: How Children and Parents Cope with Divorce*, New York: Grant MacIntyre.

Watson, K. (1986), 'Birth Families: Living with the Adoption Decision', *Public Welfare*, Spring, 24–8.

Winkler, R. and van Keppel, M. (1984), *Relinquishing Mothers in Adoption: Their Long Term Adjustment*, Melbourne: Institute for Family Studies Monograph, No. 3.

)

Name index

Page references for author entries in the bibliography are italicised.

213

Subject index

The Children Act *1989*:
Putting it into Practice

Mary Ryan

This book provides a practical guide to those parts of the Children Act 1989 that relate to the provision of services by local authorities to children and families; the powers and duties of local authorities in such circumstances; care and supervision proceedings; and child protection issues.

The book is a unique combination of information on the legal framework contained in the Act, regulations and guidance and information on good social work and legal practice, relevant research and recent case law. It is grounded on the author's practical experience of providing an advice and advocacy service for families; providing training for social workers, lawyers and other child care professionals; being involved with the development of the legislation from the consultation period in the early 1980s, through the parliamentary process, and the subsequent consultation on regulations, guidance and court rules.

Mary Ryan, the Co-Director of the Family Rights Group, is a solicitor who after working in private practice as a family lawyer, was the Family Rights Group's legal advisor for 10 years.

1994   256 pages

Hbk   1 85742 192 2   £30.00   Pbk   1 85742 193 0   £14.95

Price subject to change without notification

arena

CHILD PLACEMENT:
PRINCIPLES AND PRACTICE
SECOND EDITION
June Thoburn

"...will be warmly welcomed by social work practitioners, teachers and students alike... promises to become a popular and well-thumbed text."
Dr Jean Packman, Dartington Social Research Unit

This is the second edition of a practice handbook which has proved popular with those who work with children and families or who are training to do so. It offers guidance to social workers about how to plan for, and work with, children who are looked after by local authorities, including children who have been abused or neglected.

The book emphasizes the importance of balancing the duty to safeguard the child's welfare with the duty to enhance the ability of parents to fulfil their parental responsibilities. It endorses the partnership philosophy of the Children Act 1989, and provides practical guidance on how this principle can be put into practice, whether the child remains at home, lives in residential care, or moves to a permanent foster or adoptive family. The text combines research findings, case material, social work values and practice wisdom to provide a coherent base from which to practice.

June Thoburn is Senior Lecturer in Social Work at the University of East Anglia. She is an acknowledged expert of international standing on child protection and family placement.

1994   **189 pages**   **1 85742 119 1**   **£9.95**
Price subject to change without notification

arena

Child Care in the EC

A country-specific guide to foster and residential care

edited by M J COLTON & W HELLINCKX

"This book will be a valuable resource on our small European library shelf."
Community Care

Despite the current uncertainty about the future development of the European Community (EC), there is increasing recognition among child welfare administrators, researchers, practitioners and students across the EC that much can be learned from the policies and practices of other member states.

This book offers a systematic description of residential and foster care in each of the constituent countries of the EC. In addition, a concise account of the research on residential and foster care undertaken in each country is presented. The book is, therefore, unique in that it represents the first coherent account of policy, practice and research in the field of residential and foster care in all the countries of the EC.

M J Colton is Lecturer in Applied Social Studies, University College of Swansea, and is a member of the Executive Committee of the European Scientific Association on Residential and Foster Care for Children and Adolescents (EUSARF). **W Hellinckx** is Professor at the Section of Orthopedagogics, Faculty of Psychology and Educational Sciences, University of Leuven, Belgium, and is President of EUSARF.

1993   272 pages
Hbk   1 85742 178 7   £32.50   Pbk   1 85742 179 5   £14.95

Price subject to change without notification